DEMOCRACY WITHOUT SECULARISM:
A PRAGMATIST CRITIQUE OF HABERMAS

DEMOCRACY WITHOUT SECULARISM:
A PRAGMATIST CRITIQUE OF HABERMAS

VRIJE UNIVERSITEIT ACADEMISCH PROEFSCHRIFT

ter verkrijging van de graad Doctor aan
de Vrije Universiteit Amsterdam,
op gezag van de rector magnificus
prof.dr. L.M. Bouter,
in het openbaar te verdedigen
ten overstaan van de promotiecommissie
van de Faculteit der Wijsbegeerte
op donderdag 20 december 2012 om 13.45 uur
in de aula van de universiteit,
De Boelelaan 1105

by

Daniel Michael Mullin

geboren te Toronto, Canada

promotor: prof.dr. R. Kuipers
copromotor: prof.dr. W.L. van der Merwe

This dissertation is in partial fulfilment of the requirements for a conjoint Ph.D. degree program offered by the Institute for Christian Studies, Toronto and the VU University Amsterdam.

Democracy Without Secularism: A Pragmatist Critique of Habermans

Mullin, Daniel Michael

Published by:

Vandeplas-Grether Publishing b.v. – November 2013

Haarsteegsestraat 51
5254 JN Haarsteeg
The Netherlands

www.vangre.eu

Copyright © 2013 by Daniel Michael Mullin

All rights reserved.
No part of this book may be reproduced, stored in a retrieval system, or transmitted by any means, electronic, mechanical, photocopying, recording, or otherwise, without written permission from the author.

ISBN: 978-94-91533-00-6

ABSTRACT

Jürgen Habermas has argued that democracy depends on all citizens recognizing the legitimacy of the law. Therefore, political argument must appeal only to public reason which is secular. Religious citizens must translate their reasons into a secular language accessible to the public. This dissertation argues that religious arguments are justified in public discourse if they refrain from dogmatism. Moreover, there is nothing inherent in secular reasons that make them publicly accessible or likely to generate consensus among members of a pluralistic society. If we treat religious arguments as simply arguments with controversial premises, it becomes less clear why religious arguments are singled out as particularly problematic for liberal democracies, since many secular political arguments share this feature. Granted, religious reasons are unlikely to secure consensus, but this does not count against them if consensus is not the goal of democratic discourse. This dissertation makes the case that Habermas, and other liberal theorists such as Rawls, have placed too much emphasis on consensus as the goal of democracy. Moreover, what they refer to is not practical consensus achieved pragmatically through compromise, but an idealized consensus that is the achievement of secular reason. This is problematic for two main reasons: there is no normative reason to think we ought to attain such consensus and such consensus is unlikely to be achieved in practice. Thus, there seems to be no normative force to the claim that religious citizens ought to translate their arguments into secular language.

TABLE OF CONTENTS

Acknowledgments x

Introduction: Charting the Territory 1

Chapter 1: Modernity and Its Discontents 13

    Exploring the Secularization Thesis 15
    Preliminary Objections to Religious Discourse in Public 21
    Secularization and the Public Sphere: A Historical Excursus 31
    Habermas on the Rise of the Public Sphere in England 34
    Rethinking the Secularity of the Public Sphere in the Modern Period .. 45
    Secularization: So What Happened? 55

Chapter 2: Competing Narratives of Secularization:
    Habermas and Taylor 61

    Secularization as Disenchantment: Empirical and Normative Aspects. 63
    Secularization, Postsecular Society and the Translation Requirement. 67
    Taylor's Phenomenology of Secularism 78
    Rethinking the Translation Requirement 90

Chapter 3: Habermas vis-à-vis Rawls on Religion in the
    Public Sphere: Promissory Notes or Cognitive Contents? 113

    Religion and the Public Sphere: Habermas and Rawls 116
    Habermas's Institutional Translation Proviso 124
    A Proposed Revision to the ITP 134
    Contestable Premises, Comprehensive Evidence, and
    Immanent Critique 138
    Balancing Burdens: The Pragmatics of Translation 145
    Balancing Burdens Again: A Utilitarian Analysis 150
    Objections Answered 153

Chapter 4: Religion as Abnormal Conversation Starter:
    Considering Pragmatist Alternatives to Rorty 163

    The Three 'R's': Reason, Rhetoric, and Reeducation 165
    Is Religion a Conversation Stopper? 172
    Rorty's Reconsideration 182
    Immanent Critique and Translation 191

**Chapter 5: Freedom and Future Transcendence: Beyond
   Kulturkampf to Redemptive Critique** 205

    Soft Naturalism and Substantive Commitments 206
    Is Postmetaphysical Thinking Untenable? 212
    Postmetaphysical Responses to Meyer 216
    Transcendence Today 222
    Death as a Boundary Condition 228
    The Future as Possibility 234
    The Future as Praxis 240

Conclusion: The Way Forward 251

Samenvatting 258

Bibliography 263

ACKNOWLEDGMENTS

A project like this is never a solo effort. I owe a debt of gratitude to the many people who helped make this dissertation a reality. First and foremost, I must thank the faculty and staff at the Institute for Christian Studies which has been my intellectual home for the past seven years. ICS occupies a unique and valuable place in the North American academic landscape. The rare combination of Reformed Christian roots and engagement with contemporary Continental philosophy made it an ideal place in which to undertake this project. I honestly can't imagine producing this dissertation anywhere else.

I especially wish to thank my supervisor, Ronald A. Kuipers. He nurtured my work at every step of the way, from inception to completion. He devoted countless hours to carefully reading manuscript drafts and making helpful suggestions. He also displayed a great deal of patience and understanding, and always encouraged me when I became frustrated with the difficult and time-consuming process of writing a doctoral dissertation. His encouragement has been invaluable. I also learned a great deal relevant to the thesis in the many courses I took from him at ICS. He deserves the credit for introducing me to the work of Habermas and Taylor and helping me see connections between their work that would form an integral part of my thesis. In short, Ron is a model of humble, sympathetic, and critical scholarship and I owe him more than I can express in these few words.

I also wish to thank the other members of the faculty at ICS for their contribution to this project. I took several courses from Lambert Zuidervaart and his insight and expertise in critical theory gave me much needed background on Habermas's intellectual influences. It would have been a pleasure to have taken more courses with him. Another senior member of whom this can be said is Nik Ansell. Perhaps one the most creative thinkers I've encountered, he always had something novel to contribute to a conversation. I wish to also thank Robert Sweetman. Although I never took a course with Bob, he was always up for a conversation in the hall or the lounge. It didn't take long to realize that he had encyclopedic knowledge of philosophy – and most other subjects – and I always found our conversations stimulating. I didn't have the privilege of taking any courses with Shannon Hoff either, as my coursework was finished by the time she arrived at ICS. However, I know that she's been very active in scholarship and has made valuable contributions to the already impressive achievements of ICS. I fully appreciate the role that every senior member has played in contributing to the intellectual fecundity of ICS and fostering an environment in which good scholarship cannot help but thrive. Without such a supportive environment, I could not have completed this dissertation. Thank-you to all who made this possible.

Of course, this includes not only the faculty, but also the staff of ICS. Without their tireless dedication to keeping ICS running smoothly, the scholars could not do their work. Speaking of tireless dedication, I must thank Shawn Stovell. Shawn is always available to junior members to answer any query about the many practical details of completing a graduate degree. He's also the first to offer congratulations on any accomplishment in a junior member's life, personal or professional. Sometimes graduate study can seem like a thankless calling, but in those times, Shawn always provides a voice of encouragement. For this, I'm grateful. I wish to also thank Isabella Guthrie-McNaughton for her help regarding the printing of the manuscript and for refreshing my memory on all the formal requirements that had to be met. I wish to also thank Daryl Kinsman. I don't think I ever required his technical expertise for any particular problem, but that's simply a testament to how well he does his job. He's always a fun conversationalist and has done a lot to promote ICS online. The information available online helped bring me to ICS and since that's Daryl's department, he deserves some of the credit for my being here. I apologize for not naming every staff member, past and present, who has helped me get to this point. Be assured that your efforts behind the scenes are appreciated.

As my previous remarks indicate, ICS is not just a graduate school. It's also a community. I've been welcomed into the homes of many of the senior members and everybody socializes together in the pub after seminars and at the yearly ICS retreat. All of these activities make ICS more than simply a place to earn a degree. It's this sense of community that I most appreciate about ICS.

I would also like to thank Willie van der Merwe for being my co-promoter and the faculty at the Vrije Universiteit who served on the reading committee and made several helpful suggestions. I also wish to thank René van Woudenberg for being the liaison between ICS and the VU. The VU is to be commended for partnering with ICS in offering this conjointly conferred degree. It is a wonderful opportunity for ICS students.

On a personal note, I would like to thank the late Theodore Plantinga. It's difficult to overestimate the influence Theo had on my life including, but not limited to, my decision to pursue a PhD in philosophy. I'm only saddened he cannot celebrate this accomplishment with me.

Finally, I would like to thank my parents. Their support, both emotional and financial, over the course of my education has been overwhelming. During the time in which I've written my dissertation, I've been away from home a couple of times, including sojourns in Australia and Saskatchewan, but I always knew I had a place to come home to. They never made me feel as though I'd overstayed my welcome and they always genuinely believed in the importance of the work I was doing. For their love and support I am grateful beyond words.

Introduction: Charting the Territory

This project is an examination of the place of religious language in public discourse. There are very few settled questions in philosophy; however, one might be tempted to say that the question of the proper relationship between religion and politics is one of them. The consensus seems to be that it is good for both religion and politics if the two of them remain separate. The state should remain secular, neutral with respect to the competing claims of sectarian faiths. This arrangement prevents any particular faith from exercising a monopoly on public power and affords individuals the freedom to practice any faith or none at all. Although this principle is an idealization, it is a general principle which most proponents of liberal democracy would affirm, although perhaps with qualification. However, within this general, idealized framework, the practical details of the often complex interplay between religion and public discourse need to be worked out. To say that the state must remain secular is not a very useful statement, since 'secular' could mean many different things. Furthermore, to separate the business of religion conceptually from the business of the state is quite different from doing so in practice. To say that a person's religious faith will not influence her political actions is naive. To say that it ought not is a substantive normative claim that would require some justification. So beneath the thin veneer of consensus lie many deep and complex issues upon which people with a robust commitment to democracy can and do disagree. This project is concerned with just such issues.

More specifically, I will engage these issues in conversation, as it were, with the works of Jürgen Habermas. He is well known, at least in philosophical circles, for advocating his theory of communicative action, which is a sophisticated articulation and defense of the principles of the Enlightenment – as well as a diagnosis of where it went wrong and how to rehabilitate it. Habermas is impressed by the power of giving reasons, the capacity of human rationality to build consensus through the forceless force of the better argument. For Habermas, rational argument is the only legitimate force in political decision making. However, for rationality to do its work it has to be publicly accessible – its legitimacy must be recognized by all citizens, irrespective of particular faith positions. Therefore, a consequence of Habermas's theory of communicative action is that the secular language of Enlightenment rationality is the only normative language in which we can conduct political discourse and decision making.

In recent years, however, Habermas has begun to soften his position with respect to the legitimacy of religious language in public life. To what extent his newer writings represent continuity with or departure from his earlier work is a matter of debate and will be taken up in this volume. Suffice it to say, that whether religious language can play a legitimate role in the public sphere is now an open question for Habermas. He has, over the last decade or so, been working out some of the details of his modified position. My project, in large part, is to chart this progress and extrapolate my own conclusions from it. I often go further than Habermas seems willing to go, but nevertheless believe that my conclusions in most cases represent the logical entailments of his statements to date. To that end, I have also placed Habermas in conversation with several interlocutors in the following chapters. These interlocutors, in my judgment, push the argument in interesting directions, some of which Habermas is reticent to take, but nevertheless are often fruitful paths for our exploration. With that in mind, let us turn to a more detailed outline of the chapters themselves.

The first chapter deals in some depth with the narrative of the Enlightenment and secularization. There are several reasons for devoting the first chapter to the historical background of our subject. Firstly, it is where Habermas himself begins. His first major published work, *The Structural Transformation of the Public Sphere*, is an important examination of the cultural background in which our modern notion of "public" was formed. Indeed, his magnum opus, *The Theory of Communicative Action*, assumes much of the history addressed in the previous volume.

Secondly, the narrative is important with respect to assessing Habermas's thesis about the normativity of secular public language. The traditional narrative that describes the rise of liberal political structures during the Enlightenment as purely the result of disinterested, secular reason may be challenged. The narrative as standardly told has a tendency to ignore or drastically underplay the role that Christianity played in shaping the principles that became the bedrock of modern liberal democracies. Retelling the story of secularization does not necessarily undercut the normativity of secular reason, but it does allow us to infer that the exclusive normativity of secular language was not assumed at the birth of the modern liberal nation state. This observation may also cast doubt on whether we must affirm the normativity of secular language in functioning democracies today.

Thirdly, Habermas's conclusions are indebted to a certain interpretation of Western intellectual history called the secularization thesis. As an empirical thesis, it predicts that religion will inevitably decline in the face of challenges from secular reason, such as the explanatory power of science. However, this prediction does not seem to be coming to pass. Certainly, something that merits the name "secularization" has happened since the modern period, at least in most industrialized Western nations, but religion has experienced a resurgence in recent history that the secularization theory did not anticipate. Indeed, there is a growing suspicion that the Enlightenment narrative is not simply a neutral description of the march of reason. Rather, it may be argued that it is a value-laden description, an attempt to derive an 'ought' from an 'is'. The empirical version of the secularization thesis, now largely discredited, quickly gives way to a normative version: the language of secularism is simply the normative, public language of Western democracies. To be clear, I am not disputing the necessity of giving reasons and arguing for the political positions that we hold. Rather, I am questioning the substantive secularism that claims exclusive access to the public domain. I believe that it is legitimate to look for another idiom in which to cast public arguments.

However, it is important to do more than simply critique the standard narrative of secularization. Therefore, I offer a positive narrative that I believe provides a corrective to the one-sided history that too often forms the background of our contemporary political debates. In contrast to the disenchantment account of secularization that Habermas inherits from Weber, in which religious ways of thinking fall away as they are replaced by scientific modes of thought, I argue that factors within Christianity itself facilitated the secularization process and that a secular worldview was made possible by preconditions within Christian thought. Moreover, secularism is not simply a matter of eliminating religious modes of thinking, but is itself a positive philosophical position that serves many of the same functions as the religion it allegedly replaces. In these respects, I am indebted to Charles Taylor's massive study in *A Secular Age*. More specifically, I argue that figures like John Locke, who is often portrayed as a progenitor of the modern secular state, borrowed many of his arguments, especially in his *Letter Concerning Toleration*, from Christian sources. Thus, it is plausible that the foundations of the modern liberal state in the seventeenth century are deeply Christian; they may not arrive as the invention of an inherently secular philosophy. It is also plausible to see the emergence of secularization in the seventeenth century as a practical response to religious pluralism, rather than a process of disenchantment. This reconstructed narrative can help us make an important distinction between secularization and secular*ism* that is useful in discussing our contemporary political situation.

The second chapter deals in greater detail with Habermas's reevaluation of the secularization thesis and his translation requirement – the requirement that religious citizens translate their potential contributions to public debate from a private, religious idiom into a publicly accessible, secular language. This translation requirement, however, can be construed in stronger and weaker terms. Part of the aim of this chapter is not only to explore what Habermas means given his re-evaluation of the secularization thesis and his diagnosis that we live in a postsecular society, but also to show that stronger formulations of the translation requirement are problematic.

To be fair, Habermas now acknowledges that the overreaching predictions of the secularization thesis need to be pruned back. He recognizes that we live in a postsecular society, which means not only that we must anticipate the continued existence of religion, but that we must also acknowledge that religious language has meaning that can be appropriated by secularists. However, in order to appropriate that meaning, such language, according to Habermas must be translated into the language of public reason. While he is sensitive to the fact that this places a burden on religious citizens that has no counterpart for secular citizens, he nevertheless maintains that there is an epistemic difference between claims that rest on religious presuppositions, on one hand, and statements that any rational person would accept on the basis of secular reason, on the other.

As a pragmatic method of brokering agreement in a pluralistic context, the translation requirement makes good sense. However, the claim that religious reasons must be translated into secular ones, because only the latter count as epistemically normative, is a more problematic position. The implication that secular reasons are simply based on empirical givens can be challenged through understanding the substantive philosophical positions underlying contemporary secularism. Again, Taylor's study provides a helpful assessment of what we might call a phenomenology of secularism. If 'secular reason' is not simply reasoning without the metaphysical baggage of religion, but carries substantive philosophical baggage of its own, then we might question its alleged epistemic primacy in matters of public debate. Moreover, Habermas has come to recognize that secular language may not have the philosophical resources necessary to sustain a robust commitment to the human rights we all wish to affirm. Indeed, he has stated that religious language still has semantic power in this domain that to this point has resisted translation into secular terms.[1]

The third chapter deals in greater depth with the notion of 'public reason' and compares Habermas's position with that of Rawls. The latter argues that citizens owe each other a duty of civility which includes offering only secular reasons, or reasons that any rational person would accept regardless of whatever comprehensive doctrines they may hold. Rawls considers religious rationales to be merely promissory notes for these public reasons.[2] In my judgment, this position differs from that of Habermas, who has come to see that religious reasons may in fact contain cognitive insights from which secularists can learn. Needless to say, Rawls's contention that public reason consists of reasons that any rational person would accept is problematic. Rational people disagree about many issues, and in political argumentation especially there are very few premises that compel rational assent. Nevertheless, it is vital in a liberal democracy that everybody understands the reasons for legislation; the citizens must understand themselves as both authors and addressees of the law. For this reason, Habermas, while allowing the exchange of religious reasons at the level of the informal public sphere, believes that religious reasons must be kept out of the official chambers of political will-formation, such as parliaments. Therefore, Habermas introduces an institutional translation proviso: at the level of law-making, one must translate any religious insight into exclusively secular language. In other words, all coercively enforceable political decisions must be justifiable in a language accessible to all citizens. I agree that any liberal state must protect citizens from a religious majority gaining a monopoly on public power. Democratic citizenship, therefore, places certain restraints on the kind of legislation one advocates. Nicholas Wolterstoff calls such constrictions

---

[1] "[T]he unbelieving sons and daughters of modernity seem to believe that they owe more to one another, and need more for themselves, than what is accessible to them, in translation, of religious tradition – as if the semantic potential of the latter was still not exhausted." Jürgen Habermas, "Faith and Knowledge," in *The Frankfurt School on Religion*, ed. Eduardo Mendieta (New York: Routledge, 2005), 334.
[2] John Rawls, *Political Liberalism* (Columbia University Press, 1993), li – lii.

"restraints of content."³ However, it is less clear that one should advocate epistemic restraints on the decisions and debates of citizens, i.e. the reasoning by which they arrive at conclusions about what is best for the polity. Wolterstorff argues that this is true at the formal, as well as the informal, level. Again, reasons to which all rational persons would assent are hard to come by in political discourse. According to Wolterstorff, to single out religious reasons in these contexts is a red herring. The distinction is between reasons that would be accepted by all informed and rational people and those that would not be so accepted. However, when one looks at political arguments on controversial subjects, one finds very few, if any, premises that would qualify as 'public reasons'; they are simply not acceptable to all rational persons. I therefore argue, following Wolterstorff, that there is no justification for imposing epistemic restraints on political debate.

What then of the issue of protecting minorities from a sectarian monopoly on public power? In other words, how does one preserve the neutrality of the state? I propose a modification to Habermas's institutional translation proviso that allows a diversity of epistemic considerations but nevertheless preserves religiously neutral language in the legislation as drafted. For example, when debating prospective laws in both the informal and formal public spheres, we should be willing to let a thousand epistemic flowers bloom. But the genuine insight behind the institutional translation proviso is a good one: the official language of state should be translated into as neutral a language as possible in order to preserve its legitimacy for all citizens. The secular state must not be officially Christian or Jewish or Muslim, although the laws, though neutral in language, will likely reflect the views of actual citizens who may well credit religious rationales in their political decision making. In my judgment, this modified institutional translation proviso ensures the neutral character of the state, while allowing religious citizens to fully participate in public debate. I conclude the chapter with some reflections on the pragmatics of argumentation and consensus-building which, in my judgment will sometimes require translation, sometimes immanent critique, and other times religious premises. I make a case for being open to a multilateral approach to public discussion that

---

3   Nicholas Wolterstorff, "The Role of Religion in Decision and Discussion of Political Issues," in Robert Audi and Nicholas Wolterstorff, *Religion in the Public Square: The Place of Religious Convictions in Political Debate* (Rowman & Littlefield Publishers, Inc., 1996), 69.

avoids the flat, monochromatic insistence on an abstraction called "public reason."

Since my approach to public deliberation is indebted to pragmatism, the question arises: do pragmatists object to allowing religious arguments into the public sphere? In order to address this question, chapter four deals with Richard Rorty, who has raised objections to religious arguments in public, notably in an essay called "Religion As Conversation-stopper." Rorty contends that raising religious considerations in public contexts is in "bad taste"[4] because politics is the domain of public arguments, not private feelings. In addition, he claims that religion, at least in the American context, already receives more public respect than it deserves. However, I suggest that one should not reduce the issue to whether or not certain private considerations should receive more respect in public than other private considerations. I argue that Rorty, in setting up the problem in such a way, misconstrues the real issue. I would agree with him that arguments should not receive more respect simply by virtue of being religious. Rather, they must vie for respect critically and dialectically like all other arguments. But to say that religious arguments should not be afforded more respect is not tantamount to saying that they should be excluded from the dialetical process at the outset. Rorty frames the issue correctly, though perhaps unintentionally, when he says that "voices claiming to be God's, or reason's, or science's are put on par with everybody else's."[5] Of course, putting voices that claim to be God's on par with everybody else's is not identical with eliminating voices that claim to be God's. The former is the more democratic option, though not the one Rorty takes in developing his argument. Rather, like Rawls, he talks about religion limiting itself to the private domain and religious citizens limiting themselves to premises held in common.

Even if one grants Rorty's premise that religion is a conversation stopper, it is by no means clear that it has a monopoly on doing so. He acknowledges that the conversation has to stop somewhere, and that his Darwinian, pragmatic, antirealist reasons beg all the important questions, as do his opponents' Platonist, idealist, and realist reasons. The reason these appeals stop conversation has nothing to do with being public or private. Rather, it is simply the nature of argument. Eventually, we all appeal to what Rorty calls 'final

---

[4] Richard Rorty, "Religion As Conversation-stopper," in *Philosophy and Social Hope* (Penguin, 2000), 169.
[5] Rorty, 172.

vocabularies'. Thus, religion is not unique in this regard. As Wolterstorff says, it is not that religious reasons "are 'private' in any clear sense of that term, but that they are not shared by the citizenry in general."[6] However, such consensus is seldom achieved. Even in the best democracies, conversation always ends before consensus has been achieved which is why all democracies observe majority rule.

Rorty has since reconsidered some of his more critical statements about religion, however he still wants to make a case for translation, namely that religious citizens should find another language in which to express their convictions. He admits that he cannot find a general principle in which to couch this requirement. I would agree; translation is largely a matter of the pragmatics of concrete situations, rather than being a philosophically justifiable principle. Rorty has a point, which Jeffrey Stout also makes, when he says that religious citizens should refrain from faith-claims or mere appeals to authority. These simply do not advance democratic debate. However, given what Rorty says about the vacuity of epistemological foundationalism, it is unclear what practical, discursive purpose translation would serve. Simply switching moral rubrics from, say, divine commands to natural law would not likely convince a utilitarian like Rorty. He does not see one as more rational than the other. He simply hopes that the dominant language of public morality will continue to be couched in utilitarian terms and is committed to waging that rhetorical battle. At least for Habermas, who has a stronger conception of reason and the objectivity achieved by language, the discursive, pragmatic point of translation is clearer. Nevertheless, I look for a more pragmatically viable way to keep the conversation going than that of either Rorty or Habermas.

I conclude chapter four by looking at Stout's suggestion of "immanent critique."[7] Immanent critique attempts to make translation a two-way street, not due to any obligation on the part of either religious or secular citizens to translate their arguments, but for reasons of facilitating 'abnormal conversations' at precisely those places where we have reached an impasse due to differences in worldviews. Such an approach considers, as Habermas has recently suggested, that traditional perspectives might offer a critique of secularism that might have force for secular interlocutors. This approach suggests that nothing inherent in

---

[6] Wolterstorff, "An Engagement with Rorty," *Journal of Religious Ethics*, 31.1 (2003): 132.
[7] Jeffrey Stout, *Democracy and Tradition* (Princeton University Press, 2005), 73.

pragmatism disqualifies religious contributions to public debates. Rather, the utility of religious premises largely depends on the discursive situation.

In the final chapter, I continue to press the point that Habermas, despite his careful distinction between form and content, adopts many substantive philosophical commitments. One such commitment is foundational to Habermas's political theory; the autonomy of rational agency. Moreover, he recognizes that many substantive commitments of a secular worldview, what he calls 'hard naturalism', seriously undermine the reality of rational agency. Therefore, Habermas is quite critical of the reductionism and determinism inherent in scientism. Through exploring his recent thoughts on freedom and determinism, I contend that his commitment to rational agency is ultimately a fiduciary commitment. Regardless of how post-metaphysical we are in our thinking, we run up against the limits of our procedural apparatus and must make more substantive assumptions, whether our worldviews are religious or secular at their core.

In the remainder of the chapter, I try to articulate how we might understand our substantive commitments in a postmetaphysical rubric. I suggest, in agreement with Habermas, that metaphysics is not a useful rubric to bring to political discourse. If we see the presence of religion in the public sphere as the presence of metaphysical beliefs that secular citizens lack, then the subtraction narrative implicit in Habermas's translation requirement forces itself on our discourse. However, if we are to be post-metaphysical and recognize that religion should not be so narrowly construed and also recognize that secularists have substantive commitments, then we can see the presence of religion in the public sphere, not as the presence of 'metaphysical baggage' that we must shed, but as the presence of religious citizens who may have arguments that we ought to consider. Again, if we pay attention to the substantive claims that function as premises in arguments, the distinction is not between religious premises and secular ones, but between universally accepted premises and particular ones. I don't think we have universally accepted premises, nor for that matter a methodology that would lead us to them. All we can do, in my judgment, is work pragmatically, which may entail translation or immanent critique or some recognition of the substantive commitments we all bring to the table.

In this final chapter, I also attempt to offer a post-metaphysical understanding of transcendence which Habermas might recognize as providing a redemptive critique of some of the pathologies of modernity. Drawing upon

Moltmann and also the first generation of critical theorists, I articulate an understanding of the future as a 'paradigm of transcendence'. In the background once again is Taylor's historical narrative which chronicles the phenomenological shift in our experience of what might be called 'the boundary' between the immanent frame and transcendence. Although this experience has been cast in largely metaphysical terms (along a vertical axis, shall we say), it is now understood by moderns as located within the unfolding of time and history. This is plausibly also true for secularists as evidenced by the many utopian narratives of progress that have emerged since the Enlightenment that function as secular eschatologies. However, with the failure of these secular narratives, it is more difficult to conceptualize hope for the future as simply an expansion of the immanent order. Rather, hope must transcend the limitations of our immediate horizon of experience. Habermas also wishes to transcend the limitations of our experience and realize a better future through the ideal speech situation. His goal is a harmonious community of communicative individuals which transcends the currently antagonistic public sphere and culminates in perfect rational consensus. However, I argue that the reconciliation Habermas hopes for cannot be achieved by simply projecting the failed promise of modernity into the future, and indeed, he recognizes this. But to think of the future as a horizon of hope and possibility as Habermas does, is precisely to conceive of it transcendently upon Moltmann's schema. Thus, I detect an inherent eschatology in Habermas that does not fit comfortably within the naturalism of the immanent frame.

The relevance of the foregoing to religion in political discourse is to understand how it might offer a genuinely critical assessment of secularism and a genuinely hopeful articulation of progress. That is to say, religious modes of thinking might well perform both a critical and redemptive function in politics that transcends the boundaries of an often moribund political discourse. In saying this, however, I shoulder the burden of suggesting some practical ways this might be worked out in our contemporary political situation. For example, how does one export the Western achievements of human rights and liberal democracy in a way that respects rational communication and does not rely on the coercive power of military and market? Habermas is quite sensitive to this issue and I suggest that understanding the global citizen as a post-secular citizen is crucial to accomplishing this task. In my judgment, the post-secular citizen should not only be able to translate religious language into the widest possible discourse, but should also be able to equalize the burden that religious persons bear in public discourse, thereby allowing them to participate without naive secularism being a requirement of admission. This point is also relevant to the increased saliency of religious diversity within Western democracies. Here, again, I think that a pragmatic understanding of secularization, which admits of the resiliency of religion despite its weakening institutional presence, will serve us better than an ideological secularism that sees itself as diametrically opposed to religion in principle. In summary, I present a role for religious language that moves beyond *Kulturkampf* rhetoric; a religiosity that neither enforces orthodoxy on a pluralistic public nor claims for itself immunity from argument and rational criticism.

Chapter 1
Modernity and Its Discontents

As stated in the introduction, my project is a close engagement with Habermas on the issue of religious language in the public sphere. Thus, the first chapter concerns prolegomena to this central task. There are a number of preliminary objections to my project that I must address, such as its seeming violation of the public/private distinction that is in many ways sacrosanct to liberalism. In this chapter, I argue that this is not a formidable challenge to my thesis. In doing so, I also address concerns about the alleged epistemic differences between public knowledge and private belief. I argue that this distinction is vastly overstated. In the words of Richard Rorty, "[i]nsofar as pragmatists make a distinction between knowledge and opinion, it is simply the distinction between topics on which agreement is relatively easy to get and topics on which agreement is relatively hard to get."[8] Unlike Rorty, however, I argue that the simple lack of consensus is not a good *prima facie* reason to exclude claims, including religious claims, from the public domain. In making this case, I also explore the hidden epistemic assumptions that underlie this objection and argue that it is based on a naive evidentialism.

After dealing with these preliminary objections, I proceed with the central task of this chapter: providing a corrective to the 'subtraction story' (to use Taylor's term) of modern secularization.[9] I argue that secularization should not be equated with the disenchantment narrative that Habermas receives from Weber. Rather, I suggest that secularization is best understood as a pragmatic response to the fact of religious pluralism.

In order to make this case more concrete, I take the reader on an historical excursus through the early modern period, where Habermas and other scholars locate the rise of the public sphere. In this section, I interact with Habermas's own dissertation, *The Structural Transformation of the Public Sphere*,

---

[8] Richard Rorty, "Solidarity or Objectivity" in *The Rorty Reader*, Christopher J. Voparil and Richard J. Bernstein, eds. (Wiley-Blackwell, 2010), 229.

[9] Charles Taylor. *A Secular Age* (Cambridge, MA: Harvard University Press, 2007), 22.

in which he chronicles the rise of the modern public sphere as a major factor in social and political evolution.[10] Although Habermas deftly covers the relevant historical territory, he arguably overstates the extent to which the progenitors of secularization contributed to disenchantment, or the decline of belief in God or religious practice. This historical point is instructive, insofar as it has implications for Habermas's larger political theory. Since Habermas sees himself in the tradition of Enlightenment secularism, it is useful to ask whether or not the secularist criterion that he advocates for political participation emerges from the Enlightenment. I argue that it does not, and that the interpretation that sees secularism emerging from the Enlightenment, and indeed sees the Enlightenment itself as having facilitated the retreat of religion from the public sphere, must understate or ignore several facts about the founders of Enlightenment thought and its political progeny, liberalism.

One such founder is John Locke. Through engagement with recent Locke scholarship, I contend that the most plausible interpretation of Locke's project is a pragmatic response to religious pluralism. Moreover, tolerance does not arrive on the scene as the invention of a liberalism that is inherently and ideologically secular; rather its origins are deeply Christian. Only a forced reading of Locke would conclude that his goal is a secular, that is to say disenchanted, consensus. Perhaps modern liberal theory, along the lines of Habermas and Rawls, has overestimated the importance of consensus for the smooth functioning of democracy. In fact, if one looks to the writings of J.S. Mill, particularly *On Liberty*, one finds a trenchant critique of consensus. For these modern thinkers, we do not need a consensus, either religious or secular, in order to have a stable democracy. I suggest that contemporary liberal theorists, having correctly perceived that the search for a religious consensus in the early modern period failed, enthusiastically attempt to replace it with a secular — conceived of as disenchanted — consensus. But secularization, as a cultural phenomenon, is arguably not the result of disenchantment — the decline of religious belief in the face of reason and science — but rather a practical response to religious pluralism and the recognition that, contrary to the predictions of the secularization thesis, religion is here to stay.

None of this refutes Habermas's normative claim that religious citizens

---

[10] Jürgen Habermas, *The Structural Transformation of the Public Sphere*, Thomas Burger, trans. (Cambridge, MA: MIT Press, 1991).

must translate their religious language into a secular idiom for political purposes. That will be the goal of subsequent chapters. However, if I can complicate the subtraction story of secularization inherent in Habermas's narrative of the rise of the public sphere, this will also problematize the lessons he allegedly draws from the modern period and applies to our contemporary political discourse.

Exploring the Secularization Thesis

Modernity fostered optimism regarding the potential of non-sectarian, value neutral, critical reason to build genuine consensus among free persons. Consequently, the role of religion in the public sphere has become marginalized if not excluded. This relegation of religion to the private sphere often accompanies the attitude that only an enlightened, secular citizenry is worthy of democracy. For example, following the 2004 U.S. presidential elections, an article appeared in the *New York Times* called "The Day the Enlightenment Went Out" in which the author asks rhetorically: "Can a people that believes more fervently in the Virgin Birth than in evolution still be called an enlightened nation?" He goes on to say, "America, the first real democracy in history, was founded on Enlightenment values."[11] This statement serves to underscore both points above: the marginalization or even hostility in this case, toward religion, coupled with the assumption that 'enlightenment' is necessary for the preservation of democracy. It also serves to underscore that such strongly stated defenses of modernity, which often see modernity as monolithic, are becoming increasingly common in reaction to perceived religious fundamentalism, in this case evangelical Christianity. But this article also reveals a waning confidence in what has conventionally been called the secularization thesis. There are various versions of this thesis, but in broad strokes it denotes the historical processes, since the Enlightenment, of rationalization and differentiation that have marginalized religion from the public sphere, and which are expected to spell the end of religion as a publicly significant phenomenon, at least in industrialized nations. As a predictive hypothesis, the secularization theory has not come to pass and the article's lament for enlightenment betrays frustration that such processes of secularization have not fully come to fruition by now. But in addition to the empirical aspect of the secularization thesis, it also has a normative component: religious claims must surrender claims to public legitimacy and adopt secular

---

[11] Gary Wills, "The Day the Enlightenment Went Out," *New York Times*, November 4, 2004.

language. However, given that religion does not appear to be going away any time soon, the question of religion in the public sphere is rapidly gaining a relevance that could not have been foreseen even two decades ago.

Perhaps more than any other theorist, Jürgen Habermas has analyzed the emergence of the secular public sphere during the Enlightenment and its subsequent transformation into mass media. Habermas's early work, *The Structural Transformation of the Public Sphere*, deals with many of the themes he would later take up in his *magnum opus*, *The Theory of Communicative Action* (TCA). Chief among these themes, are the normative conditions of discourse and agreement. According to this theme: 1) all claims must be publicly accessible or rationally defensible and 2) any agreement that emerges from discourse within the public sphere must be critical consensus as opposed to mere convergence, or what pollsters often refer to as "public opinion" in our contemporary political lexicon. With these criteria in place, there is little room for religious citizens to speak the language of faith within the public sphere. However, the post-TCA Habermas, while still defending an idealized public discourse, may be allowing more latitude for religious citizens within a democracy to unlock the semantic potential of religious language within public discourse.

Under globalization, such issues have acquired increased saliency. Commenting upon the contemporary relevance of Habermas's early work on the public sphere, Nicholas Garnham argues that global markets and private corporations are eclipsing the power of the traditional nation-state. As such, he insists that "[w]e are thus being forced to rethink .... the nature of citizenship in the modern world. What new political institutions and new public sphere might be necessary for the democratic control of a global economy and polity?"[12] Furthermore, James Bohman claims that globalization and new information technologies "make it at least possible to consider whether democracy is undergoing another great transformation, of the order of the invention of representative democracy and its institutions of voting and parliamentary assemblies in early modern European societies."[13] These features of contemporary society facilitate the possibility of a globalized public discourse in which global citizens participate.

---

[12] Nicholas Garnham, "The Media and the Public Sphere," in *Habermas and the Public Sphere*, ed. Craig Calhoun (Cambridge, MA: MIT Press, 1992), 362.
[13] James Bohman, "Expanding dialogue: the Internet, the public sphere and prospects for transnational democracy" in *After Habermas: New Perspectives on the Public Sphere*, ed. Nick Crossley and John Michael Roberts, (Oxford: Blackwell, 2004), 131.

In addition to the relevant sociological considerations invoked by Garnham and Bohman, I want to add the re-emergence of religion to the list of features in our contemporary society that might well render attempts to globalize the public discourse problematic. I am not necessarily referring to religious radicalism although the challenges it poses to democracy are obvious. I refer mainly to the massive movement across international borders, mainly from the south to the north. With the exception of the United States, the historically Christian Western democracies have undergone a thoroughgoing secularization since the Enlightenment. However, the introduction of people with robust faith commitments has challenged the complacency with which such democracies dismiss religion in public discourse. Again, this does not necessarily have to do with radical demands or violence on the part of religious citizens or landed immigrants. However, the secularism of the liberal state may risk political unrest if it cannot find a way to enfranchise an increasingly religious population. Like Habermas, I would like to find a way to maintain the ideals of modernity, the formal secularism of the state and human rights, but combine these insights with the recognition that we must find a reasonable way to include religious voices in that discourse.

In my judgment, Habermas is correct in saying that the liberal ideals that emerge from the Enlightenment represent an advance over earlier methods of societal organization. And Habermas is also correct in rejecting the postmodern narrative that sees modernity as simply a source of oppression. It is instructive to note that the eighteenth century, or Enlightenment, is roughly bounded for philosophical purposes by two very important publications: Locke's *A Letter Concerning Toleration* (1689) and Kant's *On Perpetual Peace* (1795).[14] Since these works do not *prima facie* seem like tools of oppression, the burden of proof is on those who characterize the Enlightenment in this way.

The goal of classical liberalism is to reach some semblance of rational consensus amid a plurality of competing religious and metaphysical beliefs. In the background, of course, are the intramural wars of religion (Christianity) that plagued Europe, which parenthetically, account for why French, British, and Dutch colonial expansion was negligible during the eighteenth century. The major imperial forces of the time were Spain and Portugal, which were entirely

---

[14] Peter Loptson, *Philosophy, History, and Myth: Essays and Talks* (University Press of America, 2002), 76.

outside the Enlightenment culturally.[15] More to the point, the universality the Enlightenment fostered was an effort to make peace with others despite religious or metaphysical differences. The motivations, as evidenced by the titles of the above works, were toleration and peace. Over time, this had the effect of secularizing the public sphere; in order to have one's voice heard one needed to speak the dominant language of that sphere, an argumentative, rational language. The pluralities of private beliefs were invited to speak this language and gain a hearing. This public/private schema, which has been oversimplified here, has its shortcomings, which will be taken up below, but it also has its contemporary defenders, such as Richard Rorty. While critics would likely argue that insistence upon speaking the public language denies a voice to excluded minorities, Rorty sees this as symptomatic of the fact that the 'franchise' simply has not been adequately extended. We simply need more liberals and liberally-minded people. There is no doubt that Rorty's faith in liberalism is somewhat naïve. And it is true that modernity is not without its pathological elements which must be constantly criticized and reformed. However, it is also true that the link between the Enlightenment and imperialism and oppression is tenuous at best. The ethics of the Enlightenment, with liberal democracy being one of its political offspring, represent much more than a modest advance over the existing state of affairs. All of these points I happily grant, and therefore situate myself as part of the "loyal opposition" to use Charles Taylor's phrase.[16] Nevertheless, in my judgment, it is necessary to foster solidarity among religious and secular citizens, and the standard liberal model for doing so is quickly becoming antiquated as the predictions of the secularization thesis do not come to pass. I do not believe the solution to these challenges is to return to even more antiquated methods of societal organization as proposed by those whom Jeffrey Stout calls "the new traditionalists," thinkers such as Stanley Hauerwas, Alisdair MacIntyre, and John Milbank.[17] Therefore, I seek a middle ground between secularization and nostalgia for Christendom.

Despite the goods inherent in liberalism, challenges for social organization remain, not the least of which is the emerging religious voices mentioned above. The narrative of globalization may not enable us to meet the above challenges. For example, the goal of globalization is, ostensibly, to unify.

---

[15] Loptson, 78.
[16] Charles Taylor, *A Secular Age* (Belknap Press of Harvard University Press, 2007), 745.
[17] Jeffrey Stout, *Democracy and Tradition* (Princeton University Press, 2005), 11.

We want to build consensus, tolerance, and stability. We tend to think that this paradigm is in everyone's best interests. The universalizing discourse of modernity is still with us, despite its more radical postmodern critics. The global citizen, as a part of this totalizing discourse, is optimistic about the prospects of enlightened self-interest and rational communication to build a better world. The question remains, however, whether such a totalizing discourse can accommodate particularity of the kind found in religious communities. Can we foster universality at the expense of particularity as the traditional Enlightenment model advocates, or is it hopelessly outmoded in dealing with current challenges to solidarity within liberal democracies? In other words, can we promote solidarity without losses to liberty?

In venturing answers to these questions, some historical background about the rise of the secular public sphere is helpful. Thus, my first chapter will draw upon Habermas's *Structural Transformation* and its subsequent commentators, so that we may glean some of the definitive features of the public sphere and its implications for secularization.

The factors that contributed to the rise of the public sphere in the eighteenth century are numerous and the narrative is complex. Expertise in a variety of fields is required to adequately map it, making Habermas's contribution all the more impressive despite being published in 1962. However, my approach will be more modest, focusing on his assessment of the rise of the public sphere in England, particularly the contributions of Locke and John Stuart Mill to the concept of 'public opinion' as a means of brokering rational consensus within a liberal framework. My purpose in reviewing this narrative is to problematize the standard secularization thesis, particularly the concept of publicly accessible reason that is alleged to emerge from it. It is debatable, however, whether and to what extent the concept of public opinion – which Habermas takes to be synonymous with critical discourse or even achieved consensus – that emerges from the Enlightenment conforms to Habermas's stringent criterion of communicative rationality. Although he has arguably nuanced his position recently, Habermas has insisted on exclusively secular reasons within the public sphere because religious beliefs, in his view, do not admit of communicative redemption. Specifically, I want to correct what Taylor calls "subtraction stories" which he defines as "stories of modernity in general, and secularity in particular, which explain them by human beings having lost, or sloughed off, or liberated themselves from certain earlier, confining horizons, or illusions, or limitations of knowledge."[18] I will argue that Habermas's conception of public opinion as a critically achieved rational consensus is not the unequivocal stance of modern liberalism nor is it now necessary for the smooth functioning of deliberative democracy. These considerations do not necessarily refute the normativity of Habermas's construal of publicly accessible reason, but they do complicate any effort to derive a univocal definition of 'publicly accessible reason' from the Anglo-American liberal tradition.

Such a counter narrative has implications for my larger project: challenging the default status of secular reasons within public discourse in liberal democracies and the alleged duty of religious citizens to 'translate' their contributions to public debate from a religious idiom to a secular one. Indeed, it would concede too much to the normative aspect of the secularization thesis to dispense with historical reconstruction for a strictly systematic approach. This is so because the standard narrative of secularization de facto establishes the default status of secular, 'publicly accessible reason' without doing the hard philosophical work that would otherwise be necessary for establishing such a criterion as normative. This is not to say that Habermas does not go to great lengths to justify his epistemic stance with respect to what reasons count as good reasons. But the cultural acceptance of the standard secularization thesis makes such philosophical legwork almost superfluous within public discourse – the actual public discourse rather than Habermas's ideal speech situation. The narrative as it has been told establishes the priority of secular reasons largely by default. Secular reasons are simply regarded as *prima facie* plausible and any other interpretations of the world that are not purely immanent, naturalistic ones must bear an asymmetrical burden. That is to say, they must work harder to simply pull level with secular reasons in public discourse. Likening public discourse to a game of chess, religious arguments always play as black. Unlike chess, however, the rules of contemporary public discourse make it almost impossible for religious reasons to match their secular counterparts, much less gain an advantage. And in my judgment, the standard subtraction story of secularization is largely responsible for this asymmetrical exchange. The secularization thesis is a story, not a neutral description, and by challenging that story of how we got to where we are, one also challenges the default status of secular reasons in the public sphere; this situation is shown to be contingent

---

[18] Taylor, 22.

upon certain identifiable historical developments rather than purely the result of the deliverances of reason.

Preliminary Objections to Religious Discourse in Public

In what follows, I contend that secularization does not necessarily imply secularism in dealing with religious reasons in the public sphere. But what are religious reasons? One can specify at least two ways of understanding the term that are often conflated: 1) secular reasons that independently support a religious position on an issue or 2) reasons that are themselves based wholly or in part on religious premises. The first category is relatively unproblematic. It is the second that gives many liberal theorists pause.[19] So perhaps we might ask more precisely, would religious reasons in this second sense count as publicly accessible within a pluralistic public sphere? Obviously, in a pluralistic society all members cannot be expected to find the same reasons compelling. This is precisely the problem of consensus and it afflicts secular reasons as surely as it does religious ones. Despite this, secularists often allege that secular reasons are more acceptable to a pluralistic public. Furthermore, they may extend this line of argument by saying that all appeals to religion are politically illegitimate because they appeal to sources of authority that not all citizens recognize. The question of political legitimacy as it is formulated here – as relying explicitly on publicly accessible or secular reasons – begs all the important questions I wish to raise in the remainder of my project. But there is a point to be made here: on the surface, religious reasons lack scope in public debate. The authorities which they credit are often regarded as sacred and thus immune to criticism. At this point, rational argument, opponents say, is a moot point. The religionists have already made up their minds. Habermas too wants to disallow appeals to the sacredness of holy texts and other sources of religious authority. All public claims must admit of critical scrutiny. Dogmatism is not permitted.

I would agree that religious arguments should not be accorded additional respect simply by virtue of being religious. Moreover, all public claims must submit to critical scrutiny and discursive challenge. However, to set the rules of the game such that religious claims can never, simply by virtue of being religious, meet such a burden is to beg the question of rationality. Does secular thinking

---

[19] See for example, John Rawls, *Political Liberalism* (Columbia University Press, 1993).

have a monopoly on rational communication? Why should we uncritically assume that it does? I will delve further into this subject in a subsequent chapter, but first I want to address what kinds of religious arguments I will be primarily defending. I will also deal with some of the epistemic nuances attached to evaluating the rationality of claims, particularly religious ones in a public context.

As mentioned, I am broadly in agreement with Habermas and other liberal theorists who limit, albeit to varying degrees, dogmatic religious claims to the private domain (the important term here is *dogmatic* – claims that do not admit fallibility and are closed to revision in principle). This is the classical liberal compromise forged in the seventeenth century, especially in England, for safeguarding religious tolerance. We will be exploring some aspects of this narrative in what follows and its implications for secularization. For the time being, however, I will concede that stability and peace at that time did require, and perhaps still does, certain concessions by religious citizens. As Nicholas Wolterstorff admits, in seventeenth century England, "social peace did depend on getting citizens to stop invoking God, canonical scriptures, and religious authorities when discussing politics in public – to confine such invocations to discussions within their own confessional circles."[20] However, he doubts that the foundations of constitutional democracy will crumble if religious reasons are readmitted into the debate.[21]

Again, *dogmatic* claims seem *prima facie* incompatible with liberal democracy as a form of government that is perpetually open to revision at the demand of the citizenry. This is not to say that religious citizens cannot exercise their legal right to make dogmatic claims in the public sphere – excepting perhaps within formally public institutions such as parliaments. Rather, such claims, though not disallowed by law, are frowned upon by social convention.[22] Some liberal theorists, such as Rawls, have gone even further and alleged that citizens have an ethical obligation to offer exclusively secular reasons when justifying coercive legislation. Whatever the case, such religious claims achieve

---

[20] Nicholas Wolterstorff, "The Role of Religion in Decision and Discussion of Political Issues," in Robert Audi and Nicholas Wolterstorff, *Religion in the Public Square: The Place of Religious Convictions in Political Debate* (Rowman & Littlefield Publishers, Inc., 1996), 79.
[21] Arguably, in America, they were never fully barred, despite the Jeffersonian tradition of "separation of church and state."
[22] Appeals to religion are in "bad taste." See Richard Rorty, "Religion As Conversation-stopper," in *Philosophy and Social Hope* (Penguin, 2000), 169.

no consensus within a pluralistic society. Thus, expediency alone would seem to require some effort at translation. Indeed, to the extent that I accept Habermas's translation requirement, it is along pragmatic rather than ethical or legal lines.

However, when I admit that dogmatic religious claims cannot practically inform political decision making in pluralistic democracies, do I not eliminate any space for religious reasons in the public sphere? In other words, are all religious reasons dogmatic? Do they all rest on some allegedly sacred foundation and thus brook no dissent or criticism? For practical purposes, they need not. Take, for example, what philosophers frequently refer to as divine command theory. On the basis of purely anecdotal evidence, I think it highly likely that most Christians subscribe to some version of divine command theory, whether they know it or not. In the last resort, if pressed to give an account of their moral convictions, they would likely say that God commands that they act in such and such a way. This is not the place to rehearse all of the familiar philosophical objections to divine command theory summarized by the "Euthyphro dilemma" and the theological disputes over realism versus voluntarism. Moreover, one can be a Christian and reject divine command theory. For my purposes, however, it suffices to ask the question: are such arguments – that appeal to God's alleged commands – dogmatic or sacred in Habermas's sense of being immune from communicative redemption? Not necessarily.

As mentioned, even Christians disagree regarding divine command theory, but this fact alone does not necessarily affect the ethical claims they make in practice. In fact, there may be convergence even among those who disagree, because divine command theory, in philosophical terms, is a meta-ethical theory. Practically, we can agree on a particular set of moral truths without agreeing on what makes them true. Indeed, liberalism depends on the ability of people to come to this kind of practical convergence despite religious or metaphysical differences. Moreover, it is very unusual, in practice, for religious citizens to appeal directly to God's will in making ethical, and by extension, political, judgments. Notwithstanding contemporary 'enthusiasts' who allegedly receive private revelations from on high, the vast majority of religious citizens see their ethical and political decisions as mediated in various ways: through canonical scriptures, church tradition, conscience, moral exemplars, clerical authorities, etc. Not all religionists agree on how to prioritize these various strands and are free to amend or curtail the list as they see fit. In addition, they also disagree as to how 'sacred', or susceptible to criticism, each of these sources is. But to say that a source of ethical guidance is sacred, or emanates from a sacred authority, need not imply that one cannot give independent arguments in its favor. Habermas does not deny this point; in fact the thrust of his translation requirement is to get religious citizens to give reasons. My qualm with Habermas's way of putting the translation requirement has nothing to do with his insistence that we offer reasons for any public claim, rather my disagreement lies with his insistence that religious reasons be translated into a secular language that is presumably accessible to all rational people. I doubt there is such a language, thus the translation requirement strikes me as onerous. Nevertheless, religious persons can surely see the pragmatic value in trying to make their reasons accessible to a *given audience* in a pluralistic society.

Returning to appeals to religious authority, however, in what form, if any, can they inform public debate? Perhaps it is helpful to take a concrete example. Stephen Carter, in the *Culture of Disbelief*, an *apologia* for the inclusion of religion in the American political climate, suggested that a good way to end a conversation is to say that "you hold a political position (preferably a controversial one, such as being against abortion or pornography) because it is required by your understanding of God's will."[23] This admission inspired Rorty to write an essay called "Religion As Conversation-stopper" in which he argues that appeals to religious authority, in Carter's case, God's will, stop conversation. For Rorty, dragging one's private religious views into political debate does no real work. The reasons one offers for one's opposition to abortion or pornography have to be public reasons and he cites Rawls and Habermas in support.[24] While Carter may be right that, in the grand scheme of things, the will of God is relevant to moral decision making, Rorty argues that "moral decisions that are to be enforced by a pluralist and democratic state's monopoly on violence are best made by public discussion in which voices claiming to be God's, or reason's, or science's are put on a par with everybody else's."[25] I certainly agree that voices claiming to be God's should be on par with everybody else's, and equally open to criticism, but that is a far cry from saying that voices that claim to be God's ought to be excluded from the public sphere at the outset, as Rorty alleges,[26] though to

---

[23] Quoted in Rorty, "Religion As Conversation-stopper," 171.
[24] Rorty, 173.
[25] Rorty, 172.
[26] Rorty, 170.

be fair, he has since nuanced his position.[27] My point is simply that denying special privilege to religious claims is not tantamount to excluding them from public deliberation provided they remain open to criticism. In the last resort, their justification may indeed boil down to the will of God and the conversation may end there, although religion by no means has a monopoly on stopping conversation. But as Wolterstorff notes in his engagement with Rorty, there is much one can do between the time the conversation begins and when it ends. Rather than simply state our fundamental convictions, we can look for arguments that our interlocutor might find persuasive. In commenting on Carter's above-cited example, Wolterstorff notes, "I think that Carter has here offered an unusually flat-footed example of a religious argument for a political position. The speeches of Martin Luther King, Jr., were suffused with religion; I would be surprised if he ever said anything quite so flat-footed as that integration was required by his understanding of God's will, period – though in the last resort, that was his view."[28] Regarding the political efficacy of nuanced religious language, he observes, "Not all who heard King's 'I Have a Dream' speech shared his religion; those who did not, made allowances. They were moved and inspired along with everyone else."[29] I will have more to say about the accessibility and rhetorical power of religious language in a subsequent chapter, but suffice it to say that religious language need not be dogmatic nor exclude those who do not subscribe to the speaker's theological convictions; a point Habermas is increasingly recognizing.

In a poignant example of how the 'semantic potential' still latent in religious language might be realized, he takes up the issue of genetic engineering.[30] Religionists who have qualms about experimenting on human embryos often speak of them as bearing 'the image of God'. Habermas, a secularist, recognizes that one need not accept the theological underpinnings of the claim to grasp its point: that the first human to genetically reprogram another human being without consent would violate the inherent equality and autonomy of all human beings. Although offering a translation of sorts, he is

---

[27] Rorty, "Religion in the Public Sphere: A Reconsideration," *Journal of Religious Ethics*, 31.1 (2003): 141-49.
[28] Nicholas Wolterstorff, "An Engagement with Rorty," *Journal of Religious Ethics*, 31.1 (2003): 132.
[29] Wolterstorff, 135.
[30] Habermas, "Faith and Knowledge," in *The Frankfurt School on Religion: Key Writings by the Major Thinkers*, ed. Eduardo Mendieta (Routledge, 2005), 336.

careful to say that the power of the religious way of speaking is not lost on him, or even on those who might otherwise be tone-deaf to religious arguments. Thus, I do not think that all religious arguments are dogmatic in the sense of being insulated from criticism or necessarily inaccessible to a pluralistic polity.

But there is another argument for the exclusion of religious arguments from the public sphere, namely, that public claims must meet a higher evidentiary burden than private claims. Because political decisions, especially those that restrict liberty and involve the coercive power of the state, impact citizens, we owe them good reasons for why we hold the particular positions or support the policies that we do. These reasons have to be reasons that any rational person would accept independently of whatever comprehensive doctrines, to use Rawls's term, they might hold. Religious beliefs are comprehensive doctrines which not all rational people accept precisely because such beliefs fail to meet the evidentiary burden that public claims must meet, i.e., ideal rational acceptability. Of course, a claim that all rational people would accept is an ideal type; rational people frequently disagree about many things and there are very few arguments that rationally compel consent. In other words, the ideal is never, to my knowledge, instantiated in working political discussion. Be that as it may, one might still think that religious beliefs, since they are based on faith and are thus highly uncertain, make bad public reasons. This line of thinking in the liberal tradition goes back at least as far as Locke and is a species of the 'ethics of belief', although in the case of contemporary liberals, such as Rawls, the ethics of belief is modified. People are entitled to believe whatever they like within the private domain, but they have an ethical obligation to refrain from appealing to the whole truth as they see it when they enter the public domain. They must, in effect, suspend judgment on their religious beliefs. We might call this view the 'public ethics of belief'. Habermas has also spoken of public agnosticism as the default position for political debate, but has since changed his view. Nevertheless, an ethics of belief of the type outlined above is problematic.

Although 'faith' is part of any religious orientation to the world, it would be mistaken to say that it is the only available means by which to understand religious arguments, particularly those that might have public import. As Stout reminds us:

> [A] claim can be religious without being a faith-claim. It is possible to assert a premise that is religious in content and stand ready to demonstrate one's entitlement to it. Many people are prepared to argue at great length in support of their religious claims. So we must distinguish between discursive problems that arise because religious premises are not widely shared and those that arise because the people who avow such premises are not prepared to argue for them.[31]

Although some or perhaps many religious people are unprepared to argue for their premises, it does not follow that it cannot be done. There is, in my judgment, a middle ground between unqualified fideism on the one hand and modern epistemic foundationalism or 'ethics of belief' on the other. Nevertheless, one must be careful not to capitulate to modernity's flat understanding of 'faith' as a species of unjustified belief. One might instead argue that one is rationally justified in believing something without meeting the kind of evidentiary burden mandated by modern foundationalism. The view that there is an indubitable starting point from which to engage one's interlocutor and an infallible method which will lead everyone ineluctably along to a conclusion which is universally acceptable has fallen on hard times and for good reason. It is not only 'relativists' like Rorty who acknowledge "the vacuity of epistemological foundationalism."[32] Christian philosophers like Wolterstorff have also offered critiques of foundationalism. Reformed epistemology, to which he is a major contributor, argues that one is rationally justified in believing in God, for example, without necessarily offering valid arguments (although one may have them) for that belief. It is beyond the scope of this treatment to fully defend this claim, but suffice it to say that if one rejects foundationalism, there may be at least some religious beliefs that believers are entitled to have. In other words, belief need not bear a heavier burden in public discourse than unbelief. That Reformed epistemology has implications for one's assessment of the legitimacy of religious arguments in public is clear from Wolterstorff's writings on the subject. Of course, one is not epistemically entitled to any and all religious beliefs, especially those that qualify as dogmatic on our above definition. But if at least some religious beliefs are beliefs people are rationally entitled to have, it becomes difficult to impose a presumption regarding what all rational people

---

[31] Stout, 87.
[32] Rorty, 144.

would assent to for political discourse which, in the case of Rawls, not coincidentally resembles a secularist conception of religion – according to which religious beliefs that are, at best, held in tension with beliefs that a rational person would be entitled to hold.

Again, we see an implicit 'ethics of belief' at play in Rawls's position. But the problem with such an ethics of belief is that what one sincerely believes is rarely something one can switch on and off; it is not like behavior, which one can (usually) refrain from doing if one judges it unethical. One cannot simply divest oneself of beliefs at will. And if one cannot be expected to do so, it would seem that any ethics of belief violates the principle that 'ought implies can'. To put the point another way, many people find belief in God to be what we might call primitively compelling. In other words, it is difficult not to believe in God. Taylor has argued recently that our intellectual milieu in the West has made it more difficult to find belief in God primitively compelling; rather it is now one option among many, albeit a live option in Taylor's view.[33] Nevertheless, I take it to be the case that there are many people who find belief in God compelling in the way that we all find belief in other minds to be compelling; we cannot help but believe it, despite the absence of an iron-clad argument. I suppose a defender of an ethics of belief, call him Cliff, would say that religious people have a duty to investigate even those claims that they find primitively compelling. They should perhaps take a philosophy course, acquire a healthy dose of skepticism, and then reexamine their belief to see whether it is still primitively compelling. Of course, there are philosophically sophisticated religious people who persist in finding their belief compelling, although academia is often offered as an antidote for a religious sensibility. Nevertheless, I might retort that Cliff has a corresponding duty to place himself in an environment in which he might find belief in God primitively compelling, the way one might advise the tone-deaf individual to at least try and acquire an appreciation of music. Indeed, Taylor counsels the non-religious to try to inhabit a space in which they can at least consider belief a live option.[34] The religiously unmusical, however, seldom acknowledge their simple, usually unreflective, rejection of religiosity. Again, belief is not simply a matter of the will. William James, in his response to W.K. Clifford, was unfortunately misunderstood on this point. The 'will to believe' in that famous essay of the

---

[33] Taylor, 3.
[34] Taylor, 551.

same name, might have been better rendered the 'right to believe'. Persons, for whom religious belief is a live option, are entitled to believe.

But, Cliff might reply, although a religious person may be entitled to believe something privately, when one steps into the public domain in a pluralistic democracy, one has a duty to present one's arguments and justify one's political decisions on the basis of secular reason. This is roughly the line that Rawls takes and some have alleged Habermas too, although in my judgment he differs in important respects. Rorty also falls in line with Rawls and Habermas and even attempts to recruit James to his side. In Rorty's reading of "The Will to Believe," James is actually saying "we have a right to believe what we like when we are, so to speak, on our own time. But we abandon this right when we are engaged, for example, in a scientific or political project."[35] But, if religious citizens are entitled to their beliefs, and if they are unable to simply switch them off, why should we insist that they divest themselves of their beliefs in public? As we shall see, Habermas has recently taken this question very seriously. Some have argued, such as Robert Audi, that religious citizens can keep their religious beliefs in public but must, in addition, offer at least one secular reason for their position on a policy or law if it enjoins the coercive power of the state to restrict individual liberty.[36] Most religious citizens (although not all) have the capacity to offer at least one secular reason for their position on a given issue and understand the pragmatic value in doing so. Whether one can obligate them to do so, however, is another question, which I will deal with below. But the difficulty with Audi's seemingly generous proposal is that the religious citizen cannot offer just any secular reason whatsoever, but she must offer a reason that she finds motivationally sufficient apart from any additional religious reasons she might also have. This requirement is quite different from adopting a secular argument for practical purposes. For example, on the abortion issue, I might argue on utilitarian grounds that late-term abortion is wrong because the fetus has a fully developed nervous system, and is thus sentient, and has, if not rights, at least an interest in avoiding pain and staying alive. It would therefore be wrong to kill it. But I am unsure whether or not I would find this argument compelling, or motivationally sufficient, in the absence of other beliefs I hold about the sanctity of life that stem at least in part from my religious tradition. It

---

[35] Rorty, "Pragmatism as Romantic Polytheism," in *Pragmatism and Religion*, ed. Stuart Rosenbaum (University of Illinois Press, 2003), 120 – 21.
[36] Robert Audi, "Liberal Democracy and the Place of Religion in Politics," in *Religion in the Public Square*, 25.

seems impossible to discount the influence of religious beliefs when evaluating the motivational sufficiency of secular arguments for religious persons. Indeed, this is why secularists often suspect that when religious persons offer secular arguments in public, they do so to obfuscate their 'real' reasons. Far better, in my view, to be up front about what one's real reasons are and then work pragmatically from there, rather than place undue restrictions on what religious persons may be permitted to say. As for the issue of state coercion that Audi raises and the danger of it being utilized to enforce a majority religious view, I would suggest that at the level of official public institutions, laws and policies be stated in neutral language. But this is not to say, as Habermas does, that religious language must be kept out of political institutions and debate altogether; only that, after the ensuing debate, the neutrality of language is maintained in the laws as drafted.

The preceding section has served as prolegomena for many of the issues that will be taken up in greater detail in what follows. As such, the argument at this stage is still incomplete. Although I argue that secularization does not necessarily imply secularism when dealing with religious voices in the public sphere, I acknowledge that historically and contemporaneously, religious voices have posed a challenge to liberalism. The liberal state has had to find ways to maximize freedom within the boundaries of law that can be fully justified to a pluralistic polity, at least ideally. In practice, religion has usually played a significant role in shaping the constitutions and laws of existing liberal democracies, religious freedom being one the chief values liberalism has sought to secure since its inception. But in order to do so, it was thought necessary, as early as the seventeenth century, to strike a compromise between religious liberty and social cohesion. This process, which involved the privatization of religion, is part of secularization, and the narrative itself provides practical justification for suspicion of religion in the public sphere and the liberal insistence on 'public reason'. In what follows, I want to review the narrative and offer some critical commentary that might warrant some modification to our conception of secularization and 'public reason'. In what follows, I will make the case that these terms are best understood within modernity as pragmatic responses to religious pluralism, rather than responses to widespread decline in religious belief and practice.

Secularization and the Public Sphere: A Historical Excursus

So how are we to assess the processes of secularization in the seventeenth and eighteenth centuries? Ironically, as we shall see, those who are generally thought to be the progenitors of secularization did not necessarily understand the process to which they were contributing in the way that many contemporary commentators do, that is to say, along the lines of a subtraction story. In fact, the vocabulary of secularism as denoting an alternative to religion – as opposed to 'secular' in the largely neutral sense of 'temporal' – is of nineteenth century coinage. According to Michael J. Buckley, George Jacob Holyoake coined the term 'secularist' at the end of the nineteenth century to denote one who is without belief in any god but not without morality.[37] The charge of atheism was certainly bandied about liberally, especially during the seventeenth century, but this term was not used with any precision; it frequently functioned polemically.[38] It is true, however, that the seeds of secularism as a mass phenomenon were planted during the eighteenth century among elites. It took roughly another century for conditions of secularism to permeate European culture more thoroughly, yielding conditions of secularity "which takes us from a society in which it was virtually impossible not to believe in God, to one in which faith, even for the staunchest believer, is one human possibility among others."[39] The abandonment of belief in God on a large scale, however, is only one aspect of the processes of secularization, though by no means an insignificant one. It contributes to the aspect of secularization on which I focus, namely, the transformation of religion from a publicly significant phenomenon to an increasingly marginalized one. Habermas argues that any religion is a worldview or comprehensive doctrine that does not conform to the criterion of publicly accessible reason. As mentioned, my project hopes to complicate what such a criterion actually means for political praxis. One way of doing so, is to show that no general account of such a criterion, much less one as stringent as Habermas's, emerges from the Enlightenment in which the secular public sphere arguably emerges as a novel cultural phenomenon.

Although the seeds of mass secularization were planted much earlier than the eighteenth century, the Enlightenment is generally credited, at the very

---

[37] Michael J. Buckley, *At the Origins of Modern Atheism* (New Haven, CT: Yale University Press, 1987), 10.
[38] Buckley, 27.
[39] Taylor, 3.

least, with expediting the process. The Enlightenment, however, is not itself a secular age. As Buckley observes, "[i]t would be false to tax the Enlightenment with indifference to religion. It would be more discerning to say that it was obsessed with it."[40] Indeed, indifference to religion is largely incompatible with any self-understanding of secularism. As Taylor explains:

> Unbelief for great numbers of contemporary unbelievers, is understood as an achievement of rationality. It cannot have this without a continuing historical awareness. It is a condition which can't only be described in the present tense, but which also needs the perfect tense: a condition of "having overcome" the irrationality of belief. It is this perfect-tensed consciousness which underlies unbelievers' use of 'disenchantment' today. It is difficult to imagine a world in which this consciousness might have disappeared.[41]

Following Max Weber, 'disenchantment' means "that there are in principle no *mysterious, incalculable powers at work*, but rather that one could in principle master everything through *calculation*."[42] The disenchantment of the world as a key component of secularization is, for Taylor, only one aspect of the processes of secularization, and its explanatory power has been overstated within various versions of the subtraction story. Although it may not be possible to understand secularization without some account of disenchantment, it is certainly possible to view it as one factor among many, and perhaps not even the most decisive one. As we shall see, we might better understand secularization as a pragmatic response to religious pluralism, rather than a response to a world cleansed of the supernatural. The contested nature of religion, manifested by pluralism, necessitated a criterion other than religion in order to broker consensus. Thus secularization – the process of finding discursive grounds for agreement – should not necessarily be identified with secularism, which takes the 'disenchantment' of the world as simply a given. However, even if we give disenchantment a greater role in our account of secularization, it does not follow that disenchantment is accomplished from 'outside' as it were. For Taylor and

---

[40] Buckley, 37.
[41] Taylor, 269.
[42] Max Weber, "Science as a Vocation," in *Max Weber's 'science as a vocation'* ed. Peter Lassman, Irving Velody, and Herminio Martins (Routledge, 1989), 13.

Buckley, it is less a product of scientific rationality and more a consequence of Christianity's own 'self-alienation'[43] or 'excarnation'.[44] In Buckley's estimation, Christian theologians, such as Leonard Lessius (1554 – 1623), made a fateful move when they suggested that the Christian faith could justify itself on the basis of natural reason alone. It is then a short step from the sufficiency of reason to the deism and then atheism of the modern period. The Enlightenment, in moving away from confessional religion, often expanded upon elements already nascent within Christianity thereby setting a trajectory for secularization. Although it is beyond the scope of this project to delve into the many Christian precedents of modern unbelief – here I recommend Buckley's fine study – I believe that the unintended consequences of religious modes of thinking have more to do with secularization than the disenchantment theory of secularization usually appreciates. This will be apparent in many of the modern thinkers taken up below.

In another more concrete sense, Christianity was also the instrument of its own alienation from the modern public sphere. I refer principally to the infamous wars of religion. Buckley ably summarizes:

> Catholics and dissenters were hunted out of England; France revoked the Edict of Nantes and expelled thousands of Huguenots into the Dutch Republic; heretics were burned by the Spanish Inquisition and witches in the German principalities, the United Kingdom, and the early American religious colony of Massachusetts. Each major nation could tell of its slaughters in the wars of religions whose hatred had turned great portions of the earlier centuries into horror for Germany and France and the Netherlands. As the Enlightenment developed, first in England, then in France and Germany, and finally in the British colonies, the Western conscience found itself deeply scandalized and disgusted by confessional religions …. Religious warfare had irrevocably discredited confessional primacy in the growing secularized sensitivity of much of European culture.[45]

---

[43] Buckley, 341.
[44] Taylor, 554.
[45] Buckley, 39.

For this reason, among others, the progenitors of the Enlightenment taken up below decried religious fanaticism and enthusiasm and called for "a simpler, doctrinally less elaborated religion, and one more accessible to reason."[46] Accompanying the loss of credibility by confessional religion was the need to replace it with something else. If consensus could no longer be secured by a common religious confession, it would have to be accomplished by an appeal to public opinion. The phenomenon of public opinion acting as a legitimate political arbiter depended upon the newly emerging public sphere, facilitated by print, which effectively extended the franchise of the 'republic of letters' from elite circles to the emergent bourgeois class. This phenomenon, the rise of the public sphere as a novelty within modernity, is the subject of Habermas's *Structural Transformation*. He reads the emergence of the public sphere in the eighteenth century as bringing about a fundamental shift from confessional public self-understanding – which does not admit of communicative redemption – to a communicative public based on discursive reason. But importantly, public opinion is not an unambiguous, unequivocal conception during this period. Moreover, its limitations as a means of building rational consensus were recognized by those, like Locke, who advocated it.

Habermas on the Rise of the Public Sphere in England

David Zaret suggests that "the liberal model of the political public sphere can best be described as a historical accretion of print culture, lay bible reading, actuarial calculations, experimental science, and capitalist enterprise."[47] As succinct descriptions go, this one is quite accurate. In Zaret's estimation, as well as Habermas's, England in the seventeenth and eighteenth centuries serves as the model for this convergence of factors. Craig Calhoun agrees:

> Britain serves Habermas as the model case of the development of the public sphere. It was there, for example, that the elimination of the institution of censorship first marked a new stage in the development of public discourse. The free provision of information was, alongside

---

[46] Taylor, 224.
[47] David Zaret, "Religion, Science and Printing in the Public Spheres in Seventeenth-Century England" in *Habermas and the Public Sphere*, 230.

education, crucial to putting the public sphere in a position to arrive at a considered, rather than merely a common, opinion.[48]

The elimination of censorship in England with the Licensing Act of 1695 is difficult to overestimate as an impetus for the rise of the public sphere. The demise of censorship allowed the British press to enjoy unique liberties compared to the rest of Europe. Habermas also cites the appointment of the first cabinet government as a major achievement of representative democracy. The public sphere was greatly facilitated by the parliamentary system in which perennial debate between the government and the opposition became the model for political discourse in the public sphere. In the English case, the importance of critical reason serving as the arbiter in political matters emerged as the aristocratic conception of Parliament evolved into one in which the opinion of the citizenry had a legitimate place. As Habermas summarizes: "Until then political opposition had been possible only as the attempt to push one's interests by resorting to violence .... Now through the critical debate of the public, it took the form of a permanent controversy between the governing party and the opposition."[49]

Furthermore, one might suggest another reason for focusing this analysis on England. In addition to the elements enumerated above, this rise of the public sphere was also nurtured by a number of intellectual developments, notably the political theory that flows out of British empiricism. And while the Kantian architecture of Habermas's conception of public reason is so well established in the literature that it is routinely taken for granted, his indebtedness to the British liberal tradition from Locke through Mill is underdeveloped. By focusing upon what he draws from the British tradition in political philosophy, I hope to supplement this lack in Habermas scholarship. In addition to uncovering some previously underappreciated connections between Habermas and the English political tradition, this strategy enables me to place the Continental and Anglo-American traditions into conversation with each other. Ideally, such conversation will, in a modest way, make Habermas more accessible to an

---

[48] Craig Calhoun, "Introduction: Habermas and the Public Sphere," in *Habermas and the Public Sphere*, 14.
[49] Jürgen Habermas, *The Structural Transformation of the Public Sphere: An Inquiry into a Category of Bourgeois Society,* trans. Thomas Burger and Frederick Lawrence (Cambridge, MA: MIT Press, 1991), 64.

Anglophone audience. In my judgment, the challenges confronting democracy in the United States and Canada, which trace their political lineage to Britain, could greatly benefit from Habermasian insights. Anglo-American political philosophy has been unduly influenced by Rawls, in my judgment, and although he and Habermas are often mentioned in the same breath as though their positions are interchangeable, Habermas, especially recently, has sufficiently differentiated himself from a Rawlsian stance that he can provide a fresh perspective on the North American political landscape. This is crucial, because those moderate religionists who feel marginalized from public discourse need to hear a sympathetic secular alternative to the false dilemma of Rawlsian liberalism and the new traditionalism.[50]

Returning to our narrative, Habermas credits Locke with liberating the conception of opinion "from its polemically devalued association with pure prejudice."[51] Locke placed the "'Law of Opinion' as a category of equal rank beside divine and state law."[52] In so doing, Locke cleansed 'opinion' of its association with vulgarity.[53] In contrast with Rousseau, Locke viewed legislation "to be the result not of a political will, but of rational agreement."[54] According to Habermas, "*Public debate was supposed to transform voluntas into a ratio that in the public competition of private arguments came into being as the consensus about what was practically necessary in the private interests of all.*"[55] Such a perspective resonates with Habermas's later theory of communicative action which sets out criteria for formal argumentation with the aim of building consensus. Locke's epistemological fallibilism, for example, is also concerned

---

50   This is Stout's term for the movement represented by thinkers such as Hauerwas, MacIntyre, and Milbank. See *Democracy and Tradition*, 11.
51   Habermas, 92.
52   Habermas, 91.
53   It retained this connotation in France. Pierre Bayle, for example, differentiated between 'opinion' and 'critique'. The Encyclopedists adopted the polemical connotations of 'opinion' identifying it with "a mental condition of uncertainty and vacuousness" (Habermas, 92). As such, 'opinion' in the French case – even given Rousseau's adoption of the term – never enjoyed the same public authority or recognition it did in England following Locke. Indeed, Habermas contrasts Locke and Rousseau on their respective valuations of opinion. Rousseau does not rehabilitate the term, but simply takes a position against the Encyclopedists that preserves its polemical charge. Rousseau's public opinion, associated with the general will, "was more a consensus of hearts and minds than of arguments" (98).
54   Habermas, 82.
55   Habermas, 83, italics in original.

with determining what claims count as good reasons in public debate. As mentioned briefly, Locke is generally interpreted as saying that religious beliefs, due to their high degree of uncertainty, do not make good public reasons. In other words, we should proportion the publicity of our claims to the degree of certainty they enjoy. Indeed, recent scholarship has situated Locke within the ethics of belief tradition.[56]

Thus, Locke's conception of the "Law of Opinion" encouraged the devaluation of religion in public discourse. In Locke's *A Letter Concerning Toleration*, for example, the exercise of reason is seen to be a more promising avenue to the resolution of public differences than appeal to religion. Although Locke is often pigeon-holed as an empiricist, his rationalist methodology in the *Letter* is quite clear. Patrick Romanell states: "Like a typical rationalist of the seventeenth century, he uses throughout the *Letter* the deductive method of drawing conclusions from definitions and axioms."[57] Moreover, the definitions Locke offers are not simply empirical ones, reflecting their ordinary use in the culture of his time. Rather, Locke is offering normative definitions. As Jay Newman explains: "Locke does not pretend that he is simply reporting to us how people ordinarily use such terms as *commonwealth* and *church*, nor does he pretend that he is merely reporting how most people conceive of the proper spheres of political and religious authority."[58] As such, Locke is self-consciously attempting to change the way religious authority is exercised in the public sphere, replacing it with appeals to publicly accessible reason, asserting that "to this crying up faith in opposition to reason, we may, I think, in good measure ascribe those absurdities that fill almost all the religions which possess and divide mankind."[59]

It is not only in the *Letter*, however, that Locke gives priority to reason. Recent scholarship on the *Essay* also gives us reason to reevaluate Locke's contribution to epistemology. In Nicholas Wolterstorff's estimation, the traditional interpretation of the *Essay*, which places emphasis on Book II, must be rejected. Rather, the focal point, according to Locke himself, is Book IV. As

---

[56] Nicholas Wolterstorff, *John Locke and the Ethics of Belief* (Cambridge University Press, 1996).
[57] Patrick Romanell, introduction to *A Letter Concerning Toleration* by John Locke (New Jersey: Prentice Hall, 1950), 8.
[58] Jay Newman, *On Religious Freedom* (Ottawa: University of Ottawa Press, 1991), 118.
[59] Quoted in Zaret, 225.

Wolterstorff maintains, "[w]hen Book IV is given its due and intended weight, it becomes clear that Locke is one of the great rationalists of the Western tradition."[60] Only such a rationalist methodology could overcome the great crisis of uncertainty generated by the collapse of traditional sources of authority. Reason, then, must be the arbiter of which opinions we hold.[61] And, again, we should proportion the firmness of our beliefs to the weight of evidence.[62] Such a principle was certainly intended to exclude the religious enthusiasts of Locke's day from public influence. The solution to the intramural wars of religion, for Locke, was to conduct one's opinion or belief forming activities – or to use Wolterstorff's term, "doxastic practices" – critically and cautiously.[63] From this it follows that a vibrant public debate, conducted on the basis of sound doxastic practices, is essential for the maintenance of the civil order. If we abandon such an ethics of belief, we are left with the conflicting, uncertain opinions of enthusiasts who do not proportion their beliefs to the evidence or fanatics who threaten to upset the civil order. Such an ethics of belief led to the galvanization of public opinion as the result of rational-critical processes and further facilitated the increasing marginalization of religious rationales which in turn helped to enshrine secular reasoning as public knowledge.

Of course, the way had been prepared for this stance by developments within religion itself. Habermas argues that the Reformation, in identifying opinion and conscience, had paved the way for the role opinion would later play in the public sphere. Both conscience and opinion were considered to be accessible to the lay person, and thus constituted a common basis for faith. But the model of consensus within Protestant Christianity differed from the liberal model of the public sphere. Michael Warner states: "Its (religion's) model of the public sphere presupposed an ideal of determinate truth and collective agreement. But the usual means of brokering such a consensus were already strained in the period of the Glorious Revolution. And by the 1730s and 1740s they suffered considerable erosion in the face of the Great Awakening."[64] The

---

60   Wolterstorff, xv.
61   See also Chapter 1 of Ronald A. Kuipers, *Critical Faith: Toward a Renewed Understanding of Religious Life and its Public Accountability* (Rodopi, 2002).
62   Wolterstorff states the "principle of proportionality" as follows: "Adopt a level of confidence in the proposition which is proportioned to its probability on one's satisfactory evidence," 79.
63   Wolterstorff, xvii. He borrows the term from William Alston.
64   Michael Warner, *The Letters of the Republic: Publication and the Public Sphere in Eighteenth-Century America* (Harvard University Press, 1992), 56 -- 57.

problem for religion, as Warner diagnoses it, was that formerly professional issues among clergy now became publicly debatable. This anti-clericalism undermined the authority of religion in the public sphere. The impact of this shift may have affected the British colonies in America more rapidly than the mother country. To quote Warner once again: "No matter how much religious contention the colonists experienced during the Awakening, religion continued to pull against the normalization of social division, eventually requiring a separation of church and state that would mark a key victory for the cultural forces of the public sphere."[65]

But to whatever extent the revival of Protestant Christianity created space for convicted opinion to trump authority in religious matters, so-called Natural Religion in England played a much greater role. Natural Religion removed the limits that traditional Protestantism placed on the exercise of reason, namely the idea that fallen reason had to be corrected by revelation. According to proponents of Natural Religion, there were no such limits on the free exercise of reason. On the contrary, "[t]here could be nothing in religion that was not compatible with reason – so argued leading members of the Royal Society, the Latitudinarian Churchmen, and the Cambridge neo-Platonists. So did the Whig ideologues, such as Locke, Shaftesbury, and Sidney, who had complex ties to the scholars and scientists."[66] Indeed, Locke was greatly indebted to the Latitudinarian Churchmen, such as William Chillingworth, John Tillotson, Thomas Sprat and fellow members of the Royal Society, John Wilkins and Joseph Glanville; he owed much of his theory of limited certainty to these predecessors, many of whom were moderate Anglican theologians and key proponents of Natural Religion.

In 1649, Wilkins, warden of Wadham College, Oxford, created a group called the Invisible College, which would evolve into the Royal Society in 1662. This group consisted of such luminaries as Robert Boyle and Christopher Wren and others who were interested in the relationship between the new science and religion. Wilkins most important work, *Of the Principles and Duties of Natural Religion* (1675), sought to provide "a basis for reasonable religion, science, and law."[67] The ideas contained in this work, published posthumously, would be

---

65 Warner, 58.
66 Zaret, 225.
67 Richard H. Popkin, *The History of Scepticism: From Savonarola to Bayle*, Rev. Exp. (Oxford University Press, USA, 2003), 209.

popularized by Glanville, to whom Richard Popkin refers as "a propagandist for the Royal Society."[68] Locke's principle of proportionality – that we must proportion the firmness of our belief to the degree of probability based on the available evidence – is certainly indebted to Wilkins and Glanville. As Wolterstorff notes:

> The Royal Society group.... argued that since assent to the content of revealed religion did not and could not have the highest degree of truth-likelihood – at best it could have 'moral certainty' – we ought to hold such assent with an appropriately tempered firmness. Such tempered firmness, they insisted, is quite sufficient for religious life; and it would stimulate such social virtues as love and toleration, thereby promoting social peace.[69]

The differentiation of moral certainty from the indubitable certainty furnished by the sciences further marginalized religious arguments from the public sphere.[70] However, in order to do justice to the complex narrative of the rise of the public sphere, we require more than an account of the marginalization of religion. In Taylor's words, we need more than a "subtraction story." We need to add to our story the success of experimental science to fully explain the enthusiasm concerning the public exercise of reason to build consensus. The well-publicized successes of experimental science produced confidence that critical debate, such as that modeled by the Royal Society, could be extended to political and religious debate. The scientific community, then as now, served as the model of an idealized discourse which produced consensus due to the community's adherence to the dictates of reason and evidence. The knowledge that came out of the Royal Society, for example, was more than mere conviction or opinion; according to Thomas Sprat (1635 – 1713), a clerical supporter of the Royal Society, it was "public knowledge."[71] As Taylor points out, Restoration theologians, such as Sprat and Tillotson frequently appealed to reason, resulting in a less theologically elaborate conception of religion, stripped of many of the superfluous doctrines of the enthusiasts. In conjunction with this development,

---

[68] Popkin, 209.
[69] Wolterstorff, 82.
[70] See also Henry G. Van Leeuwen, *The Problem of Certainty in English Thought 1630-1690* (Springer, 1970).
[71] Zaret, 228.

these clerics understood the exercise of public reason, as modeled by the new science, as an effective tool to rebut the spurious claims of religious fanatics and enthusiasts of both Protestant and Catholic persuasions. Thus, the Anglican establishment thought the deliverances of the sciences to be compatible with so-called Natural Religion. Sprat, for instance, argued that those who put their trust in "implicit faith and enthusiasm" should fear scientific progress, but "our church .... can never be prejudiced in the light of reason, not by the improvements of knowledge, or the works of men's hands."[72] Here we see the ideal of knowledge that is accessible in principle to everyone and that should carry more weight in the open forum of political debate than appeals to conscience or faith. The impulse toward a doctrinally unelaborated religion eventually manifested itself in works of a more explicitly deistic orientation, such as John Toland's *Christianity Not Mysterious* (1696) and Matthew Tindal's *Christianity as Old as the Creation* (1730).[73] Although most members of the Royal Society, such as Glanville and Boyle, and their clerical allies, would not carry the argument this far, their emphasis on reason as a hedge against enthusiasm and fanaticism laid the groundwork for the theological minimalism seen in what Taylor calls "Providential Deism" and eventually, "exclusive humanism."

The accretion of these historical factors produced a respect for rational debate and, among parliamentarians, respect for the considered opinion of the public. The public sphere became an independent check on the governing power. In the context of representative government and social contract theory, the public sphere became an important venue for political discussion. The government needed the continual consent of the governed; the social contract was seen, in effect, as always open to review at the demand of the citizenry. Again, the parliamentary paradigm of government and opposition served as the model for debate in the informal public sphere.

It is instructive to note, as Habermas points out, to what extent the legitimacy of "public opinion" was largely created, not by liberal philosophers, but by Tory opposition under Henry St. John Bolingbroke in the first decades of the eighteenth century. Since the sympathies of the major newspapers were with the Whigs, it became politically necessary for the opposition to publish journals and pamphlets, such as the *Craftsman* and the *Gentleman's Magazine*. Bolingbroke's innovation did more than simply tap into latent public sentiments:

---

[72] Quoted in Taylor, 226.
[73] Buckley, 38.

it established public opinion as a legitimating force recognized by the government. Bolingbroke used the term "public spirit" to denote the opinions of the public which held the government to account. This term did not yet embody the ideal public sphere which Habermas alleges emerged in the eighteenth century, but it was certainly a forerunner. Habermas says that in Bolingbroke's notion of public spirit "a piece of anticipated Rousseauism was strangely fused with the principles of public criticism. Both were still united in the 'public spirit'; the direct, undistorted sense for what was right and just and the articulation of 'opinion' into 'judgment' through the public clash of arguments."[74] Habermas, following convention, treats Edmund Burke as the major conservative philosopher of the time although unlike Bolingbroke, Burke served Parliament as a Whig.[75] He clarified and refined the notion of "general opinion" as he called it, which would evolve into "public opinion." Habermas explains that for Burke, "The opinion of the public that puts its reason to use was no longer just opinion; it did not arise from mere inclination but from private reflection upon public affairs and from their public discussion."[76] The sovereignty of the state depended upon the considered opinion of the public. For Burke, "Only publicity inside and outside the parliament could secure the continuity of critical political debate and its function, to transform domination, as Burke expressed it, from a matter of will into a matter of reason."[77] Thus, by the end of the eighteenth century one finds Burke arguing that all citizens in a free country have a legitimate interest in public matters. These sentiments exerted considerable force until the importance of public opinion was formally introduced in Parliament in 1792 by Charles Fox, a Whig member, who claimed that "it is certainly right and prudent to consult the public opinion."[78] This represented a significant departure from earlier conceptions of government, and the transformation of public opinion from a place of vulgarity to one of esteem happened gradually. But, as Habermas explains:

---

[74]　　Habermas, 93 – 94.
[75]　　Burke's relationship to Bolingbroke is quite a bit more complicated than Habermas's account suggests. Burke wrote his *Vindication of Natural Society* in parody of Bolingbroke shortly after the latter's death. Burke was not a Tory, even after falling out with leading members of the Whig party, including Charles Fox, over his views on the French Revolution.
[76]　　Habermas, 94.
[77]　　Habermas, 100.
[78]　　Quoted in Habermas, 65.

> [B]y the turn of the nineteenth century, the public's involvement in the critical debate of political issues had become organized to such an extent that in the role of a permanent critical commentator it had definitively broken the exclusiveness of Parliament and evolved into the officially designated discussion partner of the delegate. Fox's speeches were made with the public in mind; "they," the subjects of public opinion, were no longer treated as people whom, like "strangers," one could exclude from the deliberations. Step by step the absolutism of Parliament had to retreat before their sovereignty.[79]

Thus, in the English case the transformation of the public sphere into an extra-political, independent, constant check on the accountability and legitimacy of the government simply confirmed the importance of critical debate and publicly accessible reason to the exercise of democracy. This atmosphere of increased public debate was indebted to the 'republic of letters' that had been created in both England and on the Continent. Now, the discussion of the savants was effectively extended to the general reading public through the proliferation of print media.

At this juncture, an important feature of the public sphere emerges: its meta-topicality. Of course, issues had been debated in coffee houses, salons, and the more formally public space of Parliament, but in the eighteenth century the discourse became more abstract. Through print media it became possible to participate in a larger discourse, not limited to the common spaces mentioned above. Taylor calls this non-local common space "meta-topical."[80] Warner calls it a "meta-discourse."[81] Both terms convey the novelty of the public sphere in the modern period. Although it is true, as Taylor notes, that the Church had existed as a meta-topical space in previous centuries, the novelty of modern meta-topicality lies in the separation of the public sphere from power, or the separation of state and society in Habermasian terms. It therefore allows the public sphere to speak to power as an independent observer: the ideal of freedom and impartiality of the press is central here. Moreover, the voices within the public sphere are often anonymous. Warner takes up both of these features in some detail. For example, the *Spectator* in England embodied the

---

[79] Habermas, 66.
[80] Taylor, 187.
[81] Warner, 65.

abstraction of the public discourse. Addison and Steele often used the fictional literary character, called the "Spectator," to convey ironic detachment from the events they commented upon. In the modern public sphere, a self-conscious effort is made at "a certain impersonality, a certain impartiality, and eschewing of party spirit."[82] This aspect of the public sphere, an abstract discussion among impartial citizens linked by print, is unique to the modern secular public sphere. It is meta-topical in that it transcends local spaces in which discussion of this kind occurred previously. It is also a meta-discourse in that it transcends the 'official' political discourse and hopefully keeps it honest. It is outside the political, properly speaking. As mentioned, it keeps power in check. Again, this is not new in and of itself. Rather, its novelty comes from the means by which power is regulated and by whom it is regulated. Prior to the public sphere, power was allegedly kept in check by the will of God or the Church or natural law. However, in the modern period the people themselves are the ones who hold the rulers to account. Moreover, they do so, not through an appeal to the will of God or natural law, but via an appeal to reason. This formally secular dimension of the public sphere is what differentiates it from earlier meta-topical spaces, like the Church. And it is this secular dimension that Habermas considers to be essential to any genuinely public discourse.

This provisional analysis, though far from exhaustive, allows us to glean a number of features of the public sphere as it emerged in the modern period: 1) the public sphere denotes a critical consensus rather than a mere convergence of opinion; 2) it is extra-political and independent and serves to regulate power; 3) it is a meta-topical discourse that is in principle universal; 4) it is secular in the sense that power is not kept in check by God, Church, or natural law but by an enlightened citizenry. This idealized conception of the public sphere embodies the Habermasian virtue of publicly accessible, secular rationality.

However, is the ascendancy of publicly accessible reason, defined in Habermas's sense, as straightforward as his account suggests? In my judgment, it is more complicated. The thinkers to whom he appeals are rather more ambivalent with respect to their evaluation of 'public opinion' and the secularity of the public sphere. In what follows, I want to develop a counter-narrative that supplements the 'subtraction story' implicit in Habermas's account.

---

[82] Taylor, 190.

Rethinking the Secularity of the Public Sphere in the Modern Period

Despite Locke's aforementioned contributions to the modern public sphere, he has an ambivalent attitude, at best, toward opinion. For example, in the *Essay*, Locke claims that "there cannot be a more dangerous thing to rely on" than "the opinions of others."[83] Of course, one could argue that Locke is referring to de facto opinion rather than the idealized opinion derived from a process of rational debate. And, indeed, the context makes such an interpretation plausible. However, Habermas may overstate Locke's "Law of Opinion" as being of equal rank with divine and state law. Indeed, Habermas may well be confusing two separate projects within Locke's epistemology. For example, Wolterstorff notes that while the application of Locke's ethics of belief to revealed religion, such as that alleged by the enthusiasts, has been widely received and adopted by Western intellectuals, his moral project has not.[84] And it is precisely this project in which Locke's distinction between the divine law, the civil law, and the law of opinion is embedded. In Locke's view "[b]y the relation they bear to the first of these, men judge whether their actions are sins, or duties; by the second, whether they be criminal, or innocent; and by the third, whether they be virtues or vices."[85] According to Wolterstorff, Locke's theory of moral obligation is a divine command theory.[86] The law of opinion, far from being of equal rank, is a much weaker conception denoting the force of social approval and disapproval. Although conventional morality of this kind can be quite effective in regulating our conduct, it is by no means the source of moral obligation. To be sure, Locke is a key figure in the rise of what Taylor calls the "order of mutual benefit"[87]: an extensive process of reform designed to bring about a well-ordered, "polite" society. And this process, probably contrary to the intentions of its progenitors, made grounding morality on human, rather than allegedly divine sources possible, thereby paving the way for exclusive humanism. However, Locke does not adopt such a stance; quite the contrary. Although utility is an important factor for Locke – God's providential design makes morality beneficial for us – the primary source of moral obligation resides in divine law. And although Locke differentiates divine law from civil law, and in the *Letter* certainly objects to the

---

[83] John Locke, *An Essay Concerning Human Understanding*, ed. Peter H. Nidditch (Oxford University Press, USA, 1979), IV. xv. 6.
[84] Wolterstorff, 148.
[85] Locke, II. xxviii. 7.
[86] Wolterstorff, 136.
[87] Taylor, 256.

civil magistrate prosecuting alleged breaches of divine law, he does not necessarily rule out appeal to divine law in public discourse. To quote Wolterstorff again: "That there are civil and social laws is obvious. Locke took it as scarcely less obvious that there is divine law ... Both reason and revelation tell us that we have obligations to God."[88] Of course, it is difficult to imagine such an overt appeal to divine law in our contemporary political discourse – certainly Habermas would object – but Locke does not consider himself in violation of his epistemic responsibilities in invoking it. Publicly accessible reason obviously meant something quite different to Locke than it does to Habermas.[89]

Furthermore, Locke does not profess any confidence in opinion in religious matters. In the *Essay*, for example, Locke states: "And if opinions and persuasions of others, whom we know and think well of, be a ground of assent, men have reason to be heathens in Japan, Mahumetans in Turkey, Papists in Spain, Protestants in England, and Lutherans in Sweden."[90] Moreover, not all of these opinions are to be tolerated. When we turn to the *Letter*, we find more ambivalence with respect to the value of opinion and public accessibility in the narrow sense. Here Locke does not so much insist upon rational criteria for regulation of our beliefs but, like Hobbes and Spinoza, subordinates religious authority to that of the state. It is also far from obvious that Locke's state is ideally neutral with respect to competing religious conceptions. For example, it is evident that Locke's definition of church – "a voluntary society of men, joining themselves together of their own accord in order to the public worshiping of God in such a manner as they deem acceptable to Him, and effectual to the salvation of their souls"[91] – is not a neutral description of 'church' but clearly reflects a repudiation of the historic Catholic position.[92] If this is to be the civil authority's definition of 'church,' it has the practical consequence of extending religious liberty only to those denominations – whether Anglican or nonconformist – with

---

[88]   Wolterstorff, 139.
[89]   One may argue that intellectual and social conditions have changed since Locke such that Habermas's interpretation is justified. However, it may be equally the case that Habermas tacitly subscribes to the disenchantment version of the subtraction story and thus sees religious modes of language as less than live options in our current situation. Habermas has arguably softened his position here, which will be taken up in the next chapter.
[90]   Locke, IV. xv. 6.
[91]   Locke, *A Letter Concerning Toleration*, ed. Patrick Romanell (New Jersey: Prentice Hall, 1950), 20.
[92]   Newman, 118.

which the magistrate is sympathetic. Moreover, Locke's functionalist definition of church with its implications for the privatization of religion "treats the attainment of salvation as if it were some mysterious technical exercise that has little, if anything, to do with the business of living a good life."[93] These weaknesses notwithstanding, the *Letter* does represent an advance over the religious enthusiasm and fanaticism that Locke criticizes, although at times he is heavy-handed in his exclusion of religious orientations with which he disagrees.

However, I want to return to the issue of state neutrality with respect to religion in the *Letter*. Many readers – not the least of whom were the framers of the *U.S. Constitution* – have interpreted Locke as advocating the separation of church and state. And while he does conceptually distinguish between their respective functions, it is not clear that he is opposed to the established Church of England, although he maintains that no religion should wield civil authority in the name of orthodoxy. Locke, like many of his Royal Society fellows, was an Anglican Whig who had a certain agenda in excluding those he deemed fanatics or enthusiasts. The Anglican clergy, cited above, in their support of reason and Natural Religion functioned as a defense against the alleged revelations of the enthusiasts who, according to Locke, were shirking their epistemic duties and fanatics who were willing to resort to violence to defend and promote dogmatic claims for which we could at best marshal "moral certainty." As such, the established church was a great ally of Locke's program and the rhetoric of clerics like Wilkins, Tillotson, and Sprat was certainly not neutral with respect to other denominations and Locke's principle of tolerance was in effect withheld from the latter.

Nevertheless, there is a tension here between Locke's professed Anglicanism and his sympathy for dissenters and, from an Anglican perspective, heterodox views. He had sympathy for the plight of persecuted minorities, such as Quakers and Unitarians. Some members of these groups, in turn, saw Locke as a great ally. For example, William Popple, who translated Locke's *Letter* from Latin to English in 1689, was a Unitarian.[94] Moreover, Locke may not have been a Trinitarian either. The aforementioned effort to articulate a less doctrinally elaborate Christianity, one more amenable to reason, brought many of the Latitudinarians, including Locke, under suspicion of Socinianism, a movement founded in Italy by Faustus Socinus (1539 – 1607). Among the tenets it denied

---

[93]   Newman, 120.
[94]   Romanell, 6.

were: the Trinity, original sin, predestination, eternal punishment, and the atonement.[95] Regardless of the orthodoxy of Locke's Christianity, scholars have noted that many of the arguments for tolerance he employs in the *Letter* were borrowed from dissenters, such as Anabaptists, Socinians, and Dutch Arminians.[96] As one might expect, these arguments are religious, rather than secular, in character. Locke employs many of these biblically derived arguments throughout the *Letter*, which are by no means original to him.[97] According to Perez Zagorin, the modern foundations of religious tolerance in the seventeenth century are deeply Christian; they do not arrive as the invention of a liberal philosophy that is inherently secular.[98] This point not only serves as a corrective to the 'wars of religion' narrative that usually accompanies the secularization thesis, but also demonstrates that Locke felt free to appeal to explicitly religious sources, in addition to secular reason.

From these considerations, it becomes clear that purely secular reason and separation of church and state – key components of modern political organization and crucial for Habermas's understanding of public accessibility – are lacking in Locke's theory. Although Locke's subordination of religious to political authority makes possible the kind of shift the standard secularization thesis describes, it is safe to say that Locke's subsequent interpreters are more responsible for this shift than Locke himself. This is not to say that we are not justified in modifying or expanding Locke's insights and appropriating them pragmatically in our contemporary political context, but any honest interpretation should take into account his religious motivations even if we do not share them.[99]

---

[95] Kim Ian Parker, *The Biblical Politics of John Locke* (Wilfrid Laurier Univ. Press, 2004), 17.
[96] Perez Zagorin, *How the Idea of Religious Toleration Came to the West* (Princeton University Press, 2003), 258.
[97] By my count Locke explicitly appeals to Scripture no less than eight times, citing chapter and verse, and alludes to it many more times.
[98] Zagorin, 289.
[99] For a fuller exploration of the theological underpinnings of Locke's political theory, see Jeremy Waldron, *God, Locke, and Equality* (Cambridge: Cambridge University Press, 2002). Waldron says the following with regard to the liberal value of equality, but one might well substitute "tolerance": "Equality cannot do its work unless it is accepted among those whom it consecrates as equals. Locke believed this general acceptance was impossible apart from the principle's foundation in religious teaching. We believe otherwise. Locke, I suspect, would have thought we were taking a risk" 243.

Likewise, the religious motivations of the natural theologians of the Royal Society are quite complex and do not support a straightforwardly secularist interpretation of public reason arising in the modern period. On the contrary, it was almost taken for granted by these thinkers that the new science, represented most perfectly by Newtonian mechanics, is eminently compatible with religion. Indeed, many of the most recognized members of the Royal Society were intent to show that the new science proved the existence of God and refuted the claims of materialists and atheists usually identified with the likes of Hobbes and Spinoza.[100] Boyle, for example, left a large sum of money upon his death for an annual series of lectures "to prove the truth of the Christian religion against the infidels, without descending to any controversies among Christians."[101] Wilkins claimed that astronomy in particular "proves of a God and a providence and incites our hearts to a greater admiration and fear of his omnipotency."[102] And Samuel Clarke, an apologist for Newton, staunchly defended the claim that Natural Religion provides no succor for the materialists. The most religiously eccentric member of the Royal Society, however, was Glanville who made a case for the existence of witches that served as a major authority for witch hunters in England and New England.[103] Glanville was concerned to prove not only the existence of witches, but the existence of a spiritual world more generally, and thereby to refute materialism. Whatever one makes of Glanville's religious eccentricities, the common thread running throughout the early Society's publications is their confidence in the harmony between theism and science and the apologetic use of Newton to refute materialism. This is especially true of Clarke, who was to take Newton's fragmentary thoughts on natural theology and develop an elaborate apologetic project. The public use of reason for these thinkers included theology in no uncertain terms. Granted, as Buckley points out, the unintended consequences of these developments aided and abetted Christianity's self-alienation and contributed to, rather than refuted, modern atheism. Nevertheless, the apologetic intent of these thinkers is undeniable. This complicates the narrative of the standard secularization thesis that has religion retreating in the modern period before the advance of science.

The preceding narrative is intended to show that the evaluation of public opinion by relevant modern thinkers is rather more ambivalent than Habermas

---

[100] For example, in Clarke's 1704 Boyle lectures, Buckley, 170.
[101] Quoted in Buckley, 170.
[102] Buckley, 129.
[103] Popkin, 211.

maintains. Moreover, the association of public accessibility with secularism is likewise less obvious upon closer examination. To his credit, Habermas allows that the golden age of public opinion as critical discourse in England was short-lived, effectively coming to an end in the nineteenth century. I merely contend that the demotion of public opinion among elites happened earlier; a case could even be made that 'public opinion' never quite lost its "polemically devalued association with pure prejudice." Successors, such as J.S. Mill, whom Habermas sees as primarily facilitating the demotion of public opinion in the nineteenth century, were simply extending the liberal tradition they inherited. Indeed, the currency "public opinion" enjoyed during the eighteenth century was largely the achievement of the conservative opposition. It is more than a little ironic, then, that aspects of the public sphere such as its meta-topicality and its role as an independent check on power, so often associated with liberal political theory and secularization more generally, were largely the product of Tory opposition and conservative elements within the Whig party, like Burke. Habermas, again to his credit, recognizes this quite clearly.

Despite the conservative origins of the term 'public opinion' in the English case, it would be a mistake to construe public opinion as denoting a singular voice in the eighteenth century. The opinion of the public does not acquire a monolithic understanding until the nineteenth century and it is during this time, especially under the pen of Mill that 'public opinion' comes under criticism for being oppressive and stifling genuine critical debate rather than facilitating it. According to Habermas, the demotion of public opinion is roughly coextensive with Mill, although once again, it is possible to locate it earlier. But Mill does offer a more developed critique of 'public opinion' than his predecessors in the liberal tradition, largely because public opinion came to enjoy such a prominent place.

Mill's utilitarian predecessor, Jeremy Bentham, for example, held that "the greater the number of temptations to which the exercise of political power is exposed" the more the government requires "the superintendence of the public."[104] Thus Bentham spoke of the "regime of publicity." The legitimacy of the public opinion was, for him, simply a given.[105] For Bentham, then, as his utilitarianism would suggest, majority opinion served as the criterion for whether a political decision was made in the public interest. By contrast, Mill

---

[104] Habermas, 100.
[105] Habermas, 100.

saw public opinion as oppressive. Laws passed under 'public' pressure did not necessarily reflect a reasonable consensus of private individuals, but often served the competing interests of the powerful. In other words, public opinion represented only a narrow public, that of propertied individuals; the franchise was still effectively withheld from a wider population that did not count as constituting the 'public' under the existing definition. So while Bentham could perhaps complacently understand public opinion as identical to the general interest, Mill spoke of the "yoke of public opinion"[106] as something to be thrown off. According to Mill scholar, Alan Ryan, "public opinion is a valuable ally of utilitarianism, but may be simply despotic .... Unlike Bentham, he (Mill) thinks the pressure of public opinion so dangerous that we need a countervailing doctrine of individuality and independence of mind to ensure that social pressure is kept within bounds."[107] Thus Mill condemns public opinion as a "yoke" and a "means of coercion."[108]

One can interpret Mill's *On Liberty*, which makes a plea for tolerance of a diversity of opinions in the public sphere, in light of his aversion to the dominant opinion. He offers four basic arguments that no opinion should be suppressed: 1) the opinion that is compelled to silence might nevertheless be true; 2) even though an opinion may be in error, we might nevertheless learn from it; 3) the common opinion, even if true, will only be considered mere prejudice if not vigorously contested to uncover its rational grounds; 4) if unchallenged, the meaning of the prevailing opinion will be lost and it will become an empty dogma. Habermas asserts that Mill's argument proceeds by analogy with religious tolerance; he is not very confident in the efficacy of rational criticism among the masses to vindicate minority opinions. Therefore, *On Liberty* represents a plea, not for criticism, but for tolerance. In other words, Mill does not aim for consensus which may well be dangerous, but, as the title suggests, for liberty. However, Mill does not throw reason to the wind; he speaks of the rational grounds of the majority opinion and argues that such grounds should be challenged if for no other reason than to convince those who disagree with the dominant opinion that it is not a mere prejudice. The arbiter for Mill is still reason, but not the calculating reason of the 'public' which can function as a tool of private interests. He recognizes the power of majority opinion and the power

---

[106] Habermas, 133.
[107] Alan Ryan, introduction to *Utilitarianism and Other Essays* by John Stuart Mill and Jeremy Bentham (Penguin Classics, 1987).
[108] Habermas, 133.

that rhetoric plays in manipulating that opinion, to the extent that the 'majority opinion' was no longer necessarily in the interests of the majority. The bourgeois class did not constitute the majority in nineteenth century England, but it still constituted the 'public'. Mill sought to separate reason from private competing interests and make it truly public. But doing so entailed allowing equal voice for all opinions, even those deemed unconventional or harmful to majority interests. In Mill's estimation, when faced with a compromise between consensus and liberty, liberalism should err on the side of liberty. For Habermas, Mill's appeal to liberty, ironically, spells the end of an era in liberalism; the golden age of public opinion as rational-critical discourse was over, assuming it ever existed. Of course, this reading of Mill can no doubt be questioned, but it suffices for my purposes to establish Habermas's position on consensus *vis-à-vis* liberty. Habermas follows Locke, for whom rational consensus is not only possible but desirable, rather than Mill for whom it is arguably neither.

However, one could also question the extent to which Mill's eschewing of public opinion within a liberal context provides any succor to those who want to bring religious arguments into public, since he was certainly no friend to religion. Indeed, he is often credited with reinforcing the public/private distinction that has become a hallmark of contemporary liberalism. For example, Rorty comments, "[it] is never an objection to a religious belief that there is no evidence for it. The only possible objection to it can be that it intrudes an individual project into a social and cooperative project, and thereby offends against the teachings of *On Liberty*."[109] However, this understanding of the requirements of democracy has been challenged by Rorty's fellow pragmatist Jeffrey Stout. Like Rorty, Stout also eschews the notion of a common basis upon which all reasonable people must agree. But he questions the reliance in many liberal theories, Habermas's included, on social contract theory. Why should we expect to be able to find up front, as it were, a common basis for politics which is contractually binding on all rational people? Stout takes a Hegelian direction on the development of social norms; they are not discovered 'up front' but are developed dialectically. He invites us to consider any social practice such as art, science, or sport. Norms, as products of social practices, constrain behavior, but they also allow, upon a Hegelian interpretation, for novel performances that have the potential to transform the practice, and thus, its norms. This opens the door to expressive freedom within norms. Once this dialectical point is in place, it is

---

[109] Rorty, "Pragmatism as Romantic Polytheism," 120 – 21.

"no longer clear why we need to tether our social and political theory to the search for a common basis."[110] We are not all likely to agree on which principles to accept or reject because we occupy different dialectical locations depending upon the social practices in which we have been able to participate:

> Among these practices will be religious practices, which carry with them their own styles of reasoning, their own vocabularies, and their own possibilities of expressive freedom. If the thoroughly dialectical view of epistemic entitlement is correct, why expect all socially cooperative, respectful persons to have reason to accept the same set of explicitly formulated norms, regardless of dialectical location?[111]

Stout sees no reason to expect such a basis to be forthcoming. The problem with social contract theory is that it feels the need to police the expressive freedom of citizens. It seeks to avoid both the communitarian threat to individual autonomy and the anarchist threat of war of all against all. The former achieves stability but at too steep a cost and the latter fails to achieve it at all. So the social contract theorist wants to fix the rules of public expression. But this is problematic from the standpoint of expressive freedom, including religious expression. The expressivist would never be tempted, says Stout, to consider King's speeches, for example, as mere IOUs for secular reasons and, accordingly, sees no reason for self-censorship or restraint on religious expression in public. Without stretching too much, I believe it is possible to see Mill, despite his secularism, in the tradition of expressivist freedom along with the American examples Stout cites such as Walt Whitman and Ralph Waldo Emerson. The above quotation from Rorty comes in his essay "Pragmatism as Romantic Polytheism," so perhaps it is fitting to note the Romantic influences on Mill that provide a counterbalance to his secularism.

Like other figures of the nineteenth century such as Carlyle, Mill rebelled against the order of mutual benefit with its leveling out of humanity.[112] They felt

---

[110] Stout, 79.
[111] Stout, 79.
[112] For Taylor, the order of mutual benefit is based upon the idea of providential order, later impersonalized in deism. Socially, the order of mutual benefit is expressed in the virtues of "civilization": politeness, discipline, and benevolence. However, some

cross-pressured, in Taylor's term, between the rational world order and a Romanticism that allowed for heroism and greatness. This rebellion against the order of mutual benefit can be seen as a major cause of Mill's breakdown at the age of twenty and his subsequent disaffection from Bentham and father James Mill. What saved Mill, according to his own account, was Romanticism, particularly that of Coleridge. Raised a religious skeptic, Romantic sources of meaning took the place of traditional religious ones for Mill. Ryan provides insight into Mill's assessment of a thoroughly secularized society:

> Mill contrasted the men of the eighteenth century and the men of the nineteenth. The men of the eighteenth century were skeptical, unemotional, objective in their outlook. They saw the folly and superstition of the *ancien régime* but they did not see the emotional supports which tradition and religious sentiment had provided .... what Coleridge asks of an institution is 'what does it mean?' – looking, of course, not at the literal meaning, but looking to uncover the attachment which it sustains. Mill resolved to try to combine the virtues of the eighteenth century and the insights of the nineteenth.[113]

Taylor recognizes this same impulse to reconcile skepticism and Romanticism in many of the poets of the era, such as Arnold and Hardy. They embodied the tension between unbelief and nostalgia for what had been lost through disenchantment. Through the creation of a "subtler language"[114] they attempted to replace the meaning lost by abandoning traditional religious language. Without straying too far into a fuller exposition of Romanticism, it suffices to say that secularization in the form of the rationalization of the public sphere and the order of mutual benefit was not without its countervailing responses, culminating in what Taylor calls the immanent counter-enlightenment.

Habermas does not make room for such aesthetic counterpoints to modernity, because the aesthetic, like the religious in his judgment, is non-

---

thinkers chaffed under the disciplinary requirements of such a social order (Taylor mentions Friedrich Nietzsche, 256) and sought to recapture the greatness and heroism of the past.
[113]   Ryan, 36.
[114]   Taylor, 353.

rational and non-communicative. Indeed, Habermas denies, unlike Weber, that modernity and disenchantment has occasioned a loss of meaning. In a fully rationalized society, for Habermas, the 'malaise of modernity' would disappear because all three forms of rationality would be fully unleashed: the normative and expressive, as well as the instrumental.[115] Nevertheless, he has recently allowed that not all of human experience can be adequately captured through the monopoly of secular language within the public sphere. Hence religious language still has great semantic power, a power that has, at least as of yet, no secular counterpart. It suffices for now to note that the historical wellsprings of modernity to which Habermas appeals are not without religious and Romantic undercurrents.

Secularization: So What Happened?

The foregoing discussion enables us to modify our understanding of the secularization thesis. I have been arguing that Habermas, at least in his early work, adopts a version of the secularization thesis that amounts to a subtraction story. In effect, the rationalization of society brought about a decline in religious worldviews, or the disenchantment of the world; religious belief was forced to retreat from the public sphere. More recently, however, Habermas has questioned the disenchantment narrative of secularization he received from Weber. There are a number of reasons for thinking such a narrative inadequate, both from a purely historical point of view and from the perspective of its potential for political praxis.

In general, such a narrative describes religious ideas, such as God, retreating from the public sphere and being replaced by a rationalistic, scientific worldview. This is a classic subtraction story. Although Taylor does deal with the notion of disenchantment in his narrative of secularization, he is scrupulous to avoid describing it in terms of humanity having divested itself of certain confining religious perspectives. Indeed, such an account does not do justice to the complexity of the processes of secularization. To be sure, Taylor is concerned with how belief in God lost its default status and came to be regarded as one option among many, and perhaps not even the most plausible possibility. But he does not interpret this decline in belief as human beings simply outgrowing the

---

[115] See Habermas, *The Theory of Communicative Action, Vol. 1: Reason and the Rationalization of Society*, trans. Thomas McCarthy (Beacon Press, 1985), 238 – 39.

notion of a supreme being when faced with a scientific, rationalized worldview. Rather, traditional religious sources of meaning are replaced with other, secular sources. There will be more on this in the next chapter.

Stout provides additional insights into the meaning of secularization. According to him, the primary cause of secularization is not that religiosity declined in the modern period, or that the world was disenchanted, or the public sphere emptied of God as some have contended.[116] Rather, it was the intensity and plurality of religious devotion that made secularization a practical necessity. He cites historian Christopher Hill's study of the use of the Bible in seventeenth century English politics. He argues that by the 1650s, the Bible had lost its authority as a public arbiter: "Twenty years of frenzied discussion had shown that text-swapping and text-distortion solved nothing: agreement was not to be reached even among the godly on what exactly the Bible said and meant."[117] Importantly, the dethroning of Scripture as a public arbiter had little to do with the Bible losing its credibility among the majority of the citizenry. Stout distinguishes between two meanings of 'authority' in relation to Scripture: its authority over an individual's conscience and its public discursive authority. The Bible maintained the former but lost the latter. Authority over an individual's conscience, however, is an inadequate basis for public persuasion. Since the authority of churches were demoted following the Reformation, individuals were left with private interpretations of the Bible, or even private "revelations" as in the case of Locke's "enthusiasts," upon which there could be no consensus.

There is a connection here with Warner's discussion of anti-clericalism in the English colonies in America. Since popular Protestant revivals, such as the Great Awakening, encouraged ordinary believers to read and interpret Scripture for themselves, theological discussion began to take place among lay persons in the meta-topical space, rather than exclusively among professional clergy in seminaries and disseminated in churches. As a result, religious authority became decentralized. In such a climate of religious pluralism – or one might even say individualism – appeals to Scripture become far less useful for brokering consensus than appeals to shared public reason. It is not that Scripture lost its authority in the minds of the citizenry or that religious devotion declined; quite the opposite. Rather, it simply became impossible to build political consensus on the basis of contested readings of the Bible. So while the Great Awakening may

---

[116]   Stout, 98.
[117]   Quoted in Stout, 94.

have increased religious devotion in America, it decreased religion's utility as a consensus builder. Thus, citizens realized that fruitful public discourse could not presuppose any specific theological framework. Secularization, in the American case, was not a process of disenchantment but a function of pragmatism; citizens had to find a way to broker agreement in the absence of a presupposed theology. Given the plurality of American religiosity, political arguments had to be sufficiently generalized or secularized, in order to achieve wide support, but that is not to say that they lost all ties to the religious imagination and moral outlook of the citizenry.

Thus, Stout's account of secularization sees it as primarily a practical political consequence of religious pluralism, rather than a process of disenchantment. Moreover, in Stout's estimation, the contemporary secular public sphere does not presuppose or produce citizens who have no robust theological commitments.[118] Secularized public discourse involves the pragmatic efforts of citizens as they engage in actual communication and has nothing whatsoever to say about humanity having outgrown religious worldviews or a cosmos devoid of religious significance.

The narrative I have been telling above is certainly compatible with this thesis. One can see clearly in Locke's *Letter*, for example, that the impetus for tolerance is the plurality of religious interpretations that lacked the practical means of brokering consensus by appealing to religion itself. Locke almost certainly did not make his arguments on the basis of the alleged disenchantment of the world occasioned by the march of science. As we have seen, Locke and his Royal Society fellows were optimistic about the prospects of reconciling science and religion. But in offering this narrative, I am not merely aiming to correct a mistaken historical thesis, but to challenge the way in which the subtraction version of the secularization thesis has been employed to exclude religious language from public discourse.

Like Stout, I see public discourse happening at the level of praxis rather than in an ideal speech situation or a Rawlsian contractarian framework. The only account of secularization we need is a pragmatic one which allows citizens to understand each other, while suspending judgment on the epistemic status of religious worldviews. This is a weak account of secularization as opposed to a strong account, which makes epistemic judgments regarding the rationality of

---

[118] Stout, 98.

religious worldviews. We might also describe this distinction as the difference between secularization and secular*ism*. The former need not entail any presuppositions regarding the plausibility of religious claims, whereas the latter usually does.[119] In my judgment, such a weak account of secularization is preferable to a strong account that marginalizes religious citizens from the public sphere by placing upon them a deontological requirement to translate their language into strongly secular terms as in some interpretations of Rawls and Habermas, although both thinkers have been careful to nuance their respective positions. In my judgment, and that of pragmatists such as Stout, there is no normative restriction on religious arguments; it is simply the case that in pluralistic contexts, it does not often advance one's rhetorical purposes to appeal to them. However, sometimes it does. Stout has talked about secularists engaging in imminent critique with religious interlocutors in a pragmatic effort to persuade them using arguments religious citizens would find convincing. I will have more to say about pragmatist responses to Habermas below, and admittedly, I have not refuted the normative status of publicly accessible, secular reason, strongly conceived. That will be the project of the following chapters. For the meantime, however, it is instructive to note that secularization does not imply secularism historically. If this is the case, the secularist cannot rely on a subtraction story of secularization as disenchantment to justify the exclusion of religion from the public sphere. In my judgment, the secularist's narrative simply cannot perform that kind of philosophical heavy lifting, as I have argued above. In this chapter, I have sought to complicate efforts to arrive at an unequivocally secularist conception of publicly accessible reason from the modern period. Since the publication of *Structural Transformation*, Habermas has also reevaluated the subtraction story implicit in his account of the rise of the public sphere. Through interweaving the historical counter-narrative in this chapter with Habermas's early thinking on the public sphere, I have tried to give us a sense of where Habermas has come from and where he is going in thinking about religion and the secularization thesis. This historical background will position us to pursue these questions in more detail and to closely engage Habermas's more recent contributions to the debate over religion in the public sphere.

In the next chapter, I will examine Habermas's reevaluation of the secularization thesis and his translation requirement – the requirement that religious citizens translate their potential contributions to public debate from a

---

[119] Stout, 97.

private, religious idiom into a publicly accessible, secular language. Continuing the theme of this chapter, I will argue that the translation requirement, construed as a normative requirement, gains its purchase from the subtraction story of secularization that Taylor criticizes. Insofar as one can offer a plausible alternative description of the phenomenological conditions of contemporary secularism, one can weaken the rationale behind the translation requirement. This translation requirement, however, can be construed in stronger and weaker terms. In what follows, I will explore not only what Habermas means given his reevaluation of the secularization thesis, including his diagnosis that we live in a postsecular society, but also show that stronger formulations of the translation requirement are problematic. I will attempt to show that Habermas's requirement is better construed as a pragmatic move to broker practical agreement, not a normative rule to create an idealized consensus. I will also examine the semantic potential of religious language that remains in a secularized context. As we shall see, Habermas is very sensitive to this semantic potential and fears that something important may be 'lost in translation' as it were. I suspect Habermas's worry is justified and I look at some examples, including one from Habermas himself, that illustrate the semantic potential of religious language especially in the context of human rights discourse. Here Habermas stands in the tradition of the Frankfurt School in attempting to salvage the resources of religious language in a secular age. In what follows, we will look more closely at how Habermas understands his secular project and how it might actually accommodate religious sources.

Chapter 2
Competing Narratives of Secularization: Habermas and Taylor

We have seen in the previous chapter that Habermas's early critical theory subsumes a subtraction narrative of secularization. In what follows, I continue to explore this theme, particularly as his account of secularization impinges on his translation requirement. The translation requirement is the requirement that religious citizens translate their particularistic faith language into an allegedly universal secular language.[120] Religious citizens must satisfy this criterion if they are to participate in public discourse. Before offering a critique of this requirement, it is important to understand what Habermas means by 'secular' and his rationale for assuming it to be publicly accessible. In what follows, I treat this subject in depth, tracing what Habermas says about secularism, and post-secularism, in his writings. In brief, Habermas contends that secular language commits us to fewer beliefs, thus offering a better chance at consensus within the public sphere. Because of the religionists' additional substantive commitments, they have heavier metaphysical baggage, making their epistemic or justificatory predicament more difficult than that of the secularist. However, I argue that this position assumes a subtraction narrative of secularization that underestimates the weighty substantive commitments that the secularist has. In making the case that one ought not to assign epistemic advantage to 'secular' substantive commitments in the public sphere, I continue to utilize Taylor's sophisticated analysis of the phenomenological conditions of secularism. If my thesis concerning this lack of epistemic advantage for secular substantive commitments is true, it also casts doubt on the rationale behind the translation requirement, because it casts doubt on one of the primary motivations for recommending it in the first place.

Whether or not the translation requirement is normative has far-reaching implications for political discourse. Through a detailed study of Habermas's writings on the subject, I adduce two interpretations of the

---

[120] As I explore in chapter 3, Habermas later modifies his position, such that he restricts this requirement to the 'formal' public sphere, i.e., legislatures and the like, as opposed to the 'informal' public sphere, i.e., public opinion, the press, etc.

requirement: in the first, the requirement is construed as normative in a Kantian sense, but in the second it is construed pragmatically. I make a case that the first sense, although plausibly interpreted to capture Habermas's meaning in many contexts, is overwrought and unworkable when it comes to applying it to political praxis. Here I look at Maeve Cooke's critique of Habermas along pragmatic lines and extrapolate some further criticisms. In my judgment, if the translation requirement is to function usefully in democratic discourse at all, it must be construed pragmatically. But this suggestion seriously weakens, if not completely undermines, any normative force Habermas claims for it. Moreover, construing the translation requirement pragmatically entails giving up consensus as the main goal of democratic discourse. However, I argue that this is consistent with what Habermas wants to say about discourse in a postmetaphysical context. Here, in my judgment, a pragmatic interpretation of the translation requirement is more consistent with Habermas's project than the stronger construal.

Finally, toward the end of this chapter, I look at problems inherent in the task of translation, regardless of which construal we choose. There are several cognitive contents that are arguably 'lost in translation'. In this context, I use the recent work of Nicholas Wolterstorff to illustrate the public accessibility that yet remains in religious language, and the violence it suffers when translated into the reigning secular idiom. Habermas has expressed similar sentiments in his recent writings. In this final section, I explore the ways in which what I call 'transcendent moral sources' might still have public import. In addition, I argue that religious belief is never purely private; it is fair to subject it to scrutiny and, hence, there is no reason for excluding it from public discourse on the grounds that it's insufficiently 'accessible' to reason. I conclude the chapter by showing how theistic and pragmatic approaches to the question of religion's public accessibility, despite their differences, dovetail nicely, as seen in the work of Wolterstorff and Stout.

While I will go into greater depth on all of these issues in this chapter, first we must start, as they say, at the beginning, with Habermas's early accounts of secularization. We will then be in a position to appreciate how his understanding of the term 'secular' informs his statement of the translation requirement.

Secularization as Disenchantment: Empirical and Normative Aspects

We have seen in the previous chapter that Habermas's account of the rise of the public sphere, though constructive in many ways, implicitly subsumes a subtraction narrative of secularization. He continues this disenchantment narrative more explicitly through his work in TCA, particularly volume two, in which he takes up "the linguistification of the sacred."[121] By this he means the process whereby the authority of the sacred, usually mediated through rituals and non-linguistic symbols, gives way to the authority of an achieved consensus through communicative action. Habermas closely follows Weber and Durkheim in linking this process with secularization conceived as disenchantment. As Habermas says: "the aura of rapture and terror that emanates from the sacred, the *spellbinding* power of the holy, is sublimated into the *binding/bonding* force of criticizable validity claims and at the same time turned into an everyday occurrence."[122] He recognizes that the monotheistic, or Axial, religions were a stage in the "rationalization of worldviews," as does Weber, but this process of rationalization culminates in "shrinking down the domain of the sacred" and leaving "behind a nature bereft of gods."[123] Thus, "rationalized worldviews have to compete with the authority of a fully secularized science."[124] Again, this is a classic subtraction story. We have already noted some flaws in Habermas's historical reconstruction of this narrative, but his normative arguments for the priority of secular reason merit closer attention, which is the purpose of this chapter.

However, we will not be leaving the socio-historical questions behind entirely as the normative and descriptive halves of the secularization thesis, although conceptually distinct, often mutually support each other. It is slightly misleading to speak of the secularization thesis in the singular; there are different versions and determining precisely what secularization as a phenomenon entails in any detail is a daunting task. I suggested above, following Stout, that secularization, which nobody seriously denies is a real phenomenon, should be conceived as a pragmatic response to pluralism rather than the pronouncement that science has revealed a universe "bereft of gods." Such a

---

[121] Jürgen Habermas, *The Theory of Communicative Action, Vol 2: Lifeworld and System: A Critique of Functionalist Reason*, trans. Thomas McCarthy (Beacon Press, 1985), 77.
[122] Habermas, 77.
[123] Habermas, 83.
[124] Habermas, 83.

materialistic assumption is no more necessary for the smooth exercise of discursive democracy than are the theistic assumptions of previous generations. If Taylor is correct, secularization is not primarily a matter of materialistic assumptions replacing theistic ones, but of a proliferation of positions along this axis. Of course, difficulties surrounding definitions of "secularization" are analogous to those surrounding definitions of "religion." There seems to be a great deal of latitude when it comes to defining these terms, and given a sufficiently wide definition of religion we can make secularization seem like a marginal phenomenon and vice versa. I do not want to minimize the extent to which something that merits the name "secularization" has occurred, but I suggest we ask anew the "how" and "why" questions.

Generally, the secularization thesis, at least in its orthodox version, contends, at the very minimum, that religious belief and practice have declined under conditions of modernity broadly conceived (the Enlightenment, and the Scientific and Industrial Revolutions). Again, we must be wary of construing religion too broadly, for example as one's ultimate concern, lest we conclude that nothing meriting the description "secularization" has actually happened. Although it is the case that religion is a resilient phenomenon and has changed in response to pressures from the challenges of exclusive humanism and a plethora of other options along the axis, it would be disingenuous to claim that religion is so infinitely malleable that it can withstand any conceivable revision. Taylor settles upon Roy Wallis's and Steve Bruce's definition of religion: "actions, beliefs, and institutions predicated upon the assumption of the existence of either supernatural entities with powers of agency, or impersonal powers or processes possessed of moral purpose, which have the capacity to set the conditions of, or to intervene in, human affairs."[125]

Wallis and Bruce are defenders of an "orthodox" theory of secularization against what could be called "revisionist" theories which contend that, while secularization may have occurred, it is a more marginal phenomenon, even in the West, than orthodox theorists contend. In some cases, revisionism also entails the suspicion that orthodox secularization theory is ideologically over-determined, that is to say, motivated by the very materialist assumptions that (allegedly) neutral social science is supposed to describe. Again, I have no interest in contending that secularization is a marginal phenomenon; neither, for

---

[125] Roy Wallis and Steve Bruce, "Secularization: The Orthodox Model," in Bruce, ed., *Religion and Modernization*, 10 – 11, cited in Taylor, 429.

that matter, is religion, in my judgment. The ideologically over-determined line of some revisionists is, in my view, a gross overstatement. Nevertheless, as Taylor rightly points out, scholarship in this area is often circumscribed by certain kinds of "unthought"[126] or hidden substantive assumptions on both sides of the debate. This observation is a cautionary one and should not be equated with a postmodern hermeneutics of suspicion, despite Taylor's unfortunate use of that Foucauldian term. Indeed, awareness of our substantive assumptions, and those of our interlocutors, should allow us to widen our sympathies and vocabularies rather than attribute ideological blindness to one another.

Returning to the decline of religion that orthodox secularization theory describes and predicts in Western society, Taylor distinguishes three overlapping explanations for religion's decline: "a) because it (religion) is false, and science shows this to be so; or b) because it is increasingly irrelevant now that we can cure ringworm by drenches; or c) because religion is based on authority, and modern societies give an increasingly important place to individual autonomy; or some combination of the above."[127] At this point, it is instructive to ask which explanatory option(s) Habermas favors. In TCA, it seems, on the basis of the above quotations, that he favors combining all three, with special emphasis on (a) and (c). In his more recent writings, however, he has backed away from (a), which is to say, the descriptive half of the secularization thesis, but has maintained emphasis on (c) which I see as roughly coextensive with the normative half of the secularization thesis. Religion's loss of authority comes from its inability to legitimize itself discursively. Thus, authority shifts to consensus which is achieved communicatively. The dilemma facing religious worldviews, in the face of communicative rationality, is to either submit to discursive reason, with the erosion of credibility such a move entails from the perspective of science, or to place religious worldviews beyond discursive reason, thereby forfeiting any claim to public legitimacy under conditions of secular morality and law. In addition to Weber, Habermas depends upon Emil Durkheim's sociological analysis. Durkheim describes the linguistification of the sacred as follows: "One begins by putting articles of faith beyond discussion; then discussion extends to them. One wishes an explanation of them; one asks for

---

[126] Taylor, 427.
[127] Taylor, 429.

their reasons for existing, and, as they submit to this search, they lose part of their force."[128] Habermas further cements the point:

> The structural aspects of the development of religious worldviews, which Durkheim and Weber sketched in complementary ways, can be explained by the fact that the validity basis of tradition shifts from ritual action over to communicative action. Convictions owe their authority less and less to the spellbinding power and the aura of the holy, and more and more to a consensus that is not merely reproduced but *achieved*, that is, brought about communicatively .... The validity basis of norms of action changes insofar as every communicatively mediated consensus depends on reasons. The authority of the sacred that stands behind institutions is no longer valid per se.[129]

Although Habermas is operating here in the descriptive mode, echoing the sociological research of Durkheim and Weber, there is clearly a normative substratum to his description of the consensus achieved by communicative rationality. It is not simply the case that in the course of societal development the authority of the sacred will recede before secular reason, but it *should* recede, precisely because religious worldviews do not admit of communicative redemption. Therefore, they cannot serve as a legitimate basis for consensus once the disenchantment of the world is fully accomplished. Notwithstanding arguments that question the emphasis on disenchantment in his account of secularization, the normative core of Habermas's case for the priority of discursive reason in a fully rationalized society remains. I do not necessarily disagree with Habermas that discursive reason, the ability to validate one's claims via reason, is a practical necessity within a pluralistic democracy. However, I do not necessarily agree that one's reasons must be limited to Habermas's stringent definition of publicly accessible, i.e. secular, reasons. In my judgment, it is precisely the prioritizing of secular reasons that assumes the broad contours of the subtraction narrative of secularization that needs to be challenged. I shall return to this point in more detail in what follows.

---

[128]   Quoted in Habermas, 84.
[129]   Habermas, 89.

Secularization, Postsecular Society and the Translation Requirement

In my judgment, Habermas, despite caveat, still assumes the broad contours of the subtraction story of secularization. Although he has been careful to qualify his position on religious language vis-à-vis public reason, there is a latent subtraction story which still needs to be confronted. To clarify, I am not charging Habermas with being ideologically motivated in marginalizing religious worldviews in public debate. On the contrary, I think this would be unfair at best and mistaken at worst. Despite those who would characterize Habermas as an unqualified Enlightenment secularist, he has always been exceedingly modest in his construal of secularization (process) and even secularism (outcome), and he is aware of the latter's potential for ideological distortion. His understanding of secularism has arguably evolved, albeit in a manner consistent with his work in TCA, in which he argues for the formal secularism of the public sphere and, by extension, that the state be based upon profane sources of morality and law. This is a natural outworking of a societal discourse based upon communicative action which draws upon the eclectic philosophical resources of Kantian autonomous reason and morality, speech act theory, and pragmatism. Importantly, however, Habermas is extremely reticent to specify the content of his secularism; it remains simply a formal requirement for genuine consensus. This reluctance to specify content has not changed, but it has broadened in his more recent work. Indeed, his secularism has evolved into something called "postsecularism" which we will explore below. Habermas's rigid adherence to the form/content distinction – in addition to ample textual evidence that could be marshaled – suffices to dispel the notion that he is an ideological secularist who is opposed to religion in principle. To be sure, Habermas has self-identified as a "methodological atheist," but this label simply means that as a matter of philosophical *procedure*, he does not presuppose a theological framework. Whether or not he subscribes to a more substantive secularist or atheological position is a matter of debate, but such a position is certainly not necessary for achieving intersubjective consensus in his view. Nevertheless, citizens must agree upon some common ground, a shared basis upon which to broker consensus. Thus, beliefs or claims that fall under the purview of discursive reason or admit of communicative redemption in principle are allowed, otherwise they are not. In Habermas's judgment, religious claims, as they stand, do not meet this criterion. As such, if they are to achieve public legitimacy, they must be translated into the public, secular language. This translation requirement is controversial, and is precisely what I want to challenge by closely engaging both Habermas and Taylor. Although he does not address Habermas directly in this context, Taylor suggests that something like the translation requirement is an unreasonable constraint upon religious citizens:

> Democracy requires that each citizen or group of citizens speak the language in public debate that is most meaningful to them. Prudence may urge us to put things in terms which others relate to, but to require this would be an intolerable imposition on citizen speech. As the sense of living in Christendom fades, and we recognize that no spiritual family is in charge, or speaks for the whole, there will be a greater sense of freedom to speak our own minds, and in some cases these will inescapably be formulated in religious discourse.[130]

Here Taylor, like Stout, suggests that it may be expedient for citizens to engage in some mode of translation in order to be understood by others, but to formulate this pragmatic move as a requirement, and a one-way requirement from religious to secular language, would be contrary to the democratic spirit. Given the normative weight Habermas imputes to public, discursive reason his translation requirement is generally interpreted strongly: religious citizens are normatively bound or obligated to translate their particularistic language into the shared public language if they wish to gain access to public debate. In other words, Habermas's translation requirement is generally understood in a Kantian rather than a pragmatic sense. I think there is room for reinterpretation on this matter, which I will address below. For present purposes, however, I will defer to the standard interpretation and point out, through insights gleaned from Taylor, reasons why the translation requirement as outlined above stands in need of revision. In my judgment, the translation requirement, strongly construed, is too heavily indebted to the mainstream secularization thesis inherited from Weber and Durkheim, insofar as it presupposes the priority and authority of exclusively secular reasons in a rationalized society.

As we have seen, Taylor disputes the mainstream secularization thesis and this may well influence his evaluation of something akin to the translation requirement. Lately, Habermas has also questioned the subtraction story as received through Weber, and has acknowledged criticism of too readily accepting the secularization thesis in TCA and other earlier work:

---

[130] Taylor, 532.

> I would also admit that I subsumed rather too hastily the development of religion in modernity with Max Weber under the "privatization of the powers of faith" and suggested too quickly an affirmative answer to the question as to "whether then from religious truths, after the religious world views have collapsed, nothing more and nothing other than the secular principles of a universalist ethics of responsibility can be salvaged, and this means: can be accepted for good reasons, on the basis of insight."[131]

This confession has its limits, of course: Habermas still sees religious language as needing to satisfy the translation requirement; in other words, religious persons must translate their particularistic faith language into more generally accessible secular or public language. Although Habermas makes many qualifications to this position, it is a fair statement of his position to date.

It is important to note, however, that the translation requirement is a salvage operation rather than a demolition. In other words, Habermas follows Kant's project of grounding the valuable aspects of religion, not in a particularistic tradition, but in a shared universal, public reason. As Habermas points out, I think correctly, the Kantian "*critique* of religion is bound up with the motive of *saving* appropriation."[132] Habermas expresses interest in Kant's philosophy of religion "from the perspective of how one can assimilate the semantic legacy of religious traditions without effacing the boundary between the universes of faith and knowledge."[133] For Kant, religious and metaphysical statements must surrender all claims to knowledge. He famously said in his first *Critique* that he must "remove knowledge to make room for faith."[134] This means that dogmatic religious claims must retreat from the public sphere, but in turn, religion is insulated from the corrosive effects of science which has a monopoly on knowledge. Although religious claims *qua* religious claims must withdraw

---

[131] Jürgen Habermas, "Transcendence from Within, Transcendence in this World," in *Religion and Rationality: Essays on Reason, God and Modernity*, ed. Eduardo Mendieta (Cambridge, MA: MIT Press, 2002), 79.
[132] Jürgen Habermas, "The Boundary between Faith and Knowledge: On the Reception and Contemporary Importance of Kant's Philosophy of Religion," in *Between Naturalism and Religion: Philosophical Essays*, trans. Ciaran Cronin (Polity, 2008), 211.
[133] Habermas, 211.
[134] Preface to the second edition of the *Critique of Pure Reason* by Immanuel Kant, trans. Norman Kemp Smith (New York: St. Martin's Press, 1968), Bxxx.

from the public sphere, their rational content may well be salvaged. Habermas sees this project as essential to Kant's moral philosophy which "can be understood in general terms as an attempt to reconstruct the categorical ought of divine imperatives in discursive terms."[135] Elsewhere, he goes even further, arguing that "Kant cannot be understood without recognizing the motive of conceiving the essentially practical contents of the Christian tradition in such a way that these could perdure before the forum of reason."[136] According to Habermas, Kant sees religion as both a "heritage and opponent,"[137] salvaging those semantic contents that admit of rational justification while removing the obscurantism and dogmatism that attaches to many religious claims. Habermas continues in this Kantian tradition and the tradition of critical theory; as he points out, Adorno, Benjamin and Bloch[138] also translated the semantic potential of religious language into secular terms.[139] Kant's skepticism regarding metaphysics, which brought about the "death of metaphysics" in subsequent German philosophy, for Habermas, is a *fait accompli*. We are now living in a "postmetaphysical" age. Habermas understands "postmetaphysical" as both an important methodological or procedural principle for all post-Kantian philosophy, and "to describe agnostic positions that make a sharp distinction between belief and knowledge without assuming the validity of a particular religion (as does modern apologetics) or without denying the possible cognitive content of these traditions (as does scientism)."[140] In my judgment, this statement is also very close to what he means by "postsecular," which we will take up shortly.[141] Furthermore, he says: "All semantic contents count as 'cognitive' in this sense which can be translated into a form of discourse decoupled from the ratcheting effect of truths of revelation. In this discourse, only 'public' reasons count, hence reasons that have the power to convince also beyond the boundaries of a particular religious community."[142] As mentioned in the last chapter, the Kantian architectonics of Habermas's thought is widely

---

135   Habermas, 228.
136   Habermas, "Transcendence," 68.
137   Habermas, "The Boundary between Faith and Knowledge," 227.
138   Habermas's interpretation is debatable. Jacob Taubes, for example, argues that Benjamin's messianism was much more substantial and less secularized than that of Adorno or Bloch. See Jacob Taubes, *The Political Theology of Paul*, trans. Dana Hollander (Stanford University Press, 2004), 74 – 76.
139   Habermas, 232.
140   Habermas, 245.
141   Habermas, 245.
142   Habermas, 245.

acknowledged, and there is nothing particularly novel about these observations. It is instructive to note, however, that Habermas views translation as non-destructive of religious meaning, even if the formal language must change to accommodate a wider public.[143]

We are now in a better position to unpack Habermas's understanding of "postsecular" vis-à-vis secularization. Regarding the latter, he has arguably nuanced his position since TCA with respect to the subtraction narrative. He argues that the two models of secularization – which we can roughly equate with the "orthodox" and "revisionist" positions outlined above – are both misguided: either secularization is construed by its defenders as the legitimate replacement of religious authority in the public sphere or it is construed by its critics as the illegitimate appropriation of resources which properly reside in a substantive faith tradition. Both views treat secularization as a zero-sum game in which gains by one side can only be achieved at the expense of the other. Habermas contends that "this image is inconsistent with a postsecular society which adapts to the fact that religious communities continue to exist in a context of ongoing secularization."[144] In my judgment, this is a significant revision of Habermas's position on the disenchantment narrative. Indeed, he suggests that the replacement view of secularization sees disenchantment and the subsequent decline of religion as simply a given. However, he is no longer prepared to accept even a qualified version of secularism which sees nothing of value in religious worldviews. That is to say, Habermas, in his recent work, does not affirm the ontological validity of either substantive religious worldviews or a purely materialistic, disenchanted worldview. In our postmetaphysical context, dogmatic claims on behalf of either view warrant our suspicion. Nevertheless, for practical purposes in a pluralist society, we need to get on with the job of discursive democracy. Therefore, we need to position ourselves, as a matter of methodology, as agnostic about such matters in public and employ public reason – arguing from premises any rational person would accept – in making our claims.

The above reading suggests that Habermas sees postsecular society as a condition necessitated by pluralism. Under postsecular conditions, "religious consciousness must, first, come to terms with the cognitive dissonance of

---

[143] Habermas, "Faith and Knowledge," in *The Frankfurt School on Religion: Key Writings by the Major Thinkers*, ed. Eduardo Mendieta (Routledge, 2004), 336.
[144] Habermas, 329.

encountering other denominations and religions."[145] The consequences of such cognitive dissonance seems to be roughly equivalent to Taylor's third sense of secularity – conditions under which belief in God comes to be seen as one option among many. Habermas would probably agree with this definition as reflecting postsecular societal conditions. Moreover, he says that believers must come to terms with the fact that they are no longer the dominant voice in society, just as nonbelievers must contend with the fact that religion is not fading away, despite the predictions of the secularization thesis. Nostalgia for either condition does not serve citizens of a discursive democracy well. For Habermas, postsecular society does not merely mean that we must anticipate the continued existence of religious communities, but has normative implications for discursive democracy as well: namely, both sides must take each others' cognitive claims seriously in a "complementary learning process" that will reflexively transform all participants, religious and secular.[146] Religious communities must take seriously the consequences of secularization such as religious pluralism, the authority of the sciences, and purely secular foundations for public morality. The secular liberal state, however, must also acknowledge its indebtedness to that religious discourse which belongs to the genealogy of human rights. Although Habermas sees religious citizens as having additional burdens, not shared by their secular counterparts, as we shall see, he nevertheless advises non-religious citizens of liberal democracies to be similarly cautious in their adoption of the secularization thesis and especially wary of specifying the content of secularism lest it become ideological and incapable of learning from the religious traditions that continue to shape our discourse. For example, Habermas states:

> As long as secular citizens are convinced that religious traditions and religious communities are, as it were, archaic relics of premodern societies persisting into the present, they can understand freedom of religion only as the cultural equivalent of the conservation of species threatened with extinction. Religion no longer has any intrinsic justification in their eyes …. In the secularist reading, it can be anticipated that religious views will ultimately dissolve in the acid of scientific criticism and that religious communities will not be able to withstand the pressures of advancing cultural and social modernization. Clearly, citizens who adopt such an epistemic stance toward religion can no

---

[145] Habermas, 329.
[146] Habermas, "Prepolitical Foundations of the Constitutional State?" in *Between Naturalism and Religion*, 111.

longer be expected to take religious contributions to contentious political issues seriously or to participate in a cooperative search for truth to determine whether they may contain elements that can be expressed in a secular language and justified by rational arguments.[147]

Habermas's use of the term 'postsecular' arguably fleshes out his earlier formal definition of 'secular' and his hesitance to specify the content of secularism. Postsecularism ostensibly reserves judgment about the ontological validity of religious claims and is more modest in its assessment of the extent to which modernity has eroded any possible foundations for a religious worldview. As such, Habermas continues to be a methodological atheist rather than a metaphysical one. But, importantly, postsecularism also remains open to the possibility that religious language can fund public debate if it can be translated into more publicly accessible language. This burden of translation – at least ideally – falls equally on all citizens: religious citizens must translate their particularistic language into a more universal one and secular citizens must be open to the semantic potential of religious language to disclose the world in a manner that purely philosophical language cannot (yet?) accomplish. Such mutual translation is Habermas's way of avoiding the charge made by some of his critics that translation places an asymmetrical burden on religious citizens. Although postsecularism is ostensibly more modest in what it claims ontologically for modernity – for example, modernity should not be simply equated with metaphysical naturalism – Habermas maintains that there is an epistemic asymmetry among secular and religious claims. In other words, "Under the conditions of postmetaphysical thinking, whoever puts forth a truth claim today must, nevertheless, translate experiences that have their home in religious discourse into the language of a scientific expert culture – and from this language retranslate them back into praxis."[148]

Thus, religious citizens bear a burden of translation in such contexts that secular citizens do not. Moreover, religious citizens must adopt a stance of public agnosticism which stands in contradiction to their private religious convictions, whereas public agnosticism, in the case of secular citizens, will likely not be

---

[147] Habermas, "Religion in the Public Sphere: Cognitive Presuppositions for the 'Public Use of Reason' by Religious and Secular Citizens," in *Between Naturalism and Religion*, 138 – 39.
[148] Habermas, "Transcendence," 76.

substantially different from their deeply held beliefs. For example, Habermas states: "To date, only citizens committed to religious beliefs are required to split up their identities, as it were, into their public and private elements. They are the only ones who have to translate their religious beliefs into a secular language before their arguments have any chance of gaining majority support."[149] Habermas recognizes this asymmetry of burdens but argues that it is justified insofar as it parallels an epistemic asymmetry between religious and secular claims.[150] That is to say, religious claims do not have the same epistemic status – status as knowledge – as do secular claims. Nevertheless, he argues that secularists must be sensitive to the "force of articulation inherent in religious languages"[151] and warns that secular society, in excluding religion from the public sphere, runs the risk of cutting itself off from important sources of meaning. He suggests that even secular citizens engage in the process of translation and, like Kant and the critical theorists, find a way to appropriate the cognitively salvageable aspects of religious language while uncoupling it from its metaphysical moorings. For example, we can reformulate the language of humans' bearing the image of God into the language of the equal dignity of all human beings, without serious loss of cognitive content or damage to the spirit of religious language.

'Mutual translation' is the shorthand I will use to designate Habermas's approach to secular vis-à-vis religious language. He indicates that there has been a double standard in secular society which militates against religious rationales being taken seriously in the public sphere. Rather than insist unilaterally that religious rationales be translated into secular rationales, he appears open to mutual translation among members of the postsecular society. As he notes, often the "boundaries between secular and religious reasons are fluid."[152] Secular society runs the risk of denying itself important resources, or meaning potentials, if it rejects out of hand religious rationales, especially when such rationales can mediate intercultural, and sometimes hostile, narratives. The religious believer might be tempted to see the repudiation of such a double standard as opening up space for the legitimacy of faith commitments within the broader intellectual and cultural discourse. However, religious citizens must be careful not to read

---

[149] Habermas, "Faith and Knowledge," 332.
[150] Habermas, "On the Relation between the Secular Liberal State and Religion," in *The Frankfurt School on Religion*, 346.
[151] Habermas, "Faith and Knowledge," 332.
[152] Habermas, 332.

Habermas's modified liberalism as an unqualified endorsement of the legitimacy of religious worldviews. There is still an "asymmetry of epistemic claims" between religion and secular philosophy and science. In other words, the dichotomy between faith and knowledge survives in the postsecular context. Moreover, the purpose of mutual translation, such as rendering the insights of religious language publicly accessible, is not to promote a particular religious worldview within the public sphere, but rather to open up paths of communication within a pluralistic society and to build consensus – the same task public reason assumes in old-fashioned secular societies – among citizens, both religious and secular. The backdrop of this process is the neutrality of the liberal state which also survives in the postsecular society, but in a more self-conscious way; there is to be no generalization of a broadly secularist worldview either. The place of religious worldviews in the postsecular context, though expanded, will not be expansive enough to satisfy those religionists who insist upon employing religious arguments in the public sphere. Nevertheless, the disallowance of ideological secularism and the potential for religious sources of meaning to inform the public discourse is an attractive feature of the postsecular condition for the moderate religionist. It should be noted, however, that although Habermas encourages mutual translation, secular citizens are not required to translate religious beliefs into secular beliefs as are religious citizens. In other words, Habermas, while thinking it prudent for secular citizens to participate in translation, does not say they are obligated to do so. Assuming for the time being that the translation requirement be read strongly as a normative obligation, it is borne by religious citizens alone.

The burden of translation that religious citizens uniquely bear is related to the epistemic burden they bear in secularized societies. This additional burden is justified because believers have additional beliefs, namely religious beliefs in addition to the thin, minimal presuppositions of public reason. Sometimes, these additional beliefs can come into conflict with even the minimal assumptions of the secular state. For example, liberalism is predicated on the priority of the right over the good. One's rights, construed from the vantage point of a public conception of justice, take priority over any substantive notion of the good. This fact alone can bring about unequal burdens for believers, but such a situation seems impossible to avoid precisely because religious citizens have heavier metaphysical baggage than their secular counterparts. As Habermas points out: "For the consciousness of the secularized citizen traveling with light metaphysical baggage who can accept a morally 'free-standing' justification of democracy and human rights, the 'right' can without difficulty be accorded priority over the 'good.'"[153] By contrast, "for the believer who travels with heavy metaphysical baggage, the good enjoys epistemic primacy over the right"[154] precisely because the believer draws her ethical self-understanding from religious beliefs that claim universal validity. These additional beliefs, such as the authority of holy texts in addition to public conceptions of justice, make it more difficult for the believer to accept the priority of the right over the good and, therefore, the believer bears an additional cognitive burden, namely that of reconciling her religious beliefs with those of a wider public. Such cognitive dissonance is not likely to haunt the secular citizen who travels light. For example, Habermas suggests that "liberal regulations on abortion place a greater burden on devout Catholics or on any supporter of a pro-life position based on a religious worldview than on secular citizens, who, even if they do not share the pro-choice position, can live more easily with the idea that the right to life of an embryo may be trumped by the right to self-determination of the mother under certain circumstances."[155] The unequal burdens religious citizens bear in the public sphere are simply the price religious citizens pay for tolerance – a compromise that has always been at the heart of liberalism – although Habermas admits that it is debatable whether or not such a price is too high.[156] When it comes to tolerance of practices in a liberal democracy, religious citizens bear the heavier burden, and reconciling one's substantive conception of the good with the liberal conception of the right is not something all religious citizens are able to do successfully. As Habermas says, religious citizens are the only ones required to split their respective identities into a religious and a secular ethos. To be fair, he does acknowledge the existential pull of religious identities and the practical difficulties that result from attempting to unload one's metaphysical baggage, nevertheless, asymmetry remains a practical consequence of secularization. But perhaps measures can be taken to remedy this inequity to some extent:

> This asymmetry between the burdens borne by believers and by unbelievers is counterbalanced at most by the fact that religiously tone-

---

[153] Habermas, "Equal Treatment of Cultures and the Limits of Postmodern Liberalism," in *Between Naturalism and Religion*, 309.
[154] Habermas, "Religious Tolerance as Pacemaker for Cultural Rights," in *Between Naturalism and Religion*, 263.
[155] Habermas, "Equal Treatment of Cultures," 286.
[156] Habermas, 308.

> deaf citizens confront an expectation of tolerance of a different kind .... For the expectation of an ongoing lack of agreement between rational factual knowledge and religious tradition deserves the predicate "reasonable" only when religious convictions are accorded an epistemic status that is not merely irrational from the perspective of secular knowledge.[157]

However, "factual knowledge" is accorded a *prima facie* plausibility upon my reading of Habermas that "religious tradition" must work harder to achieve. This caveat seems to be simply a given under postsecular conditions. Therefore, Habermas has not strayed from his concern in TCA to establish the validity – one might more properly say 'truth' in formal pragmatic terms – of all public claims, including religious ones in this context. In his view, religious claims do not meet his criteria for validity, hence the translation requirement. Therefore, Habermas, though his position has evolved to one of more openness toward religious language informing public debate, remains consistent with many of his themes in TCA and maintains the formal secularism of the public sphere as outlined above.

    I would contend that even this modified position too readily assumes the broad contours of the secularization thesis. Taylor's study of secularism is quite helpful in offering a corrective to the mainline story of secularization. He argues that we have moved, in the last five centuries, from a context in which unbelief, or what Taylor calls exclusive humanism, was unimaginable, to one in which belief must be justified, a context in which secularism is seen as the default position, at least among well educated people in industrialized North Atlantic countries. Habermas's translation requirement and the "epistemic asymmetry" of religious claims vis-à-vis secular ones, also tacitly assumes that non-belief is the default position and that religious claims, in order to be fairly assessed, must work harder to equal the *prima facie* plausibility of secular claims. Despite Habermas's caveat that all citizens, regardless of religious adherence, must work together to make the resources of religious language available to a wider audience, religious believers do bear an asymmetrical epistemic burden under conditions of what Taylor calls naïve secularism.

---

[157]   Habermas, "Religious Tolerance as Pacemaker," 263 – 64.

But it is not sufficient to translate the resources of religion into secular language; one must also "dissipate the false aura of the obvious"[158] that surrounds secular worldviews. Habermas is quite right that the formal secularism of the public sphere should not be identified with scientific materialism, but he may not go far enough. One must also offer, as has Taylor, a phenomenology of secularism: an examination of the ways in which secularism has become the default position in the modern public sphere. If one can show that a secular, functionalist interpretation of religion is not obviously true, the necessity of the translation requirement is thereby called into question as well. I can do no more than suggest a mere sketch of such a project here, but it is important, in my judgment, to expand what Habermas means by postsecular: not only should we remain open to the semantic potential of religious language, translating its resources into the prevailing public discourse, but we should also question the default status of secularism as the obvious language of that discourse. The 'obviousness' of secularism is a major assumption of the subtraction story; secularization is described as a divestment of certain 'metaphysical baggage' as though secularism is simply a matter of subtraction and does not, through the dialectical process, acquire some baggage of its own. Only an 'addition story' can help us understand how and why exclusive humanism has become the default position that religious belief must overcome – the burden of proof being on the believer. If we reconstruct our current "social imaginary" and question the default status of secularism we may be able to avoid placing an asymmetrical burden upon religious persons. Taylor's account of the rise of naïve secularism suggests a significant modification to Habermas's translation requirement in the dialogue between secular and religious citizens.

Taylor's Phenomenology of Secularism

One of the ways Taylor wants to describe the shift from 1500 – 2000 is a fundamental change in social imaginary that begins in the Age of Reason, but expands exponentially in the twentieth century. A social imaginary refers to the intellectual space that we inhabit, or the conditions for belief or unbelief. In the 1500s, for example, the social imaginary had no room for exclusive humanism – it simply was not a live option; that is to say, there was no intellectual space for it. Of course, this has changed, though not necessarily as a result of blatant unbelief.

---

[158]   Taylor, 551.

As we have seen, a number of Christian thinkers contributed to the shift without so intending. As both the spatial and temporal expanse of the universe gradually became known, people, like Giordano Bruno already in the sixteenth century could imagine an infinite universe of countless worlds, a departure from the orthodox cosmology. Likewise in the seventeenth century, people began to imagine alternative accounts of human origins, although ironically, sometimes in an effort to rescue the Genesis narrative. For example, Thomas Burnet, although willing to amend the biblical account, believed he could capture the main contours of the story, including Creation, Flood, and Apocalypse, in a 'scientific' account. In order to do so, he maintained that the world that science observes is not the one that came from the hand of the Creator, but one that has been punctuated by divine judgments, the latest of which was the Genesis Flood. Humanity's origin thus recedes into the distant and quite murky past, which goes a long way toward setting the conditions for evolutionary theory. Vico plays a similar role in the eighteenth century. In defending Scripture against Chinese chronologies, he argued that many postdiluvian peoples regressed into a bestial state and rebuilt civilization only after many years. Their chronologies were thus based on dubious memories and mythology. However, once one engages in such historical-critical theorizing, it becomes difficult to resist extending it to all histories, even those favored by religious orthodoxy. We can see how these accounts of human origins, although intended to safeguard orthodoxy, opened the intellectual space for ideas like "the state of nature" and, of course, evolutionary explanations up to and including Darwin's. Regardless of how orthodox their belief, Bruno, Burnet and Vico – and one could no doubt multiply examples – began to imagine ways in which the world might be construed differently than the received biblical narrative. In other words, they began to imagine alternatives to the Christian story, to open up space for unbelief that would expand greatly to include not only elites, but also society at large. Taylor wants to reopen intellectual space for the Christian story amid subtraction stories and a social imaginary that has opened up a plethora of spiritual alternatives to Christianity. However, he admits that this task is difficult for a number of reasons: even devout believers, regardless of the orthodoxy of their propositional beliefs, can feel cross-pressured by the modern social imaginary, they can feel its pull, and through exposure to various options, begin to imagine the world differently, whether or not they explicitly change their fundamental commitments.

Furthermore, religion has also been co-opted by the modern, secular social imaginary. For example, religion is seen by many people, whether they profess to be religious or not, as a source of meaning. However, Taylor notes that this understanding of the primary role of religion exists within the modern social imaginary. It has not always been the case that religion has served primarily, let alone solely, as a source of meaning. In an enchanted, or better, teleological world, meaning was simply inherent. It is only in the age of instrumental reason that we keenly feel disenchantment as a loss and seek some way to give our lives meaning. But this view of religion presupposes the modern, secular social imaginary. And again, we all, regardless of the strength of our religious commitment – or lack thereof – participate unawares in the modern social imaginary. Indeed, we would be hard-pressed not to participate in some capacity. In a secular age, one has to be aware of our current social imaginary's preoccupation with meaning, without acquiescing to a merely functionalist account of religion, reducing it to a provider of private meaning.

Closely related to this preoccupation with meaning is the search for adequate sources for morality. At this juncture, it becomes important to give an "addition story" of secularization. This is important for two reasons: 1) it supplements and corrects the distorted 'progress' narrative which sees religion receding before the power of modern science; 2) it locates the primary reasons for the shift in social imaginary in ethical arguments rather than empirical givens about the nature of the world. In tandem, these have the consequence of challenging the default status of secularism; it is no longer seen as simply obvious or inevitable. Let us examine these points in more detail.

Central to Taylor's discussion of secularization is the creation of the 'immanent frame' which can be best defined by briefly exploring how it comes about. Firstly, we must contend with the buffered identity that comes to the fore in the modern period. This is basically the Cartesian subject, the interior world within which reality is bounded. Taylor contrasts this with the porous self of earlier times which was more open to external influence. From the standpoint of the buffered self, however, the idea of external spirits, causal powers, supernatural agents, etc. becomes increasingly incomprehensible. The richness of the enchanted world retreats into our inner world, the depths of our psyches. As moderns, we find this general account convincing and quite natural. Another consequence of the buffered identity is the reversal of the field of fear. Within the enchanted world, unbelief was unimaginable at least in part because of the porous nature of the self. Abandoning belief in God was not to go it alone in an empty cosmos, as the modern narrative goes, but to go it alone in a world populated by non-human agents, influences to which one was vulnerable without divine protection. However, once this fear recedes, it becomes somewhat easier to relinquish faith in God. This is part of what is meant by the immanent frame: reality is considered explicable in immanent terms.

Another facet is the rigid, as opposed to porous, distinction between natural and supernatural ushered in by the buffered self. Ironically, Christian philosophers had a hand in this development. Taylor, and Buckley in his fine study,[159] has convincingly argued that the move toward exclusive humanism or atheism was unintentionally aided by the efforts of the very apologists that were trying to make room for the supernatural. However, once the buffered identity arose it was no longer inconceivable to dispense with the supernatural altogether. These two aspects, the buffered identity and the sufficiency of nature, come to form the immanent frame in which we experience the world. It also accounts for why unbelief comes to be seen as natural, or obvious within certain contexts; in other words, as bearing lighter metaphysical baggage. Taylor offers the following summary: "The buffered self feels invulnerable before the world of spirits and magic forces, which still can haunt us in our dreams, particularly those of childhood. Objectification of the world gives a sense of power, and control, which is intensified by every victory of instrumental reason."[160] Of course, there are echoes here of the coming-of-age narrative of secularization, which Taylor argues is motivated more by ethical considerations than empirical facts.[161] Moreover, the growth of civilization is seen as synonymous with establishing an immanent frame, within which human flourishing, aided by instrumental reason, can occupy its central place. However, Taylor contends that the immanent frame, as part of the modern social imaginary, is something we all inhabit. It is "not usually, or even mainly a set of beliefs which we entertain about our predicament, however it may have started out: rather it is the sensed context in which we develop our beliefs."[162] As such, the immanent frame does not necessarily, for Taylor, lead to exclusive humanism; it is not, in principle closed to transcendence – Habermas claims to reserve judgment here too –

---

[159] Michael J. Buckley S.J, *At the Origins of Modern Atheism* (Yale University Press, 1990).
[160] Taylor, 548.
[161] Taylor, 562 – 63.
[162] Taylor, 549.

although it is more difficult to think one's way to transcendence with the immanent frame in place. Nevertheless, belief, in William James's terminology, is still a live option. In fact, both open and closed orientations to the immanent frame are possible; however, the prevailing secular narrative makes it difficult to fully inhabit this Jamesian space, and takes the closed perspective as simply given.

Both the open and closed options within the immanent frame, of course, are not obvious in any usual sense. We may not be able to fully understand or imagine another person's point of view, but this has more to do with phenomenology than the givens of experience. In adopting either perspective, a leap of faith is required, or in Taylor's words, "anticipatory confidence."[163] To quote Taylor: "And so full lucidity would involve recognizing that one's confidence is at least partly anticipatory, and hence being aware of the Jamesian open space. What I am calling 'spin' is a way of avoiding entering this space, a way of convincing oneself that one's reading is obvious, compelling, allowing of no cavil or demurral."[164] So in his view, proponents of the mainstream secularization thesis have been successful in putting a closed spin on the immanent frame, making their perspective seem rather obvious, even if the available reasons are not compelling one way or another.

But let us return to the standard secular narrative for more concrete examples of closed "spin." For example, the coming-of-age narrative, that faith belongs to the infancy of humanity and our maturity entails coming to grips with reality. The courageous individual must go it alone in an indifferent, if not hostile, universe. This picture of the world, we are told, is ratified by the deliverances of science. However, as told above – and this is hardly a straw man – it is clearly a 'virtue' narrative. The virtue extolled is courage, taking one's destiny into one's own hands, having Stoic resolve in the face of adversity, ignoring the comforts of religion. In short, this narrative is based on ethical considerations, primarily, rather than purely empirical ones. There may be some who claim that this is not the case and that the empirical realities stand alone, quite independent of any implied moral outlook. But this is precisely what one would expect from the perspective of anticipatory confidence, though not recognized as such, in the closed spin. For the believer, who looks at the same world, the facts allow for a different interpretation. Often the believer argues

---

[163] Taylor, 550.
[164] Taylor, 551.

this way: there aren't any convincing arguments from science that militate against transcendence, so the unbeliever must ground his closed perspective on moral considerations, later bringing in a secular interpretation of the facts to ratify that perspective. However, both sides are getting it wrong to some extent. Both are in effect offering a subtraction account of secularization. The secularist sees religion as something that stands in need of explanation; how is it that people continue to cling to faith despite 'overwhelming' evidence to the contrary? However, this perspective may not seem so obvious from the perspective of our deconstructed social imaginary. This is why a phenomenology of secularism is so important: once the secular position is deconstructed it loses its default status. But the religionist too, makes a mistake in saying that rebellion against the Christian moral outlook alone is at the heart of making the necessary leap of faith from open to closed world systems.

There have been those, especially in the nineteenth century, (Darwin, Hardy, and Arnold) who seem to have sincerely felt the demise of faith as a loss, to be looked upon with a sense of nostalgia and regret. According to these thinkers, they preferred the Christian moral outlook, but felt they had to bow to the facts. This is more in keeping with the heroic narrative of naturalism outlined above. But I want to resist attributing to these thinkers open rebellion against a Christian moral outlook. This is why the subtraction story will not do. Rather than one model of morality falling away (subtraction) the model switched sides, as it were, under the new conditions of belief. Perhaps this is why the loss of childlike faith on the part of poets like Hardy and Arnold is seen as a tragedy; however, one can see their commitment to various Victorian virtues pulling them in the direction of closed world systems. As Taylor says, "[i]t has been noted how many of the crop of great Victorian agnostics came from Evangelical families. They transposed the model of the strenuous, manly, philanthropic concern into the new secular key. But the very core of that model, manly self-conquest, rising above the pain of loss, now told in favour of the apostasy."[165] These Victorian, neo-Stoic virtues which had formerly been cast within the Christian framework, were now seen as fitting more appropriately within a closed world system. The deliverances of the sciences, particularly Darwinian evolution, had a part, but moral motivations would appear to predominate. Indeed, Darwin's own concerns about the moral implications of his theory and Tennyson's lament about "nature red in tooth and claw" seem to bolster this interpretation. Rather

---

[165] Taylor, 564.

than lose their moral moorings, these men translated them into closed terms, and indeed the conditions for belief including the buffered identity, instrumental reason and the priority of human flourishing made this transition seem quite natural, albeit painful. Nevertheless, it is not the case, as the standard narrative goes, that "the whole thrust of modern science has been to establish materialism. For people who cling to this idea, the second order of conditions, the contemporary moral predicament, is unnecessary or merely secondary."[166] In fact, the reverse is true: the moral stance preceded the rise of materialism, and indeed was primary.

There are several themes that emerge from Taylor's analysis. Firstly, believers must address modernity's preoccupation with meaning and moral sources. Though it may be wrongheaded to see the essence of religion, or open perspectives, as bound up with answers to the question of meaning, this is nevertheless an important aspect of religion in our secular age, within the modern social imaginary. Part of the quest for meaning is modernity's continuing quest for adequate sources for morality. Problems facing particularly immanent moral sources include our failure, on a large scale, to universalize sympathy or solidarity due in part to our culture's valorization of a heroic misanthropic stance that emerges from the immanent counter-Enlightenment, those who, like Nietzsche, could not accept the disciplinary requirements of "polite society."[167] Recall Taylor's thesis that the move toward exclusive humanism is primarily motivated not by facts, scientific or otherwise, but by an ethical orientation to the world, which expresses itself in the immanent frame through the order of mutual benefit. Against this stands the narrative of the heroic individual who, in some cases, rages against the established order. Insofar as this deconstruction of secularization is accurate, and given that many of the promises of modernity remain unfulfilled – something Habermas would concede – I believe there is ample room for the exploration of other moral sources, sources that are open to the transcendent. Therefore, religious citizens are justified in criticizing the default status of closed world systems, thereby opening up space for transcendence to break through the closed spin of the immanent frame. Of course, this requires argumentation. We cannot expect our interlocutors to simply 'see' that their view is not the only rational option: we have to make that case. But the argumentation will be along historical rather

---

[166] Taylor, 561.
[167] Taylor, 184 – 85.

than metaphysical lines. I believe that Habermas is correct in suspending judgment on the truth of metaphysical propositions, religious or otherwise. Yet we cannot claim that only one side is encumbered with metaphysical baggage. Dissipating the false aura of the obvious that surrounds secular worldviews – those with substantive rather than merely procedural commitments – facilitates the postsecular stance that Habermas encourages.

Secondly, following Taylor, we must have a phenomenology of secularism. There has been a phenomenology of religion for some time, but no phenomenology of secularism, largely because religion is seen as an idiosyncrasy, or perhaps a neurosis, to be explained away from the within the closed perspective, which is taken for granted as needing no justification. Religious citizens, in a liberal democracy, must be allowed to publicly challenge the default status of this framework, deconstruct the secular narrative, and encourage the open orientation.

Finally, one of Taylor's goals is to bring his interlocutors into a space where belief can be considered a live option, not to translate religious arguments into the language of the closed spin, but to help his secular interlocutors break out of this closed spin and inhabit the Jamesian space. However, this means that we must enter the Jamesian space ourselves in a genuine, and not a contrived, way. This involves an element of risk: we risk feeling cross-pressured between the open and closed perspective, and risk feeling the pull of our interlocutor's position. We are often so averse to this risk that we never fully occupy that Jamesian space. We must actively engage in discursive reasoning, without allowing various types of 'spin' to foreclose from the outset opposing points of view. This does not mean that we enter a kind of 'no spin zone', some neutral space. The Jamesian space is not the view from nowhere, but the capacity to see, or imagine the world, from another person's point of view. It is to relinquish the 'obvious' standing of your own position and stand in someone else's shoes. So translation into a universal, neutral language is not what Taylor is offering here.

Needless to say, Taylor's strategy has met with criticism. He relies quite heavily on describing a phenomenology that secular readers will recognize as more or less their own, and also helping them imagine the world otherwise, thereby letting them appreciate the semantic potential of religious language to disclose the world in a way that secular language cannot. In addition to his critique of the immanent frame, he argues that secularization is not simply a matter of materialistic assumptions replacing theistic ones, but of a proliferation of what could be loosely called spiritual options along this axis. He goes to great pains to present these different, mostly immanent, spiritual options and what might be attractive about them against the background of the 'malaise of modernity', assuming that many or most people experience modernity as a 'malaise'. Of course, this way of framing the issue is problematic, because it can lead to the criticism that upon his view everybody is, in effect, religious. Although Taylor may find it difficult to imagine the absence of some form of religious consciousness, even under conditions of secularism – which often sees itself as emancipation from religion and thus preserves at least a minimal historical memory of religious consciousness – he recognizes that not everybody finds the absence of religion unimaginable. For example, he quotes Steve Bruce who argues that "the widespread, taken-for-granted and unexamined Christianity of the pre-Reformation period [will be] replaced by an equally widespread, taken-for-granted and unexamined indifference to religion."[168] Although Taylor concedes that such an outcome is possible, he does not consider it very likely. Rather, he wants to predict, extrapolating from empirical evidence, that the semantic potential of religious language will continue to be relevant in the future since the predictions of the secularization thesis have not come to pass. He has been criticized for offering what is essentially a theological or apologetic critique of secular culture and arguing that everyone in modernity experiences it as a malaise and that all of us, religious and secular, are looking for a sense of "fullness."[169] Taylor explores this territory in the final chapter of *A Secular Age*, entitled "Conversions." Here he highlights some recent examples of people who have 'broken out' of the immanent frame, and have felt the pull of transcendent ways of speaking. Without going into the details, suffice it to say that Taylor's sympathies clearly lie with this trajectory in understanding religious orientations to the immanent frame. This full-disclosure, in large measure, leaves him open to the above criticism.[170]

Jonathan Sheehan, for example, raises this criticism in his review of *A Secular Age* arguing that the book is an explicit theological critique of secularism.[171] Apparently, he is unable to appreciate the semantic potential of

---

[168] Taylor, 434.
[169] Taylor, 729.
[170] Ronald A. Kuipers, "An Inteview with Charles Taylor," in *'God Is Dead' and I Don't Feel So Good Myself: Theological Engagements With the New Atheism*, ed. Andrew David, Christopher J. Keller, and Jon Stanley (Cascade Books, 2010), 122 - 23.
[171] Jonathan Sheehan, "Framing the Middle,"

the religious language Taylor uses, thinking that the whole preceding argument represents a sleight of hand, leading the reader along by appearing to say something universal and then springing a particularistic faith language on him at the end. Although I do not think such a criticism is fair, it does show the persistence of the inability of many secular thinkers to hear the "potential" in religious language. The extent to which secular readers fail to appreciate this, I think, has much to do with the ubiquity of the assumption that there is one neutral language, that of secular reason, in which one can properly engage in philosophy or history or whatever, and then there are a plethora of particularistic faith languages that have very little to say to this larger universe of discourse. Taylor has since written more explicitly in criticism of this claim to neutral reason, of which Habermas, at least in his early career, has been a prime exponent.[172] Perhaps raising people's consciousness of their own latent particularistic assumptions is the best one can do to help them overcome initial resistance to occupying that Jamesian space and recognizing the potential inherent in religious language. Habermas, to his credit, has begun to do so.

But Taylor has confessed the limited success of his strategy. In a recent interview,[173] he remarks that his attempt at full-disclosure polluted the book for some people, although he does not regret being open about where he stands in the continuum of spiritual options. He also acknowledges that he settled on the term "fullness" to describe in a more or less generic way, something to which even non-religious people might be open. Now, he recognizes that trying to label what he wants to describe and affirm in a universally acceptable language is probably "mission impossible."[174] Perhaps this is a good reason to think that translation has limits and that we should be open, wherever our place on that continuum, to the semantic potential of religious language.

If Taylor is correct, there is nothing particularly normative about the default status of secular language in the public sphere. It is contingent rather than essential. This is not to say that reason is unimportant for practical political discourse – far from it. But it does suggest that the types of reasons to which we appeal are conditioned by the prevailing closed interpretation of the immanent

---

http://www.ssrc.org/blogs/immanent_frame/2008/01/14/framing-the-middle/.
[172] Taylor, "Secularism and Critique," http://blogs.ssrc.org/tif/2008/04/24/secularism-and-critique/.
[173] Kuipers, "An Interview with Charles Taylor."
[174] Kuipers, 122.

frame within secularism (which is not itself a reason, but a form of anticipatory confidence); other reasons may well be legitimate. This analysis, if correct, has implications for the translation requirement. If the closed interpretation is not obvious and if, according to Habermas, we are not to identify secularism with reductive materialism, then the translation requirement would seem to be an overly stringent criterion. In order to equalize the respective burdens of religious and secular participants in public discourse, he needs to go further than suspending judgment on the truth of closed worldviews and salvaging the useful flotsam of religious traditions; he should, in the interest of fairness, also require that secular citizens question the priority of their own reasons and even give some serious consideration to what these reasons are.

Nevertheless, Habermas insists upon the priority of secular reasons in the public sphere and equates secular reasons with publicly accessible ones, perhaps because, unlike Taylor, Habermas thinks that the reasons supporting closed worldviews justify agnosticism, at least within the public sphere. This public agnosticism also applies to religious believers. They must "develop an epistemic stance toward the internal logic of secular knowledge and toward the institutionalized monopoly on knowledge of modern scientific experts."[175] Consequently, "religious citizens must develop an epistemic stance toward the priority that secular reasons also enjoy in the political arena."[176] I have suggested, using Taylor's phenomenology of secularism, that this priority should be questioned. However, Habermas himself has acknowledged some problematic aspects of deference to scientific expert cultures, and their latent metaphysical naturalism, and suggests that religious resources may be necessary in order to preserve liberal ideals. For example, he states:

> This form of radical naturalism devalues all types of statements that cannot be traced back to empirical observations, statements of law, or causal explanations, hence, moral, legal and evaluative statements no less than religious ones. As the revived discussion of freedom and determinism shows, advances in biogenetics, brain research, and robotics, provide stimuli for a kind of naturalization of the human mind that places our practical self-understanding as responsibly acting persons in question and preempts calls for a revision of criminal law. However,

---

[175] Habermas, "Religion in the Public Sphere," in *Between Naturalism and Religion*, 137.
[176] Habermas, 137.

the permeation of everyday life by a naturalistic self-objectification of speaking and acting subjects is incompatible with any conception of political integration that imputes a *normative* background consensus to citizens.[177]

For these reasons, Habermas contends that secular society is well advised not to sever itself from religious sources of meaning which underwrite the presuppositions of the liberal state that make political integration and consensus possible in principle. Therefore, religious conceptions of identity may well have public utility. Moreover, it seems difficult, if not impossible, to translate these conceptions into the languages of scientific expert cultures without doing violence to the semantic power of these conceptions in their native context. But Habermas is ambivalent. On the one hand, he wants to withhold judgment on the ontological commitments required by a thoroughly secularized naturalism, which sees all truth claims in terms of the language of scientific expert cultures and which threatens moral, legal and evaluative claims – indeed, threatens our self-understanding as autonomous beings capable of rational action. On the other hand, he makes translation from religious to secular language a requirement of political praxis, arguably placing an asymmetrical burden on religious persons, and takes the priority of secular reasons as a given, equating 'publicly accessible' with 'secular' and seeking only to salvage the politically expedient elements of religious language in the hopes that even this project will be temporary. In my judgment, Habermas's ambivalent stance toward the secularization thesis makes his postsecular conception of an ethics of citizenship both promising and problematic for social cohesion. He seems to recognize the tension between his sacrosanct liberal principles and the practical task of getting along in society. Such tension characterizes his recent reflections on the translation requirement:

> The guarantee of equal ethical liberties calls for the secularization of state power, but it forbids the political overgeneralization of the secularized worldview. Insofar as they act in their role as citizens, secularized citizens may neither fundamentally deny that religious worldviews may be true nor reject the right of devout fellow-citizens to couch their contributions to public discussions in religious language. A liberal

---

[177] Habermas, 141.

political culture can even expect its secularized citizens to participate in efforts to translate relevant contributions from the religious language into a publicly accessible language.[178]

However, if the right to couch contributions to public discussion in religious language cannot be denied religious citizens, what remains of the translation requirement? Is it an obligation incumbent upon religious citizens as part of the social contract? Or can it be interpreted more loosely as a pragmatic gesture in which all citizens can be expected, though not necessarily required, to participate? Although developed answers to these questions will have to wait until the next chapter, I want to suggest here why the standard Kantian interpretation of the translation requirement is problematic. In addition, I want to explore what a philosophical expansion of what Taylor calls transcendent moral sources might look like while fleshing out the practical implications such a project might have for both religious and secular citizens in a deliberative democracy.

Rethinking the Translation Requirement

I want to continue to question the translation requirement construed strongly, that is to say, as an asymmetric burden borne by religious citizens. As we move forward it will be important to bear in mind Taylor's reconstructed phenomenology of secularization and the implications it has toward our public openness to transcendent moral sources. Religious citizens who allegedly travel with heavier "metaphysical baggage" may have difficulty reducing their moral sources to purely immanent ones. Habermas recognizes this existential difficulty clearly. What he may not sufficiently recognize, however, is the extent to which the translation requirement leaves religious citizens without a language, rendering suspect his claim that secular language is simply accessible; evidently not all citizens find it to be so. Maeve Cooke, however, does recognize this problem and provides some salient criticisms of the translation requirement along what I would call pragmatic lines.

Although we must reserve judgment on the truth or falsity of metaphysical claims under postmetaphysical conditions, Habermas has not given

---

[178] Habermas, "Equal Treatment of Cultures," 310.

up on truth conceived as context-transcending validity claims. Therefore, truth is at stake in democratic deliberation. Indeed, he claims that a "post-truth" democracy would no longer be a democracy.[179] However, as Cooke points out, Habermas understands context-transcending validity claims as "transcendence from within" and rules out what Cooke calls "otherworldly" points of reference. Since Habermas will only allow immanent sources of validity, he must insist upon translation. However, there are several reasons why this requirement is problematic, even within the context of his philosophy.

For example, Cooke notes that it is far from clear that Habermas can deliver on his promise of context-transcendent truth on the basis of exclusively immanent sources, and that even sympathetic commentators have questioned the success of his formal pragmatics for this purpose. Moreover, he has waffled as to whether he favors a context-transcending or contextualist position.[180] In addition, it is difficult to distinguish 'context-transcendence' from 'metaphysical' if the former is literally beyond any humanly accessible context. For example, a pragmatist would argue that Habermas's conception of an ideal speech situation is too metaphysical to be of much use. As we will see later, Rorty criticizes Habermas along these lines and Cooke likewise points out this inconsistency. For Cooke, these criticisms do not pose an insurmountable obstacle to Habermas's project, but she does question his description of it as "postmetaphysical."[181] To her initial objections, I would add that if Habermas is to maintain his postmetaphysical stance, he faces a further problem of consistency because it seems that once he makes truth as context-transcending validity a goal of deliberative democracy, he abandons a purely procedural model of communicative action. I find it hard to imagine how one could talk about context-transcending validity and avoid talking about substantive commitments insofar as context-transcending validity, for many people, involves the validity of substantive worldviews. But in order to introduce these into the discussion, we would have to surrender the claim to be postmetaphysical. The fact that Habermas sees deliberative democracy as "an epistemically demanding form of government"[182] means that it is difficult in principle to suspend judgment, even for the purposes of public accessibility, on the epistemic validity of substantive

---

[179] Maeve Cooke, "A Secular State for a Postsecular Society? Postmetaphysical Political Theory and the Place of Religion," *Constellations,* 14.2 (2007): 224.
[180] Cooke, 226.
[181] Cooke, 226.
[182] Cooke, 224.

worldviews. Thus, allowing only immanent sources of validity on the basis of publicly established truth sits uncomfortably with the suspension of judgment required by postmetaphysical thinking. If this is the case, the translation requirement, construed as a complementary learning process, seems disingenuous. Cooke also questions the translation requirement's restrictiveness and suspects that it compromises the conditions of political legitimacy for many citizens, specifically those who credit transcendent or "otherworldly" moral sources: an unwelcome consequence for any political theory.

Firstly, as Cooke persuasively argues, the translation requirement denies the transformative power of rational deliberation that Habermas elsewhere considers a central component of communicative action. For example, he has argued that because consensus is achieved, not merely produced, and because all interlocutors in a democratic process, in order to be rational, must be willing to change their minds if reason warrants, rational deliberation has great transformative power. When it comes to religion in the public sphere, however, his translation requirement preempts this transformative dialogue by having participants submit their arguments in a generally accessible, or secular, language at the outset. If arguments were simply generally accessible to all participants prior to the deliberative process, the process itself would seem to be a moot point. Moreover, because everybody is speaking the same language from the outset, transformation of perspectives is unlikely, indeed unnecessary. Therefore, Cooke argues that a generally accessible language cannot be required at the outset of the deliberative process, otherwise the search for context-transcending validity would appear pointless; we would already have the answers we need. In other words, the translation requirement preempts the "complementary learning process" that Habermas wants to achieve among religious and secular interlocutors. I would further add that it is very difficult to know what a generally accessible language would look like prior to deliberation. Therefore, as a prerequisite for deliberation, translation into a generally accessible language – whatever this might look like – is self-defeating.

Secondly, Cooke argues that neither "can general accessibility be understood as a condition that has to be satisfied *in fact* at the end of a process of argumentative deliberation."[183] Part of the intent of the translation requirement is to ensure that citizens come to decisions based on the same, rationally agreed upon, reasons. Again, Habermas thinks that democracy is an epistemically

---

[183] Cooke, 229.

demanding form of government, and that deliberation seeks to achieve rational consensus, rather than mere de facto accord, or *modus vivendi*. Such a requirement is certainly demanding, indeed it is rigorous to the point of being unworkable. In a pluralistic democracy, we can neither expect nor require that degree of consensus; nevertheless, we can often achieve a pragmatically workable solution. If we seriously insisted upon all citizens offering the same reasons for their assent to a particular proposal, political deliberation would be interminable. To be fair, Habermas probably does not seriously insist upon actual agreement of this kind; it remains for him an ideal type. In fact, he recognizes the practical necessity of the principle of majority rule in official public deliberation. However, majority rule does not terminate the ongoing epistemic process – the search for truth – but is simply the provision "that the fallible majority opinion may be considered a reasonable basis for common practice until further notice."[184] Again, the process of rational deliberation, precisely due to its fallibility, presupposes the transformative power of argumentation. Citizens of a democracy must stand ready to revise, abandon, or change their opinions as reason warrants. However, should we expect this situation to be permanent or temporary? In other words, will the epistemic process eventually come to an end or is it always in principle open to revision? In Cooke's judgment, there are severe problems attending the former option and there is evidence that Habermas favors the latter.[185] The latter option coincides with his procedural account of communicative action: the type of consensus achieved is an agreement upon the norms and principles for reaching agreement, rather than on substantive agreement itself. If this interpretation is accurate, Habermas would seem committed to the view that political legitimacy does not depend upon the kind of agreement the translation requirement seems to mandate. Indeed, such agreement, in principle, is always beyond our power to achieve. For example, one cannot expect substantive agreement on any issue in a pluralistic democracy, which is why the principle of majority rule is a fixture of democratic decision-making. But even the majority cannot be expected to agree

---

[184] Cooke, 229.
[185] As Cooke says elsewhere, "Habermas asserts a connection between the justification of validity claims and the critical evaluation of reasons in argumentation; he emphasizes, in addition, that argumentation is essentially open. He explains: "… it belongs to the grammatical role of the expression 'to justify' (*begründen*) that we cannot once and for all place reasons, or kinds of reasons, in a hierarchy in which 'final' reasons would stand at the top." *Language and Reason: A Study of Habermas's Pragmatics* (Cambridge, MA: The MIT Press, 1994), 108.

on every issue, much less agree for substantially the same reasons; everybody makes compromises and allowances.[186] Therefore, political legitimacy cannot depend on substantive agreement. Rather, political legitimacy, in Cooke's words, "is dependent only on the orientation towards the idea of norms and principles that are the object of a discursively achieved general agreement. But if this is the case, the achievement, through generally accessible reasons cannot be a condition of political legitimacy, and the translation requirement is redundant."[187] So we cannot reasonably expect generally accessible reasons to emerge even at the end of the deliberative process any more than we can make them a prerequisite for it.

Thirdly, a related point is that Habermas fails to appreciate the way in which argumentation actually works in practice. As Cooke points out, we are more often challenged by arguments that are significantly different from our own, arguments that are unexpected or unfamiliar. Moreover, arguments that are challenging for this reason tend to result, not in one being converted to another perspective, but in the emergence of an entirely new perspective. Habermas does not sufficiently grasp this Hegelian point. Thus, he is faced with a dilemma: if he makes translation into generally accessible language a requirement of deliberation at the outset, he rules out the possibility that perspectives might emerge that were unanticipated by any of the participants prior to deliberation. If he makes generally accessible language a condition that must be satisfied at the end of the process, he denies the transformative power of unfamiliar arguments that might challenge existing opinions and offer new perspectives. Both of these implications are problematic from the standpoint of decision making models, whether ideal or actual.

Cooke's criticisms aim to remedy what she sees as an unwelcome consequence of the translation requirement, namely, that it impairs the political autonomy of citizens who credit "otherworldly" reasons for political action rather than secular ones. Habermas's conception of political autonomy is based upon citizens' rational insight into the validity of the laws to which they are subject. Following Kant, citizens must see themselves as the authors and addressees of the law. But, importantly, they can only do so through rational

---

[186] As Phil Enns says: "Habermas is correct that enforceable political decisions must be in a language accessible to all citizens. Where Habermas goes wrong is in asserting that the justification for these decisions must be in the same language" "Habermas, Democracy and Religious Reasons," *The Heythrop Journal*, LI (2010), 586.

[187] Cooke, "A Secular State for a Postsecular Society," 229.

insight into the normative, context-transcending validity claims upon which it is based. Moreover, these validity claims, though context-transcending, are secular or "innerworldly" to use Cooke's term. We can only credit immanent sources of validity in public deliberation. Unfortunately, this qualification has the consequence of restricting the political autonomy of those citizens who do not see the legitimacy of their claims as resting on purely immanent sources of validity. In other words, the translation requirement weakens the political autonomy of some, perhaps many, religious citizens. This is not to say that religious citizens who do not subscribe to purely immanent reasons cannot rationally discern the practical necessity of the formal secularism of public reasons. Surely they can, and many do. But it does not follow that they regard these reasons as true in a context-transcending way. As Cooke summarizes: "Rational acceptance that secularly justified laws and decisions are pragmatically necessary in a given context (for instance in order to avoid religious strife) is not the same as rational insight into their validity."[188] But it is rational insight in precisely this sense that Habermas considers necessary for political legitimacy, according to Cooke. Moreover, unless citizens see themselves as subject to laws "for the right reasons," rather than on the basis of a mere *modus vivendi*, the constitutional state cannot secure social stability. Thus, any attempt to credit non-immanent sources of validity, in addition to carrying cumbersome metaphysical baggage, is potentially dangerous. Therefore, religious citizens need to translate their reasons into secular ones in order to achieve the same rational insight into the validity of laws and democratic decisions as their secular counterparts.

In my judgment, and that of Cooke, Habermas's concern is overstated. But I believe his point about the illegitimacy of "otherworldly" or transcendent reasons within public discourse is worth pursuing. In a pluralistic liberal democracy, it appears unfair, not to mention impractical, to insist that all citizens agree for the same reasons, even the same secular ones, and Habermas presumably knows this. Moreover, he has acknowledged that the burden of translation that religious citizens bear should not be exacerbated by denying the existential and psychological pull that religious worldviews exercise over the entirety of their lives, not just their political decisions. On this point, Cooke quotes Nicholas Wolterstorff, who reminds us that it is the conviction of religious citizens "that they ought to strive for wholeness, integrity, integration, in their

---

[188] Cooke, 223.

lives: that they ought to allow the Word of God, the teachings of Torah, the command and example of Jesus, or whatever, to shape their existence as a whole, including then, their social and political existence."[189] Wolterstorff clearly sees "otherworldly" moral sources as admissible to public deliberation. Indeed, in a recent book on justice, he goes much further, arguing that only a theistic account can ground the human rights discourse that liberal democracies cherish.[190] Although it is not necessary for my purposes to defend so strong a claim, I believe it is instructive for my project to present some aspects of Wolterstorff's case that illustrate how "otherworldly" or what I will henceforth call 'transcendent' moral sources can be rationally argued and rendered publicly accessible.

Recall Taylor's point that a sizable part of the philosophical project of modernity has been the attempt to find adequate immanent moral sources. Since the nineteenth century, particularly Nietzsche, it is far from obvious that this task has borne much fruit. Wolterstorff also takes up "Nietzsche's Challenge": whether or not any objective basis for morality is possible after the demise of religion. He quotes Raimond Gaita who alleges that we are "whistling in the dark" if we expect this challenge to be met. He argues that all secular rationales for grounding human rights, claims such as "human beings are inestimably precious, that they are ends in themselves, that they are owed unconditional respect, that they possess inalienable rights, and, of course that they possess inalienable dignity" all lack the "simple power of the religious ways of speaking."[191] Of course, this claim is contentious. But that is precisely the point: very few philosophers can agree on an adequate response to this challenge. This fact alone does not necessarily prove that there is no adequate response, but it does suggest "given that, after many attempts, no one has succeeded in giving such an account, it seems unlikely that it can be done".[192] Wolterstorff's skepticism is shared by philosophers who do not share his particular theological views. Again, this is not proof positive that all such secular attempts are "whistling in the dark", but it does justify skepticism of the claim that religious resources are completely irrelevant to modernity's task of developing adequate moral sources for liberal society. Likewise, Habermas has come to appreciate that the semantic content of religious language is not completely exhausted.

---

[189] Quoted in Cooke, 232.
[190] Nicholas Wolterstorff, *Justice: Rights and Wrongs* (Princeton University Press, 2008).
[191] Quoted in Wolterstorff, 324.
[192] Wolterstorff, 325.

Wolterstorff argues that the Kantian grounding of human rights in human capacities has serious shortcomings. It is not necessary to go into the details of those criticisms here. Suffice it to say that Wolterstorff finds the Kantian grounding of human rights in the capacity of rational agency to be unconvincing for a number of reasons, including the fact that not all humans possess it and a number of non-human animals do. There is a sense in which Habermas, in my judgment, too readily translates the Judeo-Christian notion of the image of God, for example, into universal human dignity without appropriating the conceptual resources needed to preserve the content of the claim. Although he never engages Habermas directly, I believe Wolterstorff would concur. Having sketched an account of the image of God and its implications for human nature, he poses the following question, suggested by the translation requirement: "Suppose that from the nature-resemblance construal of *imago dei* one drops the component of resembling God, keeping just the idea of human nature. Does human nature as I have all too briefly explained it, suffice to ground natural human rights?"[193] Wolterstorff argues that it does not, because it faces the same problems as the aforementioned Kantian approach: it reduces human dignity to the possession of capacities which some humans have and some do not. In the Judeo-Christian version, however, the worth of human beings is not related to a capacity they may or may not possess, but is bestowed on the basis of the relational property of being loved by God. This is the crucial point that is left out of translation from 'the image of God' to the religiously neutral 'equal dignity of all human beings'; and this difference is substantive, not merely procedural. Habermas's suspicion that something important is indeed lost by modernity's skepticism is exactly right, however, his strategy of translation to recover that semantic content falters precisely because it cannot credit the transcendent basis of that content.

Wolterstorff claims – as does Taylor to a lesser extent – that the genealogy of human rights discourse in liberal democracies, one that Habermas strives to affirm, "has its origins not in fourteenth century nominalism or seventeenth century political individualism but in the Hebrew and Christian Scriptures."[194] Perhaps this is why Habermas's attempt to credit the language of human dignity but not its traditional transcendent explanation is dubious. Habermas has indeed reflected on the question – although he offers a negative answer – "whether the pacified, secular state is reliant on normative

---

[193] Wolterstorff, 351.
[194] Wolterstorff, 388.

presuppositions that it cannot itself guarantee."[195] Perhaps it is time to reconsider our collective answer to this question. Wolterstorff in particular gives expression to an unsettling consequence of the failure to ground moral sources under secularism: "Suppose the secularization thesis is true, that modernization leads to secularization. Suppose, in particular, that the framework of religious conviction that gave birth to our moral subculture of rights is destined, under conditions of modernity, to erode and be replaced by a variety of secular outlooks. What must we then expect to happen to that subculture?"[196] His prognosis is not optimistic. He acknowledges that, in the event that religion completely erodes, a secular outlook could, in principle, take its place. Some secularists do not express any anxiety about replacing the originally religious foundation of liberal values, but others do. Rorty, for example, admits that he is a free-loading atheist,[197] whereas Habermas still sees the Kantian project as the most viable secular alternative for the creative salvaging of morality. Wolterstorff also says that the Kantian basis for human rights, despite the problems he finds there, is the only viable secular alternative that could replace religious sources with minimal damage to our moral discourse. But there would still be damage. For example, if moral consideration depends upon certain capacities, those who lack those capacities would seem to be excluded with unfortunate moral consequences. Furthermore, if the Kantian framework replaces the religious one *en masse* – a prospect Wolterstorff admits he finds highly unlikely – would it not erode our egalitarian intuitions by making rationality paramount to the extent that, to coin a phrase, 'fortune favors the bright'? I would also add that far from being accessible to everyone, Kantian morality is highly abstract. It lacks the simple power and imagination – the accessibility – of the religious vision.[198] Sometimes rationality plays a smaller role in the practical extension of moral consideration than philosophers and theorists believe. As Wolterstorff observes "*Uncle Tom's Cabin*, full of

---

[195] Habermas, 101.
[196] Wolterstorff, 389 – 90.
[197] Richard Rorty, *Contingency, Irony, and Solidarity*. (Cambridge University Press, 1989), 74.
[198] Mark Johnson argues that despite Kant's insistence on 'pure reason' as the ground for morality, Kant's moral theory is largely imaginative and metaphoric. I am sympathetic to this interpretation, but would still contend that Kant exchanges the more accessible metaphors in the Judeo-Christian tradition for more abstract metaphors that probably have much less to do with the way most people, philosophers included, practice morality. See Mark Johnson, *Moral Imagination: Implications of Cognitive Science for Ethics* (Chicago: University of Chicago Press, 1993), 75 – 76.

sentimentality, was far more effective in diminishing the violation of persons in the nineteenth century than was Kant's *Groundwork of the Metaphysics of Morals.*"[199]

However, this statement suggests another way of conceptualizing the problem of adequate moral sources, one favored by Rorty in particular. Perhaps sympathy alone can sustain our liberal values. Although these values might have emerged from a particular religious narrative, we can see narratives in general as valuable for expanding our sympathies for other human beings, as the example of *Uncle Tom's Cabin* shows. However, Wolterstoff warns that sympathy, like rationality, is not a quality found in equal abundance across the human population. Nevertheless, the point remains that rationality is not enough: one needs substantive and affective elements to sustain an adequate basis for morality. In addition, the fact that Rorty concedes that the secularist lives off inherited capital from a substantive religious worldview, reinforces Wolterstorff's worry about what happens when the capital runs out. His grim prognosis is that erosion of our religious inheritance entails the erosion of our moral subculture of human rights.

I am perhaps more optimistic about the prospects of secular morality than is Wolterstorff, and I am not defending the strong account of theistic grounding of human rights that he is, but his argument is instructive for a number of reasons. First, he is not numbered among the "new traditionalists." On a number of issues he is what liberals would call progressive despite – or perhaps because of – his theological conservatism. Second, he is not naïve regarding the other options available to the philosophical tradition for adequately grounding moral sources. He simply sees, like Taylor, that there is another, darker side to modernity that its rosier defenders seldom notice. As mentioned above in reference to Taylor's narrative, the search for adequate moral sources has been a preoccupation of modern thinkers especially given the challenge of the "immanent counter-Enlightenment": that heroic misanthropy associated primarily with Nietzsche. Most secular Anglo-American philosophers, although there are significant exceptions, dismiss the charge that, after Nietzsche, morality is meaningless, and they continue to plug away at the task of grounding morality rationally with a minimum of metaphysical presuppositions. Such attempts are contentious, evidenced by the fact that no free-standing account has so far done everything we want it to. But perhaps more importantly, and more

---

[199] Wolterstorff, 392.

subtly, such philosophers, trained as they are in rational analysis, simply fail to see how something like Nietzsche's valorization of violence might be attractive to those who cannot handle – in the absence of religion – the disciplinary requirements of modern society, a point that Taylor makes to good effect.[200] Wolterstorff also thinks that without strong substantive and affective ties, humanity's experiment in universal human solidarity will be brief, that nothing will remain to hold our tribalism in check. Again, even if one does not accept this narrative, or its implied pessimism from the perspective of the secularization thesis, I believe that its possibility permits one to say that religious resources, grounded as they are in transcendent points of reference, are not irrelevant to modernity's search for adequate moral sources. Moreover, we should not simply rule them out *a priori*, or translate their semantic resources into rationally purified secular "cognitive contents." We have already seen some of the weaknesses of such an approach.

From Wolterstorff's account of religiously grounded human rights, I believe we can conclude that transcendent sources of morality have something to offer to contemporary moral debate, but are they legitimate from the perspective of communicative redemption? In other words, are they publicly accessible? I see no reason why not. Firstly, one can make rational arguments in support of them; they are not simply suspended in mid-air, as it were. One can argue rationally that transcendent points of reference make good sense in the context of moral and political deliberation on the basis of our experience as human beings and given the ends we want to achieve as citizens working toward a more just society. Careful, analytical arguments can be made on behalf of this position, as should be clear to anyone who has read Wolterstorff's book. One might object that the fact that religiously-based arguments terminate in transcendent points of reference is problematic from the standpoint of 'public reason'. But secular arguments, especially regarding morality, also terminate at a certain point in improvable premises which often involve appeal to principles that approximate 'transcendence' to human context and experience. So I think such an objection

---

[200] Taylor, 185: "[T]he concern about leveling, the end of heroism, of greatness, has also been turned into a fierce denunciation of the modern moral order, and everything it stands for, as we see with Nietzsche. Attempts to build a polity around a rival notion of order in the very heart of modern civilization, most notably the various forms of fascism and related authoritarianism, have failed. But the continued popularity of Nietzsche shows that his devastating critique still speaks to many people today. The modern order, though entrenched – perhaps even because entrenched – still awakens much resistance."

will not do. It is especially dubious when we remind ourselves that most bases for public morality entail some robust substantive or affective account of ourselves as human beings. We are not, *contra* the Kantians, concerned exclusively with rationality. But nevertheless, religious premises can be, and have been historically, sustained on the basis of rational argumentation. Canadian Jewish philosopher Jay Newman ably summarizes many of the points I have been making thus far:

> The fact is that morality is not purely a matter of reason – or intuition – and it actually was around in the world that existed prior to the time that the ancient Greeks "invented" systematic philosophy as we know it. Secondly, the fact that a Marxist materialist or non-Christian might be inclined to dismiss a point as irrelevant does not necessarily mean that the point is an insufficiently "general" moral consideration. For one thing, an appeal to something like the doctrine of creation or the gospel of redemption can conceivably be defended by arguments in natural or philosophical theology, in which case, ironically, it might ultimately have to be regarded even by the secularist as more "objective" than non-theological moral appeals.[201]

In other words, the fact that somebody or other dismisses transcendent moral sources is no measure of their rational defensibility or public accessibility. As Phil Enns also reminds us, "People may differ on religious beliefs, but the rational grounds for those beliefs are available to all and open to rational discussion. The justification and application of beliefs are never a private matter so that religious beliefs are always open to public scrutiny and subject to criticism on rational grounds such as coherence or consistency."[202]

To be clear, I am not here adopting a classical foundationalist position with respect to the grounding of religious belief. As I mentioned in the first chapter, we may be rationally entitled to at least some religious beliefs without explicit argumentation. We may treat some beliefs as innocent until proven guilty. This approach is common to both Wolterstorff's Reformed epistemology

---

[201] Jay Newman, *On Religious Freedom* (Ottawa: University of Ottawa Press, 1991), 126.
[202] Enns, 588.

and Stout's pragmatism.[203] However, we cannot treat our entitled beliefs as indefeasible in the way the classical foundationalist would; such beliefs can be proven guilty in principle and, thus, are not immune from criticism. It is in this respect that religious beliefs are open to rational critique just like any other beliefs. They are not uniquely private or inaccessible to public scrutiny. Where I part ways with Habermas, and join ranks with Wolterstorff and Stout, is in thinking that the case against religion has not been made as decisively as its critics assume. Wolterstorff, of course, is a Christian whose philosophy often has apologetic intent, but even Stout, an unbeliever, recognizes that the critique of religion is "a harder and more complicated line of work than it has often been made out to be."[204] He continues:

> It would be a simpler process if the dialectic that led from Hume to Feuerbach had essentially completed the critique of religion as such, as Marx thought it had. But the critique of religion is a trickier business than Marx thought it was. James raises the possibility that some of the religious reasoning that Hume and Feuerbach dismissed as merely wishful thinking is better understood as pragmatically justified hopeful thinking. And some types of religion – the ones Cornell West terms prophetic – function neither as social narcotics that disable the pursuit of justice nor as justifications for existing injustices. So the sweeping dismissals and all-purpose explanations of religion that remain a staple of critical theory do not persuade me.[205]

So it is not clear that religious rationales are simply indefensible or inaccessible to 'public' reason. Of course, in practice it may require a lot of work to show that particular religious beliefs are rationally defensible and this work is usually carried out in specialized corners of academia rather than in full view of the public. But the epistemic habits of philosophers with respect to religion are probably not much more commendable than those of the average citizen. To quote Stout again:

> Philosophers who do not pay much attention to the philosophy of religion often assume that the case has long been closed on the question of

---

[203] Jeffrey Stout, "Comments on Six Responses to *Democracy and Tradition*," *Journal of Religious Ethics*, 33.4 (2005): 712
[204] Stout, 714.
[205] Stout, 714.

rational entitlement and theistic belief. It would be too harsh to assume that such philosophers are sheltering their commitments from challenge, but I suspect that they behave epistemically more or less the way theists do. We all take some commitments for granted if they seem to be serving us well. Getting on with life often takes priority over inspecting all of the conceivably relevant arguments and evidence.[206]

As such, practical considerations get in our way when it comes to seriously evaluating religious claims and counter-claims. I doubt that these debates in philosophy of religion will be settled anytime soon, but we should remember that merely charging a religious rationale with being an insufficiently general claim or lacking public accessibility is to ignore a lot of important arguments that seriously attempt to render explicit the rational entitlement to those claims. Since it is impractical on the level of political praxis to cultivate the exacting epistemic standards that even philosophers fail to exemplify, perhaps the best we can do is to cultivate a generous attitude with respect to the epistemic entitlement of citizens to express their arguments in religious language. Again, I agree with the pragmatist intuition that we should widen our vocabulary and remain willing to engage the arguments of our interlocutors in whatever form those arguments take. From the standpoint of political praxis, then, all sorts of reasons that are not strictly secular might be publicly accessible. I will have more to say about this in a subsequent chapter.

But, secondly, as for the public accessibility of a secular grounding of human rights, for example, it is not clear that the Kantian account – Wolterstorff's only secular candidate and the one Habermas favors – could practically replace religiously motivated grounds for the simple reason that it lacks the texture, imagination, and rhetorical power of the tradition it translates. To quote Gaita once again, all secular expressions "lack the simple power of the religious ways of speaking" when it comes to articulating human dignity. No doubt some philosophers will disagree with this, but there is also no doubt that religious ways of speaking have great semantic resources that may well be missing from modernity's thinned-out Kantian translation and these religious ways of speaking are themselves accessible to many citizens, religious or otherwise. Habermas has increasingly recognized the potential of religious language. For

---

[206] Stout, 713.

example, consider his following meditation on what "the image of God" regarding human embryos might mean to contemporary secular citizens:

> In the controversy, for instance, about the way to deal with human embryos, many voices still evoke the first book of Moses, Genesis 1: 27: "So God created man in his image, in the image of God created he him." In order to understand what *Gottesebenbildlichkeit* – "in the likeness of God" – means, one need not believe that the God who is love creates Adam and Eve, free creatures who are like him. One knows there can be no love without the recognition of the self in the other, nor freedom without mutual recognition. So, the other who has human form must himself be free in order to be able to return God's affection. In spite of his likeness to God, however, this other is also imagined as being God's creature .... This *creatural nature* of the image expresses an intuition which in the present context may even speak to those who are tone-deaf to religious connotations.[207]

Habermas's caveat that one need not believe in God to understand the metaphor makes the point that this way of speaking has rhetorical power and accessibility not only to those familiar with the biblical tradition but also to those who are religiously tone-deaf. Therefore, Habermas seems very much open to the possibility that as-yet-untranslated religious language can be publicly accessible in precisely the way I have been arguing above. Indeed, such language may be more accessible and efficacious than the Kantian translation of the same point, especially given the fact that one can hardly ground the dignity of human embryos on rational capacity. Habermas goes on to elaborate on the implications of this non-secularized religious insight for the issue at hand:

> Because he is both in one, God the Creator and God the Redeemer, this creator does not need, in his actions, to abide by the laws of nature like a technician, or by the rules of a code like a biologist or computer scientist .... Now, one need not believe these theological premises in order to understand what follows from this, namely, that an entirely different kind of dependence, perceived as a causal one, becomes involved if the difference assumed as inherent in the concept of creation were to disappear, and the place of God be taken by a peer – if, that is, a human

---

[207] Habermas, "Faith and Knowledge," 336.

> being would intervene, according to his own preferences and without being justified in assuming, at least counterfactually, a consent of the concerned other, in the random combination of the parents' sets of chromosomes .... Would not the first human being to determine, at his own discretion, the natural essence of another human being at the same time destroy the equal freedoms that exist among persons of equal birth in order to ensure their difference?[208]

Habermas's novel use of biblical language is, I believe, a model of the way religious language can inform public debate by offering the kind of perspectives that have transformative power. These languages cannot be expected to be 'publicly accessible' in the sense of secular; that would be to rob them of the transformative power Habermas elsewhere attributes to democratic deliberation. Therefore, I believe that the criterion of 'public accessibility' as coextensive with 'secular' needs to be rethought.

However, Wolterstorff's view can be criticized for compromising solidarity among citizens within pluralistic societies by making some sort of theism a prerequisite for the political values we all embrace. Clearly, Wolterstorff thinks a robust metaphysical foundation – a theistic foundation – is necessary for grounding human rights discourse. I do not think it prudent to defend this stronger contention. Stout, by contrast, is skeptical of any such grounding; he wants ethics without metaphysics. He says:

> The purpose served by pragmatic ethical theory ... is to make clear that a society divided over the nature and existence of God is not thereby condemned to view its ethical discourse as an unconstrained endeavor. If the God of the philosophers is dead, not everything is permitted. There can still be morally valid obligations to constrain us, as well as many forms of excellence in which to rejoice. Pragmatism comes into conflict with theology in ethical theory mainly at those points where someone asserts that the truth-claiming function of ethics depends, for its *objectivity*, on positing a transcendent and perfect being.[209]

---

[208] Habermas, 336.
[209] Jeffrey Stout, *Democracy and Tradition* (Princeton University Press, 2005), 268.

Clearly, Stout thinks that Nietzsche's challenge is misguided, as is the quest to ground the objectivity of ethical discourse in a divine being. On this point, he and Wolterstorff are deeply divided. Since the latter thinks that Kantianism is the only viable candidate to replace a theistic grounding, he is suspicious of Stout's pragmatism.

For example, he critiques Stout's Hegelian expressivism, whereby norms emerge in the course of practice. According to Wolterstorff, expressivism offers an inadequate account of moral obligation. Simply because a group has a set of practices that they regard as normative, it does not follow that one is thereby obligated to adopt those practices. As Wolterstorff puts it, "The rabbit of moral obligation cannot be pulled out from the hat of moral practice. The practices are simply too defective and incomplete for that."[210] He notes that philosophers who grant this point have essentially two options: one strategy posits a hypothetical, idealized moral practitioner and asks what such a person would require; the second strategy posits an actual morally perfect practitioner, i.e. God, and asks what this person does in fact require. "The pragmatist," however, "dislikes both options. He wants to talk about our actual practices, not about some idealized version thereof. The last thing he wants to do is commit pragmatism to theism."[211] Indeed, given the above block quote, Stout does want to avoid committing a pragmatic understanding of norms to any kind of theism. But Stout is also aware that our practices do not guarantee moral obligation. What if our practices are wrong? What if nobody desires the good? In Wolterstorff's estimation:

> Stout both resists all attempts to provide metaphysical grounding for the good and resists all attempts to ground the good in human activities of some sort. As a pragmatist, he is content to say that the good is what is approbation worthy. That's enough. Norms – the *right* norms, not the norms in force in some group – are then understood as specifying the means necessary for achieving whatever be the good in view. Norms are objective because the good is objective.[212]

---

[210] Nicholas Wolterstorff, "Jeffrey Stout on Democracy and Its Contemporary Christian Critics" *Journal of Religious Ethics*, 33.4 (2005): 641.
[211] Wolterstorff, 641.
[212] Wolterstorff, 642.

Nevertheless, positing some goods as objective still does not obligate one to achieve those goods; there are many conceivable goods I could achieve that I am not morally obligated to achieve. At the end of the day, the pragmatist must pick and choose. For Wolterstorff, then, "The ethical substance and tradition of liberal democracy do not incorporate commitment to Stout's expressive pragmatist account of moral obligations. Just as liberal democracy has to be pulled loose from the contractarian's embrace, so too it has to be pulled loose from the pragmatist's embrace."[213] He continues: "Democracy is hospitable to pragmatists; it does not require of its members that they be pragmatists."[214]

Stout admits that citizens of a democracy do not have to accept his account of moral obligation, but wants to defend the pragmatic notion that norms are the result of social construction in a way that even the Christian could countenance. Here we see Stout's aptitude for immanent critique at work:

> When I say that such norms are creatures of social practices and social relationships in which persons participate, I take care to leave open, for the purposes of this discussion, what sorts of persons exist. Suppose God exists. Suppose that God's inner life has the structure of two persons united in love, beheld by a third, whose person consists in their communal relatedness or spirit. Suppose further that the God whose inner life has this triune structure enters into a practical social covenant with human beings. Suppose this covenant involves mutual accountability oriented around a practice of promising and promise keeping. Suppose that the resulting promises go hand in hand with commands issued by one existing person to others and that the promises and commands, taken together, give rise to ethical obligations. Then it makes sense to say that the ethical obligations just mentioned are creatures of social-practical doings. If this is so, then how does Christian theism conflict with the pragmatic thesis about the genesis of ethical norms that I have put forward?[215]

Of course, as Stout makes clear, these are not his suppositions. However, they do demonstrate how a theist might be a pragmatist on a social level. The theist

---

[213] Wolterstorff, 643.
[214] Wolterstorff, 643.
[215] Jeffrey Stout, "Comments on Six Responses to *Democracy and Tradition*," 720.

simply includes another person(s) – albeit the supreme Person – in the relevant norm-forming community. Therefore, although Wolterstorff's criticisms of Stout's theory of moral obligation have merit, Stout's response indicates that the metaphysical grounding of norms in the strong sense that Wolterstorff defends is unnecessary. Therefore, we need not compromise the solidarity of citizens in a democracy by committing them either to expressivism or theism.

Despite their disagreements, Wolterstorff shares much of Stout's pragmatism on the social level; both eschew a common basis and criticize moral restraints on offering religious reasons in public. Moreover, Wolterstorff, unlike the new traditionalists, shares a commitment to democracy, as Stout acknowledges.[216] Wolterstoff is not trying to achieve consensus, either on the liberal model or on the basis of religion, as would the new traditionalists. Rather, I see his contribution as an example of a way in which religiously based ethics can be rigorously defended by philosophical arguments that are, in principle, publicly accessible. They also, in an indirect way, test the limits of the translation requirement that both he and Stout reject.

As we have seen, Habermas has staked out an epistemic territory "between naturalism and religion." In other words, he sees postsecularism as requiring that secular citizens not take for granted metaphysical naturalism when offering their arguments in the public sphere. He warns that the secular worldview should not be over-generalized; religious convictions must not be considered simply irrational compared to secular knowledge. Neither should we see the process of translation from religious to secular language as the secularization thesis has conventionally interpreted it: as society's emancipation from religion. Such a process would not only ignore criticism of the subtraction story of secularization, but more importantly, it would violate the principle of state neutrality as surely as would the establishment of some particular religion because it would be tantamount to the establishment of secular*ism*. Thus, believers and unbelievers are involved in a complementary learning process: believers must translate their particularistic language into the publicly accessible language and unbelievers must treat religion as at least a potential source of insight and meaning with value for human beings generally. However, once these epistemological points are granted, what remains of the normative weight of the translation requirement?

---

[216] Stout, *Democracy and Tradition*, 298.

The answer to this question rests on an important distinction, made by Habermas, between formal and informal public spheres. The informal public sphere is the sphere of opinion formation, independent of the official political discourse. Indeed, as our historical excursus shows, this was one of the defining features of the emergent modern public sphere. In an informal or weak public sphere, at least in a democracy, a plurality of voices, including religious ones, compete for a fair hearing. Of course, the fact of pluralism may make some translation into the most accessible language necessary for practical purposes, but translation, strictly speaking, is not required. For this reason, I believe one should interpret the translation requirement as a pragmatic consideration, rather than a formal requirement, in the informal public sphere. In the case of formal or arranged publics, however, the translation requirement is applied more strictly. This is the domain of democratic legislation, the official political discourse. The translation requirement is in place here, because of the formal requirement of the neutrality of the state. Certainly, it is important that the formal political deliberations take into consideration the informal debate in the public sphere; indeed the legitimacy of the opinion of the citizenry to inform and regulate the official political discourse is a defining feature of modern parliamentary democracy. Nevertheless, the distinction is important for preserving the neutrality of the state and the integrity of the democratic process.

Thus, Habermas seeks to preserve the normative weight of the translation requirement in the official political discourse. For example, members of parliament are not to appeal to religious arguments in their capacity as public representatives, regardless of whatever personal beliefs they may hold. Cooke and Wolterstorff question even this condition on the translation requirement; however, in Habermas's judgment, the absence of this qualification erodes the neutrality of the state by abandoning the need for at least some shared background assumptions and removing any restrictions on religiously-based arguments. Such a free-for-all strikes him as threatening democratic legitimacy. As we have seen, he argues that legitimacy derives from citizens' rational insight into the validity of the laws to which they are subject; a mere *modus vivendi* does not suffice. Thus, in the domain of official public discourse, or will formation, the translation requirement retains its obligatory, deontological status. If religious arguments entered into the formal public sphere, or were invoked in making the laws by which all citizens must abide and which state coercion must enforce, it would seriously undermine state neutrality.

In the following chapter, I will more fully address questions pertaining to state neutrality and the normativity of the translation requirement at the level of official public discourse. For my purposes in this chapter, I have endeavored to defend three main theses. Firstly, I have argued that the rationale behind Habermas's translation requirement can be questioned even on his own methodological assumptions. As we have seen, he has recently become more critical of the disenchantment narrative of secularization he acquired from Weber, and instead has come to see the task of secularization, following Kant and the critical theorists, as more of a salvage operation than a demolition. Nevertheless, he maintains that religious worldviews bear heavier metaphysical baggage. I have argued that this strain in Habermas's thought represents a remnant of the subtraction story of secularization, suggesting that Habermas's self-critique is not yet complete. A consistent extrapolation of his criticisms of Weber should culminate in something like Taylor's phenomenological description of the substantive sources of secularism. If Taylor is correct about these sources, I argue that one must question Habermas's assumption that secularism is the default language of 'the public'. Precisely because a secularist outlook does not lack particular substantive commitments, it must forego its claim to universality, and therefore also its alleged potential to secure political consensus. Once the assumption of secularism's default publicity is called into doubt, the translation requirement no longer follows as simply normative.

Secondly, I have argued in this chapter that the insight behind the translation requirement is better construed as a pragmatic concession to discourse in a democracy, rather than as a contractarian obligation. Religious citizens can certainly see the value in translating, when possible, the insights of their tradition into secular language in an effort to persuade their secular interlocutors. However, this practice is distinct from insisting that religious citizens must translate their religious language into secular language because the latter simply is the normative public language (by virtue of its rationality, epistemic normativity, or metaphysical 'lightness', etc.) I have suggested reasons for casting doubt on these assumptions and, consequently, on the strong construal of the translation requirement as well.

Thirdly, I have argued that something is indeed lost through secularism's evisceration of religious sources of meaning. Habermas has expressed this worry himself, and I have provided reasons to think that his skepticism regarding the capacity of secularism to sustain robust commitments to 'sacred' Western values, such as human rights discourse, is justified. Habermas also provides a striking example of what it means to exercise the semantic potential of religious language when dealing with contemporary political issues, such as the ethics of genetic engineering. I have argued that if Habermas can appropriate religious sources of meaning in this way, there should be no ban on religious citizens utilizing the resources of their own traditions in public discussion of such issues.

In the next chapter, I will continue to explore the translation requirement through an exposition of Habermas's essay "Religion in the Public Sphere." It will also be instructive to compare Habermas *vis-à-vis* Rawls on the rigidity of the translation requirement. In my judgment, the two positions are not simply equivalent, as is commonly assumed. I think Habermas offers a more nuanced account than Rawls, while staying within the broadly Kantian tradition in political theory. Nevertheless, even his more nuanced position is not immune from challenge. In what follows, I will continue to argue that the translation requirement should be relaxed. It is best construed as a pragmatic move in democratic discourse. Recently, Habermas has recognized that the strong construal of the translation requirement significantly impairs the political participation of religious citizens. His revised view in "Religion in the Public Sphere" is more generous with respect to religious language in public. However, Habermas is still concerned with the neutrality of the state and thinks that political legitimacy must be grounded in rational consensus rather than a mere *modus vivendi*. So while he contends that religious citizens can appeal to religious arguments in the informal public sphere, the realm of opinion formation, they ought not to do so in the formal public sphere, the realm of will formation. At the level of political will formation, i.e. Parliaments, religious arguments must be translated into secular language. Habermas believes that this revised translation proviso succeeds in extending to religious citizens the freedom to appeal to religious arguments while simultaneously safeguarding the neutrality of the state. While there is a genuine insight behind Habermas's revised translation proviso, for practical purposes it means that religious citizens must submit all of their arguments to secular translation if these arguments are to be politically efficacious. Habermas's revised proposal is arguably only a nominal relaxing of the translation requirement; in practice it remains in full force.

In chapter 3, I argue that even this revised proviso is too rigid. In order to preserve the neutrality of the state it suffices that the laws are parsed in as neutral a language as possible when drafted. It does not follow that those who debate these prospective laws, at the informal or formal level, need limit their arguments to secular ones. Again, if translation is useful with respect to brokering practical agreement, then so much the better. But it is problematic to assert the normativity of translation on the basis that secular arguments are public, and thus more likely to find assent, whereas religious arguments are private, and thus more likely to find dissent. The arguments that any given public finds persuasive is a matter of dialectical context, and defining some arguments as 'public' and others as 'private' is often simply another way of saying 'those arguments which secular citizens find persuasive and those which they do not'. The contest here is not between public reasons and private reasons, or secular reasons and religious reasons, but between those reasons that command universal assent by any rational person and those that do not. I will argue that, in political contexts, we do not have access, for practical purposes, to such universally compelling reasons. Instead, we have an array of reasons of varying degrees of controversiality. Unless we are willing to bar all controversial reasons from public debate, there seems to be no principled reason to single out religious reasons. Although religious reasons have served as the paradigm case for 'private reasons' in liberal theory, they are in principle no different from other controversial reasons. Through the use of more neutral examples, I try to demonstrate that pointing out that a reason is 'religious' or 'private' in this context is a red herring. The real issue is whether or not consensus is, or ought to be, a goal of democratic discourse. This question has been a theme throughout this project, but in the third chapter, I will deal with it in greater detail.

Chapter 3
Habermas vis-à-vis Rawls on Religion in the Public Sphere: Promissory Notes or Cognitive Contents?

In this chapter, we shall explore in more concrete terms the way that Habermas sees his translation requirement at work in political praxis. In an effort to elucidate his theory of public reason, I find it useful to compare it with that of John Rawls. Habermas and Rawls both propose theories of the way rational discourse should proceed in democracies. Although there are significant differences between the two, upon which I shall elaborate, both thinkers seem to consider the goal of discourse to be consensus, and thus the goal of any democratic discourse should be rational consensus. However, should consensus, as such, be the goal of democratic discourse? In what follows, I suggest reasons to question this assumption.

Both Habermas and Rawls insist that only 'public' or 'publicly accessible' reasons count as reasons in a secular democracy. Public reasons are, effectively, secular reasons; a paradigm example of a 'private reason' would be a religious reason, and such a reason does not count as justification in a secular democracy. The reason for this, according to Habermas and Rawls, is that citizens are both the authors and the addressees of the law; as such, every citizen, must understand (in principle) the justification of the law, and so this justification must be public, secular, and universal, rather than private and sectarian. This is especially true with respect to what Rawls calls the 'principles of basic justice', or when state coercion is invoked to restrict a particular liberty.

Habermas is aware that citizens in democracies may have religious justifications for their political views, but he insists that they must translate these justifications into secular ones in order to participate in democratic discourse. Rawls also says that citizens have a moral obligation to offer public reasons, and that private, i.e. religious, reasons act as merely "promissory notes" for public, i.e. secular, justifications.

Both Habermas and Rawls seem to couch this requirement in Kantian terms as an obligation incumbent on all rational persons within democratic discourse, at least at the institutional level in which the coercive power of the state is brought to bear. In this chapter, I continue to argue that this requirement ought to be construed in weaker, pragmatic terms. In what follows, I will present arguments which attempt to show that this weaker construal of Habermas's translation proviso secures all of the relevant protections afforded secular citizens and religious minorities under standard liberal theory, while significantly increasing the expressive freedom of religious citizens to couch their contribution to public debate in religious terms.

Taking a pragmatist line with respect to discourse, I suggest that the translation requirement, at both the formal and informal level of political discourse, is best construed as a pragmatic move in the course of argument. Religious citizens are usually capable of offering some secular reason for their view, while presumably finding it less compelling than their motivating, religious rationale. However, if we construe the goal of democratic discourse as Habermas and Rawls arguably do, namely consensus, strongly construed, we must say that merely offering a secular reason is not enough. It does not suffice that a majority of citizens agree on some concrete policy for some stated secular reason. Rather, they must first agree on premises that would count as acceptable to any reasonable person and then agree on the policy *for the same reasons*.

Robert Audi makes this principle explicit in his revision of Rawls. He argues that in addition to whatever religious reasons a citizen has for support of a public policy, one must also have a "motivationally sufficient secular reason." In other words, it is not enough for one to have a secular reason for pragmatic purposes, i.e. attempting to persuade a secular interlocutor, but one must have a secular reason that would motivate action *in the absence of religious reasons*. This seems like an undue burden to place on religious citizens as a condition for participation in public discourse.

In his more recent writings, Habermas has come to see this point and has offered a revision of his translation requirement. He now wants to say that citizens can appeal to whatever reasons they want in the informal public sphere (the domain of 'opinion formation') but must only appeal to secular, public reasons in the formal public sphere (the domain of 'will formation', i.e. Parliament). He thinks this institutional translation proviso solves the problem of excluding religious citizens in a democracy from political participation and preserves the neutrality of the state.

So far, so good, but the distinction between public and private reasons can be questioned. Indeed, as Nicholas Wolterstorff points out, the distinction is not between public reasons and private reasons or secular reasons versus religious reasons, but rather between premises that would be universally accepted by all rational people, and those that would not. Again, this would seem to follow if the goal of rational discourse, and thus democracy, is consensus: we would ideally try to find universally assented to premises for use in our political arguments. But of course, such premises are in almost all cases impossible to come by. So the distinction is not between premises that are public, in some mysterious sense of the term, and those that are private, but between universally accepted premises and contested premises. In what follows, I argue that the fact that we can't find universally accepted premises is problematic for liberal theorists like Habermas and Rawls, because there is very much reason to doubt there are such premises; moreover, I think we lack any non-question begging criteria for figuring out what those premises might be. The best democratic discourse can do is to proceed pragmatically from premises that are dialectically useful with respect to persuading a given audience, hopefully the widest audience possible in a pluralistic society.

Nevertheless, there is a sense in which Habermas's institutional translation proviso has force. The laws as written in a pluralistic democracy should not credit a particular religious tradition. The language at the level of legislation should remain as neutral as possible with respect to competing religions and ideologies.

Habermas has recently become more sensitive to the burdens that his translation requirement places on religious citizens. In the final part of this chapter, I look at his efforts to balance the burdens of religious and secular citizens such that the political participation of the former is unimpaired. I find much laudable in Habermas's efforts, while arguing that the translation requirement should be relaxed. In doing so, I present a revised proviso that I believe accomplishes everything Habermas wants to accomplish with respect to securing the neutrality of the state, while greatly balancing the respective burdens of religious and secular citizens. I then offer an analysis of this model in terms of the costs and benefits of such a scenario, concluding that it is a better system than the standard liberal model for all involved. I conclude the chapter by anticipating objections to my revisions of liberal theory and providing answers to them. But before drawing any such conclusion, we must first turn our attention to a close reading of Habermas's essay, "Religion and the Public Sphere."

Religion and the Public Sphere: Habermas and Rawls

Thus far, we have critically examined the role Habermas allows for religious arguments within the (mostly) informal public sphere. Now, we turn to a more explicit engagement of his view on the place of religion and the translation requirement in the formal realm of political will formation. The most fruitful place to begin is, unsurprisingly, an essay called "Religion and the Public Sphere."[217] Here, he argues for a middle ground between John Rawls and Robert Audi on the secular side and Nicholas Wolterstorff and Paul Weithman on the religious side. The former do not take the existential pull of religious beliefs on the rationale of citizens seriously enough, and place unreasonable burdens upon religious citizens in the process. The latter, in Habermas's judgment, erode the neutrality of the state by abandoning the need for at least some shared background assumptions and removing any restrictions on religiously-based arguments. Between these two positions, he opts for the complementary learning process model outlined above. I want to unpack his arguments in this essay in more detail before critically engaging his position as it emerges.

Important in this regard is Rawls's understanding of 'public reason' and 'ethics of citizenship', both of which inspire Habermas's analysis. Rawls's understanding of the former is only superficially straightforward: the appeal to reasons which any rational person would accept regardless of comprehensive religious or philosophical doctrines. In this way, Rawls hopes to achieve a wide "overlapping consensus"[218] in the public sphere. To quote Rawls:

> In discussing constitutional essentials and matters of basic justice we are not to appeal to comprehensive religious and philosophical doctrines – to what we as individuals or members of associations see as the whole truth …. As far as possible, the knowledge and ways of reasoning that ground our affirming the principles of justice and their application to constitutional essentials and matters of basic justice are to rest on the plain truths now widely accepted, or available, to citizens generally.[219]

---

[217] Jürgen Habermas,"Religion and the Public Sphere: Cognitive Presuppositions for the 'Public Use of Reason' by Religious and Secular Citizens," in *Between Naturalism and Religion: Philosophical Essays* (Polity, 2008), 114 - 47.
[218] John Rawls, *Political Liberalism* (Columbia University Press, 1993), 208.
[219] Rawls, 224 – 25.

I will have more to say about Rawls's conception of public reason a little later. Regarding an 'ethics of citizenship,' Rawls claims that citizens of liberal democracies have "a duty of civility to appeal to public reason."[220] Of course, all citizens have the right in a liberal democracy to appeal to religious reasons for their political decision making. Such a right cannot be reasonably withheld from citizens in liberal democracies which value freedom of religion and freedom of expression; indeed, in liberal democracies such rights are legally protected. Nevertheless, Rawls argues that civility requires that we not claim such rights when debating constitutional essentials or matters of basic justice. We have a moral obligation to give exclusively public reasons. To again quote Rawls:

> The ideal of citizenship imposes a moral, not a legal, duty – the duty of civility – to be able to explain to one another on those fundamental questions how the principles and policies they advocate and vote for can be supported by the values of public reason. This duty also involves a willingness to listen to others and fair-mindedness in deciding when accommodations to their views should reasonably be made.[221]

Thus we have a moral obligation to appeal only to public reasons, reasons that others would reasonably accept. Needless to say there is a great deal of latitude in interpreting "reasonable" in these contexts and I will have more to say about that shortly. But the upshot of Rawls's claim is that as free and equal citizens in a liberal democracy we owe one another good reasons for the political positions we support, reasons that are independent of "the whole truth as we see it." If our political decisions were based upon comprehensive doctrines, state neutrality would be compromised, since the state could be construed as enforcing religiously based principles which not all reasonable citizens would accept.

However, Rawls, like Habermas, later revised or qualified his views on this issue. After all, it seems odd to claim that while citizens have the right to appeal to any rationale they choose, including a religious one, they are never actually justified in claiming that right in practice. What then does such a freedom actually mean? Moreover, it does not seem obvious that we have a *prima facie* obligation to voluntarily surrender our rights in the way that Rawls claims. Perhaps if we were to enter into a contract that specified as one of its

---

[220] Rawls, 226.
[221] Rawls, 217.

conditions that civility requires divesting ourselves of religious rationales, we could be held to such a standard. Indeed, this seems to be what Rawls proposes. But there is no prima facie reason to think we should enter into such a contract, especially since it is more restrictive than the social contract assumed by most liberal democracies. Rawls's unqualified restriction sounds more like a rule of decorum for debate rather than a moral duty incumbent upon members of existing liberal democracies. Thus, Rawls's restriction on what counts as 'reasonable' debate in the public sphere strikes me as counterintuitive. As Wolterstorff queries, "given that it is of the very essence of liberal democracy that citizens enjoy equal freedom in law to live out their lives as they see fit, how can it be compatible with liberal democracy for its citizens to be *morally restrained* from deciding and discussing political issues as they see fit?"[222] This is not to say that we do not owe each other some justificatory basis for our political claims, but the common justificatory basis that Rawls's proposes is not itself embraced by all reasonable people.

In response to these criticisms, Rawls revisited the notion of public reason with respect to the legitimacy of religious reasons informing political decisions. His updated position says that reasonable comprehensive doctrines, religious or non-religious, "may be introduced in public reason at any time, provided that in due course public reasons, given by a reasonable political conception, are presented sufficient to support whatever the comprehensive doctrines are introduced to support."[223] In other words, religious reasons are only promissory notes for public reasons. The relevance of this "proviso" to Habermas's translation requirement is clear. Stout puts the point this way, "The amended Rawlsian view is that religious reasons are to IOUs what contractarian reasons are to legal tender. You have not fulfilled your justificatory obligations until you have handed over real cash."[224] Despite finding this proviso more plausible than the original formulation, Stout still mentions some significant problems. For example, he points out that the American abolitionists, including Abraham Lincoln, and later the civil rights movement under Martin Luther King Jr., couched their contributions to political debate in religious terms. Rawls

---

[222] Nicholas Wolterstorff, "The Role of Religion in Decision and Discussion of Political Issues," in Robert Audi and Nicholas Wolterstorff, *Religion in the Public Square: The Place of Religious Convictions in Political Debate* (Rowman & Littlefield Publishers, Inc., 1996), 94.
[223] Rawls, li – lii.
[224] Jeffrey Stout, *Democracy and Tradition* (Princeton University Press, 2005), 69.

confesses that it is unclear whether they ever satisfied the proviso to supplement their religious rationales with secular ones. For Stout, the fact that some of the most important political achievements in American history may not qualify under Rawls's proviso is good reason to question its plausibility.

Habermas also mentions the potential exclusion of King and the U.S. civil rights movement as a criticism that can be leveled even against Rawls's modified position. Furthermore, he extends the scope of the data, saying that "the deep religious roots of the motivations of most social and socialist movements both in the Anglo-American and European countries are highly impressive."[225] Echoing Weithman, he then notes that under Rawls's proviso "churches' civic engagement would, however, wane, so the argument goes, if they constantly had to distinguish between religious and political values according to the yardstick laid down by Rawls's 'proviso' – in other words, if they were obliged to find an equivalent in a universally accessible language for every religious statement they pronounce."[226] Therefore, as a practical matter, religious citizens in liberal democracies cannot be expected to meet Rawls's proviso; to do so would be to seriously compromise their political participation. But as Habermas notes, there is another, more central objection to the proviso, which he puts as follows: "the state cannot encumber its citizens, to whom it guarantees freedom of religion, with duties that are incompatible with pursuing a devout life – it cannot expect something impossible of them."[227] Since ought implies can, this is a more serious objection to the obligatory force of Rawls's proviso.

Habermas pursues this objection further by way of introducing Robert Audi's defense of the duty of civility. Audi defends a modified version of Rawls's proviso, albeit with some important differences. Audi's principle, called the principle of secular rationale, "says that one has a *prima facie* obligation not to advocate or support any law or public policy that restricts human conduct, unless one has, and is willing to offer, adequate secular reason for this advocacy or support (say for one's vote)."[228] This sounds very similar to Rawls's duty of civility, although, as Habermas notes, Audi goes even further by introducing the principle of secular motivation which says "that one has a (*prima facie*) obligation to abstain from advocacy or support of a law or public policy that

---

[225] Habermas, 124.
[226] Habermas, 125.
[227] Habermas, 126.
[228] Audi, "Liberal Democracy and the Place of Religion in Politics," in *Religion in the Public Square*, 25.

restricts human conduct, unless one is sufficiently motivated by (normatively) adequate secular reason."[229] In other words, it is not sufficient to simply offer a secular justification for political action, but that reason must be sufficient to motivate one's action independently of whatever other reasons one might have. Audi argues that his view represents an advance over other liberal theories in dealing with religious arguments. His view states that "citizens have a *prima facie* obligation to have and be willing to offer at least one secular reason that is evidentially adequate and motivationally sufficient … This allows that one also have, for the law or policy in question, *religious* reasons that are evidentially adequate and motivationally sufficient."[230] In other words, he does not exclude religious reasons from the public sphere, but says that religious citizens must have at least one good secular reason for their position when restrictions on liberty or state coercion are at stake. Thus, Audi thinks that his view actually allows more space for religious reasons than the liberalism defended by Rawls. The only asymmetry in Audi's position is the absence of a counterpart requirement – that secular citizens must have at least one evidentially adequate and motivationally sufficient religious reason. However, because there is an alleged epistemic asymmetry between religious and secular claims, such a justificatory asymmetry, according to Audi, is nevertheless reasonable.

Habermas is unwilling to go along with the principle of secular motivation: "Now, the link between the actual motivation for a citizen's actions and those reasons he cites in public may be relevant for a moral judgment of the citizen, but it has no import for assessing his contribution to maintaining a liberal political culture."[231] For Habermas, secular justifications, not secular motivations, are what count for liberal democracy. Although Habermas is inclined throughout the rest of the essay to "ignore Audi's additional requirement",[232] I think it is worth pursuing this line of argument further. Not only does difference on this score differentiate Habermas's position from Audi's, but also, in my judgment, from that of Rawls.

Remember that from Rawls's perspective, the practice of public reason demands that we abstain from referring to the whole truth as we see it when formulating reasons in public debate. This practice, however, leaves open the

---

[229] Audi, 28 – 29.
[230] Audi, 123.
[231] Habermas, 126.
[232] Habermas, 126.

possibility that the reasons we cite in public may not be our real reasons, and thus in aiming to fulfill the duty of civility we may, ironically, be disingenuous. Arguably, this is the hole in Rawls's theory that Audi is attempting to fill with his principle of secular motivation or motivational sufficiency. But it is clear that in order to be consistent, Rawls must at least implicitly assume something like Audi's principle. Although it is ambiguous whether Rawls uses 'reason' both in a justificatory and motivational sense, I believe one can make a case that he at least implicitly affirms the principle Audi renders explicit. For example, Rawls states that:

> [Democracy] implies further an equal share in the coercive political power that citizens exercise over one another by voting and in other ways. As reasonable and rational, and knowing that they affirm a diversity of reasonable religious and philosophical doctrines, they should be ready to explain the *basis of their actions* to one another in terms each could reasonably expect that others might endorse as consistent with their freedom and equality.[233]

The words I have italicized surely indicate that motivationally sufficient reasons are in play in Rawls's description of the duty we owe fellow citizens as free and equal members of a constitutional democracy. If such reasons are not in play, Rawls seems to fall into the paradox of allowing citizens to meet their respective duties by offering disingenuous reasons. But such a view would be in flagrant contradiction with Rawls's insistence that we owe one another respect in offering public reasons. If one were not offering a motivationally sufficient reason, but merely a secular rationale, in order to obfuscate one's real reasons, that would surely qualify as disrespectful manipulation. Thus, Rawls's insistence on public reason may actually undermine the respect it seeks to secure. This is ironic, especially given his claim that respect requires that we appeal only to public reason and avoid any appeal to comprehensive doctrines. It may be the case that respect requires the opposite. Wolterstorff suggests a thought experiment: "Suppose that you offer to me reasons derived from your comprehensive standpoint; and that I, fully persuaded of the moral impropriety of such behavior by the advocates of the liberal position, brush your remarks aside with the comment that in offering me such reasons, you are not paying due

---

[233] Rawls, 217 – 18, italics added.

respect to my status as free and equal."[234] He concludes that "such a response would be profoundly disrespectful in its own way."[235] Another way of putting the point, is that Rawls's view "neglects the ways in which one can show respect for another person in her particularity."[236] Stout proposes his own thought experiment that reinforces the point in a more positive way: "Suppose I tell you honestly why I favor a given policy, citing religious reasons. I then draw you into a Socratic conversation on the matter, take seriously the objections you raise against my premises, and make a concerted attempt to show you how *your* idiosyncratic premises give *you* reason to accept my conclusions. All the while, I take care to be sincere and avoid manipulating you."[237] Stout fails to see how this qualifies as disrespectful conduct, and so do I. In fact, such immanent critique is a profound sign of respect if conducted along the above lines. Furthermore, he speculates that the reason Rawls neglects this form of respect "is that he focuses exclusively on the sort of respect one shows to another individual by appealing to reasons that *anyone who is both properly motivated and epistemically responsible* would find acceptable."[238] Again, the words I have italicized suggest that Rawls needs both the notion of secular rationale and secular motivation to satisfy his requirement of public reason. However, we have noted some serious problems with the latter that actually militate against proper respect for the individual. In this regard, I believe Habermas differs from Rawls and is thus more open to the kind of immanent critique that Stout has in mind. This difference could also be expressed by saying that Habermas does not see religious reasons as promissory notes but as expressing cognitive contents from which secular interlocutors can learn.

A key to explaining this difference, in my judgment, is by way of an even more fundamental difference between the two thinkers, namely their conception of the role of truth in democratic deliberation. Rawls is careful to distinguish his political liberalism from the comprehensive liberalism of, say, J.S. Mill. Rawls's version of liberalism allegedly eschews all comprehensive doctrines, both religious and secular. Indeed, Rawls has expressed frustration with his critics for failing to make that distinction, and has emphatically denied that he is making "a

---

[234] Wolterstorff, 110.
[235] Wolterstorff, 110.
[236] Stout, 72.
[237] Stout, 72.
[238] Stout, 72 – 73, italics added.

veiled argument for secularism."[239]   However, such a charge is not entirely groundless. As Stout says, "The charge being made by both his secular and religious critics alike is that he is wrong to expect everybody to argue in the same terms, which just happen to be a slightly adjusted version of the same terms dictated by his comprehensive secular liberalism."[240] Habermas is arguably more forthright. Despite his public agnosticism regarding metaphysical certainty, he realizes that truth is at stake in democratic deliberation.   Constitutional democracy, he says, is "an epistemically demanding, 'truth-sensitive' form of government."[241] Therefore, there is no distinction between 'secular' reasons and 'public' ones as Rawls tries (implausibly) to maintain. Rather, Habermas uses 'secular' and 'public' interchangeably. It is tempting to see this aspect of his thought as counting against religious reasons in public; indeed I argued in the last chapter that we should question the priority of secular reasons in the public sphere. But there may well be a hidden benefit to religion embedded in Habermas's conception of the truth-sensitivity of liberal democracy. As Cooke explains:

> Habermas now also sees an important difference between ethical conceptions and religious convictions. Unlike conceptions of the good, which are always conceptions of the good "for me" (as a particular individual) or "for us" (as the members of a particular group), religious beliefs are deemed to have a cognitive content that is of potential relevance to everyone. This means that postmetaphysical philosophy, and postmetaphyscially-minded citizens, must be willing to learn from religious traditions and engage critically with their contents."[242]

This willingness to learn from the cognitive contents of religious worldviews is the difference between seeing religious reasons as placeholders for secular reasons and seeing them as potential sources of insight that must be regarded as at least potentially true and relevant for all. Rawls simply fails to see this difference between ethical conceptions and religious convictions.

---

[239] Quoted in Stout, 76.
[240] Stout, 76.
[241] Habermas, 144.
[242] Maeve Cooke, "A Secular State for a Postsecular Society? Postmetaphysical Political Theory and the Place of Religion," *Constellations,* 14.2 (2007): 225.

Habermas's Institutional Translation Proviso

Hence, for Habermas, all that is necessary for the standard conception of liberal democracy is that citizens be able to translate their religious convictions into publicly accessible secular language. However, he notes that even this more lenient position is often countered by the argument that some, or perhaps many, religious citizens are not able to artificially separate their political lives from their religious lives; he is sensitive to the fact that only religious believers are asked to split their identities and that this requirement increases the burden that religious citizens bear within liberal democracies. It is not only the empirical fact that some religious citizens lack the imagination to find counterpart secular reasons for their religiously motivated political decision making, although, as Habermas notes, such a fact is unsettling enough since ought implies can. Rather, the point is precisely that from the perspective of some, perhaps many, religious citizens, one's theological conceptions ought to inform the whole of one's life. Habermas is aware that the request for secular reasons may well be incompatible with such a citizen's right to live a devout life, to pursue the good as she sees fit. He quotes Wolterstorff's oft-quoted passage that for many religious citizens, it is their conviction "that they ought to allow the Word of God, the teachings of the Torah, the command and example of Jesus, or whatever, to shape their existence as a whole, including, then, their social and political existence."[243] Habermas continues, "If we accept this, to my mind compelling, objection, then the liberal state, which expressly protects such forms of existence as a basic right, cannot at the same time expect *all* citizens in addition to justify their political positions independently of their religious convictions or worldviews."[244]

Although we cannot expect all religious citizens to do so, Habermas argues that politicians and candidates for political office can reasonably be held to this stricter demand. Again, the normative force of the translation requirement is preserved at the institutional level. The separation of church and state is such an important principle for the free exercise of religion that Habermas still insists upon the translation requirement, but "to extend this principle from the institutional level to statements put forward by organizations and citizens in the political public sphere would constitute an over-generalization of secularism."[245] In other words:

---

[243] Wolterstorff, 105.
[244] Habermas, 128.
[245] Habermas, 129.

> The liberal state must not transform the necessary institutional separation between religion and politics into an unreasonable *mental and psychological* burden for its religious citizens. It must, however, expect them to recognize the principle that the exercise of political authority must be neutral toward competing worldviews. Every citizen must know and accept that only secular reasons count beyond the institutional threshold separating the informal public sphere from parliaments, courts, ministries, and administrations …. Religious citizens can certainly acknowledge this "institutional translation proviso" without having to split their identity into public and private parts the moment they participate in religious discourses. They should therefore also be allowed to express and justify their convictions in a religious language even when they cannot find secular "translations" for them.[246]

The foregoing suggests that for Habermas, *contra* Rawls, the translation requirement is not to be construed as an obligation of the social contract in the informal political public sphere, or the domain of opinion formation. In this domain, the translation requirement can be construed along pragmatic, rather than Kantian, lines, as necessitated by the fact of pluralism. However, in the formal public sphere, parliaments etc., the domain of political will formation, in which the coercive power of the state is in play, he defends the "institutional translation proviso" (henceforth ITP) delineated above. By contrast to the pragmatic understanding of translation with regard to the informal public sphere, the ITP is arguably a contractarian principle. Some preliminary evidence for this interpretation comes just prior to the introduction of the ITP in the essay. Habermas notes that "the conflict between one's religious convictions and secularly justified policies or proposed laws can only arise because even the religious citizen is supposed to have already accepted the constitution of the secular state for good reasons."[247] In other words, the religious citizen has already entered into a social contract. The benefits to the religious citizen of entering into such a contract are clear: since the religious citizen no longer lives in a religiously homogenous society with a religiously legitimated state, one's freedom of religion depends upon a secular state, neutral toward competing worldviews. Thus, one's citizenship in a constitutional democracy and one's

---

[246] Habermas, 130.
[247] Habermas, 129.

enjoyment of religious freedom obligates one to accept the legitimacy of the ITP. But as we have seen, Habermas does not see this requirement as too onerous because it does not place an unreasonable psychological burden on religious citizens; it recognizes the existential pull of religious reasons for many citizens, while maintaining that state neutrality necessitates secular reasons at the institutional level. Since religious citizens benefit from this aspect of constitutional democracy, they can surely understand the reason for the ITP, and thus have a good reason for accepting the social contract. Habermas continues:

> Even if the religious language is the only one they speak in public, and if religiously justified opinions are the only ones they can or wish to contribute to political controversies, they nevertheless understand themselves as members of a *civitas terrena*, which empowers them to be the authors of laws to which they are subject as addressees. They may express themselves in a religious idiom only on the condition that they recognize the institutional translation proviso. Thus the citizens, confident that their fellow-citizens will cooperate in producing a translation, can understand themselves as participants in the legislative process, although only secular reasons count therein.[248]

According to Habermas, even the most devout citizens usually understand themselves as members of an earthly city – by contrast with the city of God – and as such understand themselves as the authors and addressees of the law in this terrestrial domain. It is difficult to miss the Kantian language in this context. Furthermore, Habermas makes recognition of the ITP as a condition of the freedom of religious expression. Clearly, he understands the ITP in a contractarian way.

This contractarian understanding is important and, on the surface, its application to the ITP seems plausible. However, there are implications to even this revised proviso which count against its purported generosity towards public religious language. For example, in order for religious citizens to make contributions to the legislative process, their religious reasons must be translated into secular reasons *prior* to the legislative process proper. As Habermas says, "The truth contents of religious contributions can enter into the institutionalized practice of deliberation and decision-making only when the

---

[248] Habermas, 131.

necessary translation already occurs in the pre-parliamentary domain, i.e. in the political public sphere itself."[249] Therefore, although religious citizens may speak in a religious idiom in the informal public sphere, and are not expected to be forthcoming with secular translations, if they want to actually affect the outcome of the legislative process, then they must offer secular reasons. So, although citizens may appeal to whatever reasons they choose, they must appeal to secular reasons in order to be politically efficacious. For practical purposes then, only secular reasons count. Habermas seems to take back with his left hand what he gives with his right. The generosity with which he allows religious citizens to speak their own language in the informal public sphere has no direct practical consequences unless it is translated into secular language. This proviso seriously impairs the efficacy of religious language in public. It is unclear whether Habermas recognizes the extent to which his proviso, despite its apparent generosity *vis-à-vis* that of Rawls, impairs the political participation of religious citizens. Habermas adds the caveat that the translation requirement must be construed as a cooperative task, in which secular citizens will assist those religious citizens who are willing to make the effort to translate their reasons. He goes further, saying that "Even if the religious contributions are not subjected to self-censorship they depend on cooperative acts of translation. For without a successful translation the substantive content of religious voices has no prospect of being taken up into the agendas and negotiations within political bodies and of gaining a hearing in the broader political process."[250] I find it naïve in the extreme to think that religious citizens can depend on the generosity of their secular counterparts to help them translate their substantive contents into admissible secular language. Why should we not expect secular citizens to be instead hostile toward religious points of view or to take advantage of their monopoly on public power? Habermas is surely talking about an ideal speech situation! But I appreciate that he is trying to equalize the burdens borne by religious citizens. In the essay currently under discussion, he makes an almost supererogatory effort to eliminate the asymmetry of burdens that many of his critics have noted. Whether his noble attempt is successful or not, we will have occasion to address later. Now, let us return to the plausibility of the ITP.

Habermas notes that Wolterstorff wants to abandon even this modest (in Habermas's view) proviso. Naturally, Habermas sees this move as threatening

---

[249] Habermas, 131.
[250] Habermas, 132.

the neutrality of the state toward competing worldviews. He quickly draws what he believes are the illiberal consequences that follow: "Since no institutional filters are envisaged between the state and the public arena, this version does not exclude the possibility that policies and legal programs will be implemented solely on the basis of the specific religious or confessional beliefs of a ruling majority."[251] He accuses Wolterstorff of not only opening the door to this abuse, but to explicitly drawing this conclusion. He continues: "What is illegitimate is the violation of the principle of the neutrality of the exercise of political power which holds that all coercively enforceable political decisions must be *formulated* and be *justifiable* in a language that is equally accessible to all citizens."[252] Wolterstorff, by contrast, does not see the need for a general background consensus. Such a consensus is impossible to achieve, which is why all liberal democracies recognize the principle of majority rule. Wolterstorff says that there is a difference between a parliamentary session and a Quaker meeting, in which unanimity is required. Habermas takes exception to this characterization, charging Wolterstorff with "ridiculing the idealizing assumptions inscribed in the practices of the liberal state."[253] Habermas also recognizes the principle of majority rule, but says that it "mutates into repression"[254] if it imposes policies based on religious principles without justifying them to the minority on an independent basis. According to him, upon Wolterstorff's view, democracy is reduced to "coexistence in an ideologically divided society based on majority decisions only as a reluctant adaptation to a kind of *modus vivendi*: 'I do not agree, I *acquiesce* – unless I find the decision truly appalling.'"[255] He continues by arguing that it is difficult to see how such a situation is not in constant danger of falling into religious strife. Such a danger can only be avoided, according to Habermas, by a shared background consensus on constitutional principles which must be secularly grounded. However, his characterization of Wolterstorff's argument strikes me as unfair. Moreover, he seems to lack imagination regarding how one might avoid religious conflict even in the absence of the ITP. Let us take each of these points in turn.

---

[251] Habermas, 133. Here, he simply fails to see that a non-neutral, secular majority can also be abusive, as in the case of France's ban of religious symbols, such as headscarves in public and crucifixes worn by public school teachers.
[252] Habermas, 134.
[253] Habermas, 134.
[254] Habermas, 134.
[255] Habermas, 135.

First of all, Wolterstorff lists the core concepts of a liberal democracy as follows: "*Equal protection* under law for all people, *equal freedom* in law for all citizens, and *neutrality* on the part of the state with respect to the diversity of religions and comprehensive perspectives."[256] He later adds, "an equal voice for all citizens within fair voting schemes."[257] So far, there seems to be little in this definition to which Habermas or any other liberal theorist would object. Wolterstorff is quick to point out that his definition functions as an ideal type; nowhere is it fully exemplified. "No society is anything than *more or less* a liberal democracy."[258] Despite this pragmatist-sounding admission, he does not think that liberal democracy can be reduced to the competition of interests. Rather, what qualifies the liberal position as liberal is its insistence upon securing justice for all. To be sure, justice has to compete with a number of other considerations; sometimes it loses, but sometimes it wins and we manage to bring the ideal a little closer to actualization.[259] Already, we have gone a long way toward correcting Habermas's mischaracterization of Wolterstorff's position, which makes it sound as though it is unconcerned with *constitutional* democracy. What the latter questions, of course, is the restraint that the liberal position places on religious reasons in the name of justice. Again, his position is more nuanced.

For example, Wolterstorff admits that democratic citizenship involves restraint on the kind of legislation one advocates. Certainly, he concedes, there are evangelical Christians in the U.S. "who believe that American society would be better off if only evangelical Christians were allowed to vote and hold public office."[260] And obviously, a liberal democracy, for the above reasons, places constitutional restrictions on the advocacy of such legislation. We can call such restrictions *restraints on content*. Nobody even within a generously wide purview of liberalism advocates removing such restraints. What Wolterstorff objects to are epistemological restraints on religious citizens when it comes to democratic deliberation. He asks, "But what is the rationale for *epistemological* restraints on the decisions and debates of citizens? That is, why should epistemological restraints be laid on a person *when the legislation advocated by*

---

[256] Wolterstorff, 70.
[257] Wolterstorff, "Audi on Religion, Politics, and Liberal Democracy," in *Religion in the Public Square*, 159.
[258] Wolterstorff, "The Role of Religion in Decision and Discussion of Political Issues," 70.
[259] Wolterstorff, 71.
[260] Wolterstorff, 77.

that person does not violate the restraints on content?"[261] After looking carefully at the liberal position, he concludes there is no sound rationale for epistemological restraints, and I agree. Since I have been dealing with the issue of epistemological restraints in one way or another throughout, and will do so again later, I will not linger too much on this point. Furthermore, as we have seen, Habermas seems to appreciate the argument for loosening epistemological restraints on religious reasons in the informal public sphere, although he tightens them at the institutional level. I want to suggest in what follows that the same reasons for loosening them in the former case extend to the latter.

Bearing in mind that any society is only ever more or less a liberal democracy, we have to ask whether the epistemological restraint on religious reasons is either derived from or compatible with the liberal ideal above. In Wolterstorff's estimation, no liberal theorist has sufficiently answered either question. Some, like Rawls and Audi, have insisted that there is a moral obligation to refrain from religious reasons even in the informal public sphere. We have also seen reasons to think they are wrong. But either way, such a principle is not explicitly derived from the liberal ideal and there are many good reasons to think it is incompatible with it, such as the fact that the limits it places on freedom of religion and expression are more restrictive than those found in actual liberal democracies. Yet nobody would deny that it belongs to the nature of liberal democracies to protect these rights. It would be a strange situation indeed if the ideal of liberal democracy turned out to be less permissive than the imperfect exemplification of it in existing liberal democracies. As Wolterstorff points out, the concept of liberal democracy originated, presumably, "not from the speculations of theorists concerning ideal types of social order, but from the attempts of theorists to single out certain extant societies from others as constituting a certain type, the liberal democratic type."[262] Whether or not this genealogy of the concept of liberal democracy is correct, he is right, in my judgment, that we must pay attention to the historical contingencies of actual liberal democratic societies, rather than limit our focus to the ideal type. Speaking of whether or not the argument in favor of epistemological restraints on religious reasons is cogent, Wolterstorff answers that it depends, "on the particular society one has in mind and the particular stage in the history of that society. For seventeenth-century England, it quite clearly was cogent: social

---

[261] Wolterstorff, italics in original.
[262] Wolterstorff, "Audi on Religion, Politics, and Liberal Democracy," 158.

peace did depend on getting citizens to stop invoking God, canonical scriptures, and religious authorities when discussing politics in public – to confine such invocations to discussions within their own confessional circles."[263] But he wants to say that now, in twenty-first century America, with a long history of religious tolerance behind her it is not obvious that civil society will collapse if citizens invoke religious reasons for their political decisions.

None of this is to deny that the creation of liberal democracy in the seventeenth century was an historical achievement. The hard lesson of this period was that the state must remain religiously neutral. The cost of religious liberty, both positive, the freedom to live according to one's own religious views or lack thereof, and negative, protection against interference from others, was the limiting of religious arguments to the private sphere. Practical considerations, such as peace and security, meant that religious citizens had to make certain concessions. I agree with Habermas in thinking that they still do, although I differ with him over the extent and type of concessions necessary for the smooth functioning of discursive democracy. Nevertheless, the secular liberal state is the achievement of a long and bloody learning process in Western Europe's history. However, it would be problematic to suppose that the learning process is now over. Cooke, taking her lead from Habermas, thinks that this learning process is inherently open-ended. We must stand ready to revise our understanding of the place of religion in democratic politics if the standard secular paradigm becomes antiquated in the face of new challenges. Habermas's position, that political discourse is inherently fallible, would seem to suggest that no commitment is sacrosanct in the sense of being closed to revision. Indeed, to claim otherwise would fall prey to precisely the objection that Habermas makes against dogmatic religious claims. So we must stand ready to modify the way in which liberalism is understood when encountering challenges in existent democracies and our often rough-and-ready political discourse.

All of this discussion about the contingencies of existing liberal democracies speaks to Wolterstorff's question of whether or not we need consensus, or what Rawls would call a common political basis. Do we need an "abiding set of agreed-on principles to which all of us ... can appeal in deciding and discussing political issues – at least the most important among them those

---

[263] Wolterstorff, "The Role of Religion in Decision and Discussion of Political Issues," 79.

that deal with 'constitutional essentials and maters of basic justice'?" [264] In other words, do we need a common basis, other than the particular constitution itself, in order to decide these matters? He denies that such a common basis is necessary on empirical grounds. After all, no liberal theorist claims that any existing liberal democracy has achieved such consensus; rather they are submitting proposals for how such a society might achieve such consensus in principle. But for Wolterstorff, there is no compelling reason to think that we need such a consensus, and even less reason to think that we can achieve one in practice. Of course, we do aim for agreement in political discourse, but not upon some pre-established basis for political discourse from which no reasonable person could dissent. Rather, we aim to agree upon some concrete proposal, policy, or law. As Wolterstorff says:

> Our agreement on some policy need not be based on some set of principles agreed on by all present and future citizens and rich enough to settle all important political issues. Sufficient if each citizen, for his or her own reasons, agrees on the policy today and tomorrow – not for all time. It need not even be the case that each and every citizen agrees to the policy. Sufficient if the agreement be the fairly gained and fairly executed agreement of the majority. [265]

This is perhaps the best that actual functioning liberal democracies can realistically hope for, but it is enough for most practical purposes. His point is so common-sensical that it would hardly bear mentioning if not for the counterintuitive requirements placed upon democracy by those who only study the ideal type. Why these additional requirements by liberal theorists? Wolterstorff provides some helpful insights into their motivations:

> So-called 'communitarians' regularly accuse proponents of the liberal position of being against community. One can see what they are getting at. Nonetheless, this way of putting it seems to me imperceptive of what, at bottom, is going on. The liberal is not willing to live with the politics of multiple communities. He still wants communitarian politics. He is trying to discover, and to form, the relevant community. He thinks we need a shared political basis. For the reasons given, I think that the attempt is

---

[264] Wolterstorff, 114.
[265] Wolterstorff, 114.

> hopeless and misguided. We must learn to live with a politics of multiple identities.[266]

I agree that we must live with the politics of multiple identities. Indeed, accommodating and facilitating such multiplicity is one of the main objectives the modern liberal democracy was designed to achieve. I say again: the formal secularism of liberalism is best understood as a pragmatic response to the fact of pluralism. Those citizens among us who are nostalgic for a religiously homogenous population where Christianity, say, was the only game in town have to learn to live with the reality of pluralism. Habermas is correct that the fact of pluralism requires reflexivity on the part of religious citizens. By the same token, secular citizens who yearn for a homogenous secular population long promised by the secularization thesis, in which nobody appeals to religious rationales for their political decisions, are being equally unrealistic. Both camps need to embrace, or at least learn to live with, the politics of multiple identities. They seem to be here to stay and it is among the virtues of liberal democracy that it can make such diversity work. I am making a broader pragmatic point that we need to avail ourselves of the widest discourse, within constitutional limits, in making political decisions and this includes allowing religious and secular voices to speak their own language authentically in public. Those who resent pluralism, whether they are exclusive religionists or exclusive secularists will no doubt also resent this wider discourse. But the rest of us need not.

The fact that consensus of the kind hoped for by liberal theorists is not forthcoming is at least partly the point of Wolterstorff's introduction of the admittedly "stylized"[267] distinction between a parliamentary session and a Quaker meeting. What he is getting at, is that no democracy achieves anything like the unanimity sought after by liberal theory of a Rawlsian persuasion. Bracketing for the moment the issue of religion, such consensus is still practically impossible. Addressing Audi, Wolterstorff notes that the classification of "religious reasons versus secular reasons ... is misleading. The classification that the [liberal] rationale calls for is that between reasons that would be accepted by all appropriately informed and fully rational citizens, and those that would not be accepted by all such."[268] We simply cannot find reasons belonging to the former

---

[266] Wolterstorff, 110.
[267] Wolterstorff, "Audi on Religion, Politics, and Liberal Democracy," 153.
[268] Wolterstorff, 157.

category, regardless of our religious beliefs or lack thereof. Nor does the distinction between political and comprehensive liberalism seem to get us any closer as we saw above in criticism of Rawls.

I should qualify that I am not against consensus *per se*, nor do I think Wolterstorff is. Rather, I believe, along pragmatic lines, that we need to try to persuade the widest possible audience, but not on the basis of a presumed ideal rational acceptability, a common basis to which all rational people would assent. Rather, persuading the widest audience, building consensus, requires that we use different arguments in different contexts. The widest possible audience in a pluralist society will always include a subset of members who do not necessarily agree with a given policy or law for the same reasons as other members. Again, we aim for agreement on particular issues, not on an idealized basis upon which to reach consensus on any conceivable issue for all time. If Cooke's analysis of Habermas's position on finalist closure summarized in the last chapter is correct, then he would concur that we should be very cautious indeed in saying that a political issue is closed because the requisite rational consensus has been reached. To the extent that we are committed to fallibilism in our political discourse we seem to be committed to the more modest pragmatic agreement outlined here.

We now return to the relevance of these arguments to Habermas's ITP and Wolterstorff's alleged abandonment of any and all restraints on religious rationales. Is the ITP necessary for the kind of peaceful society Habermas, and presumably the rest of us, wants? What would the abandonment of this principle as applied to public officials look like? Habermas has made a slippery slope argument regarding the danger of readmitting religious rationales into official chambers, but is what is waiting at the bottom of that slope as bad as he thinks?

A Proposed Revision to the ITP

Thus far we have been concerned with the role that religious reasons should play in the duty of citizens. What about public officials? Habermas clearly denies that religious reasons should play any role, as he says "This strict demand can only be made of politicians operating within state institutions who have a duty to remain neutral among competing worldviews, in other words, of all who hold public office or are candidates for such."[269] Since I outlined his reasoning in greater detail above, I shall proceed to the question of whether or not such a "strict demand" is necessary. First of all, Wolterstorff makes an important distinction between legislators on the one hand and executives and judges on the other. Despite having the American context primarily in mind, I think this distinction is useful. "That divide" he explains, "is this: legislators play a pivotal role in the normal process whereby a democratic society reaches its decisions about the laws that shall govern the interactions of its citizens; executives and judges exercise their roles after the society has reached its decision."[270] The task, then, of executives and judges is to enforce and adjudicate the law. If they have scruples in doing so, they best get out of the role. Although each task involves interpretation, there is a stricter purview in which these tasks are performed; they are not asked for their personal opinion. Indeed, in the case of a judge, for example, precisely the opposite: she is obligated to remain impartial. The legislator, by contrast, works with *prospective* laws and thus the question of the legitimacy of her own personal views in supporting or opposing the legislation at this stage certainly enters the picture. Unsurprisingly, citizens of liberal democracies disagree on how to answer this question: Should the legislator, in her capacity as a representative, yield to the will of her constituents, either the majority or the most vocal, or, after taking such considerations into account, should she rely more heavily on her own judgment? This is one of the many issues upon which reasonable citizens reasonably disagree. Again, there seems to be no way of resolving this issue on the basis of a pre-established rational consensus. Is it then reasonable to say that it is never legitimate for a legislator's personal views, including religious ones, to enter into political decision-making? Although the representative is not a private citizen, political decision making is not a mechanical process. Should the epistemological restraints on religious reasons that Habermas concedes are unreasonable in the case of citizens be applied at the legislative level even if there is no violation of restraints on content? Not in my judgment. Despite Habermas's concern that loosening such restraints will inevitably erode the separation of church and state, I find no reason to think that such an unwelcome outcome would obtain. Perhaps an example will help clarify why.

---

[269] Habermas, 128.
[270] Wolterstorff "The Role of Religion in Decision and Discussion of Political Issues," 117.

Take a Christian socialist's defense of the welfare state.[271] Suppose her view is informed primarily by her understanding of the biblical writers' injunction to care for the poor. Is such a basis politically legitimate? It might well be objected that she could find a secular reason for the same principle. But what counts as a secular reason in this context? One might say that one could formulate the principle as supporting equal rights to adequate sustenance. All well and good, but she still has an underlying religious basis for this belief in rights, despite the fact that it contains no explicit theological presuppositions. In other words, the new formulation does not constitute a secular reason *for her*. As Wolterstorff points out, if finding secular reasons were this easy, "religious people would almost always automatically have secular reasons. The religious person opposed to abortion *because God says that abortion is wrong* is perforce also opposed to abortion *because abortion is wrong*."[272] In other words, "[t]o determine whether or not someone's reason is secular, one usually has to know the path by which it was arrived at."[273] So it is often difficult to tell, even from a first person perspective, whether one's reasons are religious or secular. What is the evidence in any case for one's moral convictions regarding the poor? Does compassion count as evidence? Although it may be a good rhetorical device in argument, I fail to see how it might be evidential. How about biblical texts that say we have an obligation to the poor? It is unclear what evidence means here. One would have to establish some criteria for evidence before one could specify what reasons count as secular in such a context. I am unconvinced that such criteria, ones that consistently admit only secular reasons and exclude religious ones can be found, but I leave it to those who disagree to produce such criteria. Thus, the line demarcating religious from secular reasons is itself difficult to establish.

However, there is a sense in which Habermas's ITP does have force. One can appreciate, for example, even as a religious believer, that the language of laws must be neutral with respect to any particular religion, otherwise they fail to represent the entire citizenry. Of course, this caveat does not entail that religious arguments should be barred from the *process* whereby deliberation becomes law, either in the informal public sphere, as Rawls argued, or in the formal public sphere of legislatures, as Habermas contends. The insight behind the ITP is that in order to preserve the formal neutrality of the state, there must

---

271	Wolterstorff "Audi on Religion, Politics, and Liberal Democracy," 162.
272	Wolterstorff, 162.
273	Wolterstorff, 163.

be a domain of the state in which the language must be neutral regarding religion. As Taylor elaborates:

> This zone can be described as the official language of the state: the language in which legislation, administrative decrees and court judgments must be couched. It is self-evident that a law before Parliament couldn't contain a justifying clause of the type: "Whereas the Bible tells us that *p*." And the same goes *mutatis mutandis* for the justification of a judicial decision in the court's verdict. But this has nothing to do with the specific nature of religious language. It would be equally improper to have a legislative clause: "Whereas Marx has shown that religion is the opium of the people," or "Whereas Kant has shown that the only thing good without qualification is a good will." The ground for both these kinds of exclusions is the neutrality of the state.[274]

As Taylor goes on to say, the secular state cannot be officially Christian or Jewish or Muslim although the laws, though neutral in their language, will likely reflect the views of actual citizens who may well credit religious rationales in their political decision making. However, so long as the laws do not credit these sources, they are legitimate. Of course, minorities dissatisfied with the law are free to try and convince the majority that the law ought to be changed, or failing that, appeal to the judiciary if the constitutionality of the law can be challenged. All of this is standard procedure in working democracies, and is relatively uncontroversial even among religious citizens. Of course, citizens, both religious and secular, disagree about the respective roles of legislatures and judiciaries as reflected, especially in the U.S., in concerns over majority oppression of minorities feared by many secularists, and judicial activism feared by many religionists. However, these are again issues upon which rational citizens disagree. The demarcation between a religious majority's will and the officially neutral language of legislation is often difficult to draw and it is often the task of the courts to do so. Such decisions seldom please everyone, but there seems to be no alternative in diverse democracies. Again, citizens of a democracy, whether religious or secular, must be tolerant of losing the vote and judicial decisions.

---

[274]   Charles Taylor, "Secularism and Critique," http://www.ssrc.org/blogs/immanent_frame/2008/04/24/secularism-and-critique/.

Thus, I would endorse a revised version of Habermas's ITP which states that religious contributions to public debate, at both the informal and formal level, must be translated into as neutral a language as possible when legislation is drawn up, in order to preserve its legitimacy for a pluralistic citizenry. That is not to say that all citizens will agree with the legislation, but they will recognize the legitimacy of the process by which it is drafted and passed into law. In my judgment, this revised proviso accomplishes everything Habermas's ITP intends without impairing the political participation of religious citizens who wish to couch their political contributions in a familiar language. Habermas, through the ITP, seeks to preserve the formal secularism of the state by ensuring that state coercion is never used to enforce an explicitly religious position. However, he wrongly thinks that in order to accomplish this goal he must restrict the kinds of arguments to which citizens, at both the pre-institutional level (since translation must occur prior to parliamentary deliberation) and in parliament, can appeal in making a case for a particular position. I have argued above that to claim that translation must occur at the pre-institutional level would be to take back for practical purposes all of the concessions Habermas has made to religious citizens. Moreover, if there are good reasons for acknowledging the existential pull of religious convictions for private citizens, those reasons should, I argue, extend to their official representatives. Indeed, it is not so clear cut where religious reasons end and secular ones begin; trying to specify a criterion to demarcate between them strikes me as unworkable and unnecessary for political praxis. Thus, all that we need to preserve the neutrality of the state is to maintain that the official language of the state be as neutral as possible with respect to any particular religion(s). This revised proviso addresses the legitimacy issues Habermas fears while allowing religious citizens to couch their contributions to public debate in a religious idiom. Naturally, such debates may lack the decorum of an 'ideal speech situation' but such is the case in a robust democracy that values freedom of speech and expression for all its citizens without favoring any particular religious or non-religious group when the laws are ratified. In my judgment, this revised proviso addresses all of Habermas's concerns and avoids all of the drawbacks of the ITP as outlined above.

Contestable Premises, Comprehensive Evidence, and Immanent Critique

In my judgment, the hesitancy on the part of liberal theorists, like Rawls and Habermas, to adopt such a pragmatic revision to their respective 'provisos' stems from two sources. Firstly, there is the issue of civility that Rawls raises. There is a tendency among academics to expect democratic debate to emulate that found in the academy. This observation leads Stout to say that Rawls's duty of civility reflects a kind of decorum that a liberal professor would want to impose on discussion.[275] But robust debate in a healthy democracy seldom conforms to such rules, nor does parliamentary deliberation for that matter. The notion that a society can have genuine debate without friction is too idealized to be of much use. I believe Habermas too falls prey to the same objection. This is not to say that we cannot debate issues in both a lively and respectful manner, but claiming, as Rawls and Habermas have at varying points in their careers, that only secular reasons count pre-empts debate by policing the expressive freedom of citizens. This is a high price to pay to avoid the kind of friction indicative of healthy democratic discourse. The tendency of contemporary liberal theory is to be 'frictophobic'. I do not see the need for the kind of decorum – in the sense of limited expression – that contemporary liberal theory wants to impose. Once again, we cannot expect consensus on every issue, but why should it matter? So long as citizens have access to fair voting procedures and the courts, we can reach compromises. In my judgment, echoing Mill, liberalism should err on the side of liberty rather than consensus.

      Secondly, there is an epistemological basis for such provisos. This in turn is supported by two underlying assumptions: 1) religious reasoning is dubious or divisive or superfluous for the purposes of deliberation in pluralistic contexts; 2) secular reason provides an adequate normative basis for political deliberation. I have already dealt with some of the objections based on the dubiousness of religious arguments in the first chapter, but I believe that it is worth reiterating the distinction between faith-claims and premises that are not universally accepted. The former of these claims, those that appeal uncritically to faith or dogmatically to authority function in practice as conversation-stoppers. In other words, there are religious persons who are unprepared or unwilling to offer reasons for their beliefs, which upon further examination are seen to rest on an uncritically held faith-claim. If such persons cannot offer reasons, then discussion quickly breaks down. Habermas, Rawls, and Rorty are quite concerned to show that the privilege of religion's immunity from criticism in the private realm disqualifies it from the discursive democratic process which is inherently critical and argumentative. If this were the only kind of religious

---

[275]   Stout, 76.

contribution to public debate, I would have to agree with these liberal theorists. However, I am unconvinced that this is the only religious contribution to debate. As Stout reminds us, there is a difference between a faith-claim, as defined above, and a premise that not all rational people will accept. Indeed, most premises, not just religious ones, are of this type. That is to say, one might be prepared to argue at great length for one's religious conclusions on a particular issue, yet be unable to convince all interlocutors of the truth of the premises one uses in supporting such a conclusion. For example, take the following argument: 1) All persons that come within the jurisdiction of the state are to be granted equal protection under the law; 2) a fetus is a person; 3) Therefore, a fetus ought to be granted equal protection under the law. This argument is sound. Of course, pro-choice advocates would simply dispute or deny the second premise. It is not universally accepted and it seems that rational people can rationally disagree about the truth of premise two. But we still have an argument as opposed to a faith-claim. But one might object that this is still a secular argument because it contains no explicitly theological premises or conclusion. As such, it would fall into the category of secular contributions by religious persons to political debate; in other words, as an example of translation. However, I would reiterate that it is not easy to demarcate religious justifications from secular ones even when no explicit theology is at play.

For example, there are two kinds of evidence one could offer for the truth of premise two which I shall call 'minimal' evidence and 'comprehensive' evidence respectively. Minimal evidence would be evidence that entails a minimal number of ontological or metaphysical commitments. This is roughly what liberal theorists refer to as 'secular reason' or reason to which no rational person could object. Thus, we are back to the problem of common basis, the assumption that there are premises which are universally acceptable. Comprehensive evidence, following Rawls's terminology, would be evidence that draws upon one's comprehensive doctrine, or view of the world, with all of the attending metaphysical baggage. Such an appeal, Rawls claims, is disallowed. But why should this be so? At the risk of belaboring the point, the criticisms of Rawls we have examined thus far and Habermas's revised position on the issue make it difficult to justify such epistemological restraints on religious citizens. Why should religious citizens not be allowed to draw on the whole truth as they see it despite the fact that the premises will not be accepted by all rational people? The secularist is able to appeal to the whole truth as he sees it and I see no good *prima facie* reason why we should assume that he travels without metaphysical baggage. The metaphysical assumption of materialism, for example, would seem to be as relevant in determining the moral worth, if any, of the fetus as would an explicitly theological formulation.

However, one might object that the allowance of comprehensive evidence is simply a veil for the readmission of faith-claims into the discussion. What would comprehensive evidence for the personhood of the fetus look like? Would one say that human life is sacred? That it is made in the image of God? That the fetus has a soul? I list these in more or less increasing order of reliance on a faith-claim and most sophisticated pro-life arguments are not stated in so bald and flatfooted a manner. But even if one cannot convince one's interlocutor of the truth of certain premises on the basis of comprehensive evidence, what does this prove? Unless the person appealing to such comprehensive evidence is unwilling to countenance criticism, such claims do not necessarily cease to be discursive. For example, the avenue of immanent criticism remains open, despite the fact the conversation cannot proceed on the assumption of a common basis. Of course not all rational people will be willing to accept the truth of these comprehensive claims, but so what? It should be noted that liberalism offers no basis, secular or otherwise, upon which to resolve such disputes. Stout cites a study by Kent Greenawalt who argues that in addition to the abortion debate, debates over welfare assistance, punishment, military policy, euthanasia, and environmental policy cannot be resolved on the basis of commonly held liberal principles.[276] The absence of universally acceptable premises is something with which both secular and religious citizens in a democracy must contend.

Moreover, religious arguments do not have a monopoly on comprehensive evidence. Many secular premises implicitly appeal to such evidence or remain unsupported. It is often very difficult to demonstrate one's entitlement to moral and political convictions and reasonable people often differ. This is especially true in cases where our beliefs have developed through acculturation rather than explicit reasoning. We may, in such cases actually have epistemic entitlement to such beliefs, but we may be incapable of practically justifying them to someone else. If we were to exclude all beliefs of this kind from public expression, we would be compelled to silence on all of the important of issues listed above.[277] According to Stout, when religious citizens find that their premises are not universally accepted they have three options: "(1) remain

---

[276] Stout, 88.
[277] Stout, 88.

silent; (2) to give justifying arguments based strictly on principles already commonly accepted; and (3) to express their actual (religious) reasons for supporting the policy they favor while also engaging in immanent criticism of their opponents views."[278] Rawls's proviso and Habermas's translation requirement seem to force a false dilemma between (1) and (2). But Habermas, and even Rawls, have since recognized that silence is dangerous for democracy and it would be contrary to liberal principles to compel particular citizens to silence. And as I have been arguing all along, (2) is usually off the table. In my judgment (3) is a viable way to proceed in such instances.

But let us take yet another example in order to clarify some of these points. Take the argument, alluded to above, for welfare assistance. A religious person might argue as follows: 1) The Bible admonishes us to care for the poor; 2) welfare assistance is an effective way of doing so; 3) Therefore, we should support such initiatives. Now, this argument does not enjoin that the Bible is the Word of God or sacred, but there is, nevertheless, a hidden premise that stated modestly would be "we ought to pay attention to what the Bible has to say regarding social policy." Once this premise is rendered explicit, it is clear that this is what the secularist will deny or at least qualify (maybe we should pay attention to the Bible in this case, but not, for example, when quoted in opposition to gay rights).[279] But as we have seen, simply because the premises are not universally acceptable, it does not mean that the argument should not be given a hearing in the public sphere. It is, after all, an argument rather than merely a faith-claim that brooks no criticism. As such, there seems to be no good prima facie reason why it should be disallowed. To see why, we might substitute a different text in place of the Bible. A secularist could argue thusly: 1) Marx admonished "From each according to his abilities to each according to his needs"; 2) welfare assistance is an effective way of achieving such transformation; 3) Therefore, we should support such initiatives. The hidden premise, once again, is that "we ought to pay attention to what Marx has to say regarding social policy" and no doubt many citizens in liberal democracies will reject this premise. But so what? Nothing prevents the secular socialist from bringing his favorite text into the public debate. Likewise, nothing prevents the religionist from bringing his favorite text. Of course, legislation cannot specify the Bible or *Das Kapital* as

---

[278] Stout, 88.
[279] See the next chapter for a discussion of this issue.

inspiration for welfare policies, but we cannot reasonably expect people to check their favorite texts at the door when they enter the public sphere.

Therefore, the claim that religious argument ought to be disallowed on the grounds of being dubious or divisive fails. With the exception of tautologies, no argument appeals to premises that are universally acceptable or could not be denied by any rational person. Moreover, we inevitably appeal to comprehensive evidence in support of our premises if challenged, which is why Habermas cautions against an "overgeneralization" of secularism as a worldview. I simply fail to see how religious arguments are unique in this regard. We all appeal to what Rorty calls "final vocabularies"[280] in the sense that we can offer no further noncircular justifications for them. This is true of religious and secular citizens alike. Rorty's "final vocabulary" is similar to what I mean by comprehensive evidence in justification of premises: persons may be entitled to their premises but unable to demonstrate their entitlement in a non-question begging way.

I have not yet explicitly addressed the claim above that religion is superfluous for purposes of deliberation in pluralistic contexts because it segues into the second claim above: secular reason provides an adequate normative basis for political deliberation. One might in fact argue that either religious reasons fail to convince because of their dubious nature and are thus divisive or one can find secular reasons that support the same conclusions and thus religious reasons are superfluous. Therefore, this trio of charges against religious arguments mutually reinforce one another. Since I have already addressed the charges of dubiousness and divisiveness, the charge of superfluity essentially hangs on the claim that we have adequate secular reasons that do the same work that religious reasons do. Such a claim is akin to Audi's principle of secular rationale and motivation: religious citizens must find at least one rationally adequate and motivationally sufficient reason for their support of a policy or position in addition to whatever religious reasons they might have. In other words, religious reasons for purposes of public deliberation are superfluous. Of course, such an argument assumes that there are adequate secular reasons that can effectively replace religious ones and it seems far from obvious that this is true. In my judgment, this is one of the reasons Audi's proposal fails and why the translation requirement should be relaxed. Habermas, despite still holding to the normative adequacy of secular reasons, has

---

[280] Richard Rorty, *Contingency, Irony, and Solidarity*, 73.

acknowledged the semantic potential of religious language to enrich public discourse.

We have already seen reasons to doubt that secular reasons are adequate in the sense of being sufficient to convince any rational person regardless of comprehensive evidence. One might argue that they are adequate in the sense of adequately explicable in exclusively "this-worldly" terms. But it is not obvious that "this-worldly" explanations are adequate to sustain the kinds of political values we want to defend and promote and I have cited Habermas to this effect previously. Moreover, as Taylor expounds:

> The two most widespread this-worldly philosophies in our contemporary world, utilitarianism and Kantianism, in their different versions, all have points at which they fail to convince honest and unconfused people. If we take key statements of our contemporary political morality, such as those attributing rights to human beings as such, say the right to life, I cannot see how the fact that we are desiring/enjoying/suffering beings, or the perception that we are rational agents, should be any surer basis for this right than the fact that we are made in the image of God. Of course, our being capable of suffering is one of those basic unchallengeable propositions …. as our being creatures of God is not, but what is less sure is what follows normatively from the first claim.[281]

To be sure, as Taylor also concedes, it may be the case that religion is founded on an illusion as various strong versions of secularism contend, in which case the premises based upon it are less than credible. But the claim that religion is fundamentally illusory is also one of those claims on which reasonable people disagree and barring some fulfillment of the secularization thesis, such debate is bound to be interminable. In the meantime, it would be naïve to say that religion no longer sustains many citizens' commitment to liberal political values. It surely does. So to claim that religious reasons are superfluous because we have adequate secular replacements immediately prompts two questions: 1) adequate in what sense? 2) How could one claim such reasons are adequate without first demonstrating that religion is illusory or that some comprehensive account of secularism is true? In terms of the first question, secular reasons are neither persuasively adequate nor necessarily adequate to ground our liberal

---

[281] Taylor, "Secularism and Critique."

commitments. Regarding the second question, the claim that they are adequate in an explanatory sense is also dubious, but even if one could make such a case, and many have tried, it is not clear that a political overgeneralization of secularism should follow especially given the importance of state neutrality and the pragmatic justificatory role that religion continues to play in sustaining many citizens' liberal political values. Following Taylor, the secularism of the state should be an "open secularism,"[282] not a secularism that sees its task as the emancipation of society from religion. Of course, even open secularism demands compromise on the part of religious citizens, such as respecting state neutrality, but it does not entail that religious citizens cannot avail themselves of religiously informed premises when making arguments in public. In my judgment, Habermas's evolving view on the place of religious language in public involves recognition of these points.

Balancing Burdens: The Pragmatics of Translation

We thus return to the question: what remains of the normative force of Habermas's translation requirement? As indicated above, I think a revised version of his ITP is defensible, namely, that religious contributions to public debate at both the informal and formal level, must be translated into as neutral a language as possible when legislation is drawn up, in order to preserve its legitimacy for a pluralistic citizenry. Beyond this fairly minimal requirement, I do not think the translation requirement carries any normative weight at either the informal or formal level. Certainly, discursive situations arise in which some measure of translation is pragmatically necessary in order to keep the discussion going, but construed as a deontological, contractarian obligation, the translation requirement fails except at the level of legislation as drafted and ratified by parliaments or other elected bodies. In my judgment, something like Stout's option (3) above, candor combined with immanent critique, is really all Habermas needs to protect the neutrality of the state while allowing for the real existential and psychological pull religion exercises on many citizens.

But since translation, even upon my revision, is still operative within liberal democracies the question remains: who should be expected to do it and

---

[282] Gérard Bouchard and Charles Taylor, *Building the Future: A Time for Reconciliation*, Abridged Report, The Consultation Commission on Accommodation Practices Related to Cultural Differences (Government of Québec, 2008), 46.

does it still impose an asymmetrical burden on religious citizens? In "Religion and the Public Sphere," Habermas is very concerned to avoid imposing such an asymmetrical burden. Thus, we should look briefly at the burden Habermas thinks is reasonable for religious citizens to bear and how he attempts to balance it with that of secular citizens. For example, he regards religious belief as entailing greater cognitive dissonance within liberal society than its secular counterpart. I would argue that such an assumption, though it may be empirically true, stems from a superficial evaluation of epistemological justification, as though secularism is based exclusively on evidence no rational person could dispute. Since I have argued against this point at length, I mention it only to underscore how prominently the Enlightenment ideal of rational consensus figures in Habermas's evaluation of religion vis-à-vis the secularity of the state. Once this ideal is challenged, many of the conclusions that follow, including the translation requirement, cease to be necessary for the smooth functioning of democracy.

However, with the assumptions of ideal rational consensus and the epistemic adequacy of secular reason in place, it follows that religious citizens must face cognitive burdens their secular counterparts do not. Habermas cites, for example, the changing self-consciousness of religion itself since the Reformation and Enlightenment, the challenges of religious pluralism, and the rise of modern science, positive law, and secular morality. Of course, none of this is news to reflective religious believers, many of whom have offered thoughtful responses to each of these historical developments that seek to preserve the viability of a religious worldview. Nevertheless, Habermas asserts: "In these three respects, traditional communities of faith must process cognitive dissonances that either do not arise for secular citizens, or arise only insofar as they adhere to doctrines anchored in similarly dogmatic ways."[283] He then goes on to delineate what concessions religious citizens are required to make: they must develop a self-reflexive stance toward competing worldviews within a pluralistic society, accept the monopoly on knowledge enjoyed by scientific expert cultures, and accept the priority that secular reasons enjoy in the political arena.[284] He acknowledges that such hermeneutical self-reflection in the face of pluralism, modern science, and secular morality and law is arduous work, which prompts him to wonder: "Within this liberal framework, what interests me is the

---

[283] Habermas, 136.
[284] Habermas, 137.

open question of whether the revised concept of citizenship that I have proposed still imposes an *asymmetrical* burden on religious traditions and religious communities."[285]

He contends that secular citizens are not spared a cognitive burden of their own that goes beyond mere tolerance of religious worldviews. Rather, we must expect from secular citizens "a self-reflexive overcoming of a rigid and exclusive secularist self-understanding of modernity."[286] Moreover, "the admission of religious assertions into the political arena only makes sense if *all* citizens can be reasonably expected not to exclude the possibility that these contributions have cognitive substance – while at the same time respecting the priority of secular reasons and the institutional translation proviso."[287] As we noted above, this point, in my judgment, differentiates Habermas significantly from Rawls: religious assertions are seen as having cognitive content, not as mere promissory notes for secular reasons which alone have cognitive content. In addition, Habermas claims that secular citizens must recognize "that they live in a postsecular society that is also *epistemically attuned* to the continued existence of religious communities … a change of mentality that is no less cognitively exacting than the adaptation of religious consciousness to the challenges of an environment that is becoming progressively more secular."[288] In other words, the fact that the predictions of the secularization thesis have not come to fruition demands a cognitive dissonance on the part of secularists that transcends mere tolerance or accommodation of religious viewpoints within liberal society. Rather, secular citizens should be open to investigating religion for any cognitive contents it might have to offer. The epistemological challenge facing secularists, occasioned by the failure of the secularization thesis, is analogous to the challenge faced by religious persons in the wake of modernity. For Habermas, "The secular counterpart to reflexive religious consciousness is an agnostic, but nonreductionist form of postmetaphysical thinking."[289] In his judgment, this requirement on the part of secular citizens equalizes the respective burdens of both secular and religious citizens. In conclusion, he states:

---

[285] Habermas, 138, italics in original.
[286] Habermas, 138.
[287] Habermas, 139, italics in original.
[288] Habermas, 139, italics in original.
[289] Habermas, 140.

> The effort of philosophical reconstruction required shows that the role of democratic citizenship assumes a mentality on the part of secular citizens that is no less demanding than the corresponding mentality of their religious counterparts. This is why the cognitive burdens imposed on both sides by the acquisition of the appropriate epistemic attitudes are not all asymmetrical.[290]

There is much that is laudable in Habermas effort to equalize the burdens borne by citizens in democracies, and I agree with much of what he says in the above quotations. He goes much further than many liberal theorists in assigning cognitive contents to religious beliefs. This concession alone goes a long way toward mitigating some of the post-religious, Enlightenment assumptions I criticize above. Of course, all this talk about equalizing burdens is difficult to reconcile with the epistemological assumption, dealt with in the last chapter, that religious citizens necessarily travel with heavier metaphysical baggage. Nevertheless, these are important qualifications to the secularism inherent in, say, Rawls's political liberalism. Also, in an effort to equalize the translation burden, Habermas states, "A liberal culture can even expect its secular citizens to participate in efforts to translate relevant contributions from religious language into a publicly accessible language."[291]

However, some believers might still object that they bear an asymmetrical burden. After all, they must still translate their language into secular language, at least at the institutional level, if it is to have any public force. There is no counterpart requirement on the part of secular citizens, nor is there an obligation to aid religious citizens in translation. Although Habermas thinks one can expect secular citizens to do so, others are more skeptical of such a prospect. James Bohman and William Rehg, however, claim that Habermas's translation requirement actually entails the least possible burden on citizens.[292] It is difficult, they argue, for secular citizens to translate religious reasons into secular ones, because they may not adequately understand the religious tradition(s) in question. Therefore, the burden is logically on those who know it best: religious citizens. Moreover, to abandon the translation requirement would

---

[290] Habermas, 143.
[291] Habermas, "Equal Treatment of Cultures," 310.
[292] James Bohman and William Rehg, "Jürgen Habermas," *Stanford Encyclopedia of Philosophy*: http://plato.stanford.edu/entries/habermas/#DiaBetNatRel.

be to abandon any appeal to public reason. The burden of translation is not obviated; rather it is exacerbated if each citizen has to translate his or her convictions into the language of every conceivable interlocutor rather than a shared public reason.

In response to the first point, Habermas implies that it is part of the secular citizen's epistemic responsibility to learn about other religious traditions in order to draw from them 'cognitive contents' that might have value to political discourse. Moreover, it is expedient for secular citizens to learn as much as possible about their religious interlocutor's point of view in order to facilitate immanent critique, Stout's option (3) above, since this option is often the most promising tack to pursue when no common basis can be established. Perhaps in learning about religious traditions, secular citizens can argue for their own position in a way that religious citizens would find persuasive on the basis of assumptions that they already hold. So not only should secular citizens learn about religion out of sense of fairness and responsible citizenship, but also for pragmatic purposes.

Regarding the second point, I do not abandon the translation requirement, but do question its stronger versions. In my judgment, it has normative force only at the level of legislation and should be construed as a pragmatic gesture in both the formal and informal public spheres, rather than a deontological requirement as it is for Rawls. But Bohman and Rehg imply that to weaken the translation requirement in this way is to abandon any claim to public reason. Here I would distinguish between reasons that are publicly accessible and a common basis of secular reason; they should not be conflated. I do reject the latter, but see no reason why this compels me to reject the notion of practical reasons that are accessible to a wide audience within a pluralistic democracy. Such reasons can be either secular or religious and their accessibility lies in their rhetorical resonance rather than in meeting some abstract criterion, such as ideal rational acceptability. It is certainly impractical to translate our convictions into the language of each and every interlocutor, but this is completely unnecessary. While we do share a common language, it draws from many sources and comes packaged in different ways. It is the insight of pragmatic conceptions of discourse that reaching the widest possible audience does not depend upon the idealized universal acceptability of certain premises. Limiting one's repertoire to a 'public' language that artificially excludes cultural realities, including religion, which could widen one's base of argument, is counterproductive for building consensus on particular issues. Better to draw upon that wider cultural base in aiming to reach a wider audience. Thus, religion is only publicly 'inaccessible' to the extent that it no longer plays a role in the lives of citizens; in other words, if the secularization thesis is true. But we have seen good reason to reject both its empirical and normative aspects. Further complicating the notion of public accessibility is that no univocal account of it has emerged historically and is nowhere instantiated in working liberal democracies. Therefore, rather than being an idealization or abstraction, public accessibility is something that is built dialectically and pragmatically.

Balancing Burdens, again: A Utilitarian Analysis

So if the translation requirement, or something like it, is not to be mandated as a deontological requirement incumbent upon religious citizens alone, but as a cooperative endeavor that seeks to balance burdens, how should we approach this task? If deontological approaches are problematic are we left with a utilitarian analysis? I would suggest that even if one does not opt for deontology, Habermas's translation requirement is still problematic on utilitarian grounds. We might begin by asking: How do we decrease pain (the burdens citizens bear) and increase pleasure (the success of our democratic discourse)? Utilitarian calculations are rarely this simple and there are reasons to suggest that such an analysis is also problematic. For example, although the notion of the "general happiness" is notoriously vague, it is difficult to determine exactly what arrangement would promote the general happiness of both religious and secular citizens. Moreover, it seems that some of Habermas's recommendations could actually make citizens unhappier than more familiar conceptions of liberalism. For instance, some religious citizens might benefit from having their arguments taken more seriously in the public sphere, but others will no doubt feel uncomfortable that their particular religious views, previously insulated within private confessional circles, will no longer be immune to public scrutiny, criticism, and even ridicule. Under the current liberal arrangement, the private/public distinction serves to protect religious liberty, which includes the negative freedom from inference by others. However, the public demands placed on religious citizens to subject their religious convictions to criticism may in fact lead to a net loss of happiness. Also, although some religious citizens might benefit from increased public influence, they may be negatively affected by the expanded influence of religious groups with which they strongly disagree. One can easily envisage this scenario in historically Christian Western nations with increasing Muslim populations. In other words, the happiness Christians derive from their increased influence may be offset by the unhappiness they derive from increased Muslim influence.

Or take, for example, the impact upon secular citizens. Upon Habermas's recommendation of 'postsecular' citizenship, secularists must work harder than in classical liberalism to understand and appreciate religious orientations. Such work, as we have seen, is analogous to the work that the religious must do in the wake of the cognitive dissonances associated with modernist challenges to religious orthodoxy. However, the effort required to mine religion's 'cognitive contents' may well make secular citizens unhappier than they are now, especially if they cannot bring themselves to take religious belief seriously in the way Habermas admonishes. Despite the efforts of Habermas, Taylor, Stout and others, to aid their religiously unmusical fellows in this task, not all of them are able or willing to participate, just as not all religious citizens are capable of translation. However, one might argue that secular citizens, and society as a whole, might benefit from religious citizens' civic engagement. Religious citizens who feel marginalized from the public sphere might participate under conditions of postsecularism and their contributions to public debate may in fact yield a net benefit. But it is also possible, some would say likely, that such openness will only empower those religionists who are already vying for political power and will use the newly transformed public sphere to further advance obnoxious social policies that will infringe upon the freedom of minorities that they deem 'sinful.' Anxiety over this outcome, for a secularist, will no doubt counterbalance any benefits, hypothetical or actual, that are likely to result from increased religious participation in public debate.

Furthermore, an increase in religion's public presence has unpredictable outcomes. On the one hand, it might promote healthy societal pluralism and competition thereby enriching democratic debate. On the other hand, it might lead to sectarian divisions that threaten the unity of the state. Again, forecasting the consequences of these actions, and relative happiness of citizens, is exceedingly difficult. Perhaps more disconcerting is the prospect of such sectarianism breeding violence and discrimination. Despite Mill's disdain of censorship in *On Liberty*, many contemporary liberals think he underestimated the extent to which some ideologies, such as sexism, racism, and other forms of intolerance, ought to be suppressed by the state. Religion, sadly, is often used as a vehicle for the promotion of such illiberal tendencies, such as a constitutional ban on same-sex unions, and the thought of it gaining influence causes secularists no end of anxiety. Less serious, but also problematic, is the notion that 'fringe' religions, such as Wicca or Scientology, will expect their arguments to be taken seriously rather than cursorily dismissed. Perhaps Pandora's Box is best left closed.

So it is not obvious that the practical implementation of Habermas's postsecular proposals will bring about a net happiness for citizens, and it may well be the case that utilitarian analyses are not useful in this case. Certainly, Habermas is not a utilitarian and the fact that his requirements for democracy are more stringent than competing conceptions, does not constitute an objection for him. Democracy is, after all, an epistemically demanding form of government. Indeed, the fact that a reform is difficult is not a good reason for failing to implement it, even from a utilitarian perspective, because the net happiness may well be greater in the long run. Of course, the 'long run' is notoriously difficult to calculate and probably would involve some consideration of posterity centuries, or even millennia, from now. The practical pitfalls attending such an endeavor are obvious, not the least of which is the severe limitation of our foresight. Nevertheless, despite the problems I raise with such consequentialist calculations, it seems that any pragmatic approach to Habermas's suggested revisions to contemporary liberalism must take into account what the likely consequences would be for human flourishing. If concrete implementation of the proposed revisions will likely detract from human flourishing, or simply balance what our current social arrangements provide, philosophers and ordinary citizens will have good *prima facie* reason to judge the cost too high. In my judgment, however, the challenges facing societal organization today with respect to religion are not radically different from those of the early modern period when our current political compromise was forged. The above revisions to that 'Jeffersonian compromise' do not radically modify liberalism; indeed, they follow from assumptions liberals already take for granted, as I shall argue below. We must also bear in mind that, if Habermas is right and democratic forms of government participate in a continual learning process that is inherently fallible and revisable, then such alterations are to be expected. We should not naively assume that seventeenth and eighteenth century conceptions of the relation between liberalism and religion should hold for all time. We do not oppose economic reforms on the basis that it conflicts with the eighteenth century classical liberal understanding of the relationship between the state and private enterprise. Why should we oppose modifying our conception of the liberal state vis-à-vis religion on these grounds?

Objections Answered

In what follows, I would like to briefly make the case that the negative consequences outlined above do not necessarily follow. Moreover, many of the above objections are not so different from objections against the extension of religious freedom more generally, many of which were dispatched in the seventeenth century. Thus, allowing religion access to the public sphere does not inherently contradict principles most liberals already accept provided the secularity of the state can be maintained. On the basis of my revised ITP, I think the secularity of the state can be maintained without further restrictions of the expressive freedom of religious citizens.

So are we to expect dire consequences, such as those outlined above, to obtain if restrictions on religious language in public are relaxed? Importantly, almost all of the fears mentioned apply to religious liberty more generally. Upon the utilitarian criterion, one could make the case that religious liberty does not tend to promote the general happiness and the state is therefore justified in restricting it. Jay Newman has in fact argued that utilitarianism does not provide unambiguous moral justification for religious freedom.[293] For example, as Dostoevsky's Grand Inquisitor claims, many people are happier if others do their religious thinking for them; the responsibilities, or burdens, associated with reflexively engaging one's faith, or lack thereof, not to mention the myriad of other religious options, often leads to anxiety. Moreover, the happiness a particular religious community derives from the right to, say, freely proselytize may be neutralized by its unhappiness when another religious community exercises the same right. Moreover, the freedom to proselytize, while benefiting those adherents who believe they are carrying out God's will, tends to irritate non-adherents who proselytizers inform are mistaken or even damned. Yet this objection is rarely taken as a serious reason for the state to withhold religious liberty. In addition, religious liberty can easily threaten the unity of the state, especially when historically Christian, or even secular, nations identify citizenship with a set of values not all religions unambiguously embrace. As

---

[293]   Jay Newman, *On Religious Freedom* (Ottawa: University of Ottawa Press, 1991), 131 – 32.

stated, many of these fears were present when Locke proposed religious tolerance. Some of his contemporaries, following Augustine, believed that error has no rights and as such the state is justified in suppressing 'error.' The seventeenth century polemicist, Jonas Proast, responded to Locke's *Letter*, arguing that the coercive power of the state is indeed justified in suppressing erroneous religious views.[294] Of course, very few, if any, citizens of liberal democracies today would see this as an argument for suppressing religious freedom. Yet parallels between this general case and the specific revisions to liberal theory that I propose clearly exist.

But let me speak more concretely about the safeguards my proposal establishes against the aforementioned deleterious consequences. Firstly, throughout this project my main concern has been the subject of religious beliefs and arguments, not religious practices. This distinction is important. Historically, in Anglo-American liberalism, religious freedom has been restricted in the case of the latter. There are certain practices we simply do not allow even if done for ostensibly religious reasons. The free exercise of religion must be practiced within the purview of secular law and this proviso remains upon my revision. Secondly, my revised liberalism does not give license to just any religious language whatsoever. Again, dogmatic claims that brook no argument or criticism are *prima facie* disqualified from democratic discourse which is inherently fallible and critical. Such language must remain within private confessional circles and religious citizens who cannot or will not offer arguments – religious or secular – should not expect to influence the political process on the basis of appeals to the authority of sacred doctrines or texts. Religious citizens who are willing and able to make an argument, regardless of whether or not the premises are commonly accepted, are free to participate, but they also thereby leave the safety of their confessional circles; their views are now fair game for criticism and religionists should not take offense or expect additional respect by virtue of the fact their views are religious. As long as religious interlocutors offer arguments which are non-dogmatic and fallible then they should not necessarily be excluded from the public sphere. Under these conditions, the opportunities for abuse are limited; my proposal includes all of the checks and balances of traditional liberalism while expanding the expressive freedom of religious citizens. Certainly, this expansion may be more modest than some religionists

---

[294] Patrick Romanell, introduction to *A Letter Concerning Toleration* by John Locke (New Jersey: Prentice Hall, 1950), 6.

would hope – not to mention more generous than some secularists would like – but it is a significant advance over the "Jeffersonian compromise"[295] that arguably impairs religious participation in public debate.

So let us reexamine some of our hypothetical consequences to individual and societal flourishing and how a revised liberalism might in fact obviate such problematic outcomes. Take, for example, the unhappiness Christians might experience as a result of the increased influence of, say, Islam. The topic of Islam's relationship to historically Christian nations and contemporary liberal values has received much interest in the popular media and the academy recently. But Christians should not expect a net loss of happiness to result from allowing Muslims to participate authentically in public debate, nor should we expect the kind of sectarian violence many secularists fear. On the contrary, I would suggest that encouraging such engagement actually minimizes the potential for violence which is, of course, a net benefit. For example, if a particular religious community feels disenfranchised by the state, if it cannot make its voice heard through words, it is more likely to make itself heard through violent acts. Habermas also recognizes the point that silence all too often results in violence. We should strive to avoid this fatal silence.[296]

Thus I propose that we enlarge the domain of public discourse, which is, as I have argued, a relatively 'low cost' way to achieve a net gain in terms of human flourishing. It is 'low cost' in the sense that it does not require us to sacrifice any of our liberal political values. The checks and balances of classical liberalism remain in place: the restraints on content, the neutrality of law, restrictions on religious practice, and the disqualification of dogmatic claims. These conditions make it very difficult for religious citizens to employ the coercive power of the state to enforce a particular doctrine to restrict the liberty of other citizens who do not share it. I simply advocate, as do other contemporary philosophers, removing epistemological restraints on the kinds of reasons religious citizens can offer for their political decisions. As I have argued, such epistemological restraints are based on a mistaken historical interpretation of the relevant thinkers, a mistaken epistemology, and are unnecessary for political praxis. Arguably, these restraints are worse than unnecessary; they are

---

[295] Richard Rorty, "Religion As Conversation-stopper," in *Philosophy and Social Hope* (Penguin (Non-Classics), 2000), 169.

[296] Giovanna Borradori, *Philosophy in a Time of Terror: Dialogues with Jurgen Habermas and Jacques Derrida* (University Of Chicago Press, 2004), 35.

ideologically imposed restraints that are an impediment to full democratic participation for many citizens and thus invite violence. A pragmatic approach to this situation calls for a reassessment of classical and contemporary liberal theory.

The expansion of the public sphere to include certain kinds of religious discourse need not result in violence or disunity. In fact, in my judgment, it is likely to decrease it. In evidence of this claim, one could contrast Islam in the United States with Islam in Western Europe. Although a detailed empirical investigation of the relevant differences is beyond the scope of this chapter and my disciplinary competence, I would suggest that Islam has become more radicalized in Western Europe than in the U.S. because in Europe the overgeneralization of secularism has imposed a culture of silence on religion generally. In the United States, by contrast, there is more public space for religion and thus Muslims, even post-911, are invited to participate in the 'civil religion'.[297] The notion of civil religion and the role it plays in explaining the 'American exception' with respect to the secularization thesis is, likewise, beyond the scope of this chapter. But a few cursory remarks are, I think, helpful. Although the First Amendment prohibits the establishment of religion, religious devotion in America actually increased throughout the period known as the Enlightenment, as we saw in chapter one. These religious communities were not homogenous, but they were understood as part of the broader church or civil religion. At first, Catholics and Jews were not included. Gradually, however, the franchise extended to them. The unity of faith amid pluralism is thus achieved through a perceived religious consensus, or civil religion. On American 'civil religion,' Taylor comments:

> [A] way that Americans can understand their fitting together in society although of different faiths, is through these faiths themselves being seen as in this consensual relation to the common civil religion. Go to the church of your choice, but go. Later this expands to include synagogues. When imams also begin to appear at prayer breakfasts, along with priests, pastors, and rabbis, the signal is that Islam is being invited into the consensus."[298]

---

[297] Charles Taylor, *A Secular Age* (Belknap Press of Harvard University Press, 2007), 524.
[298] Taylor, 524.

To be sure, this does not mean that everybody who participates in this 'civil religion' is necessarily religious. Nor does it deny that secularization is also a factor in the American experience. In the first chapter, I looked at how secularization became a pragmatic necessity in American political discourse despite growing religious devotion among the citizenry. But it seems that Americans are less inclined than Western Europeans to see secularization as emancipation from religion. Indeed, for the United States, religion was an important avenue to civic solidarity in a way that it arguably was not in most Western European countries with their history of religious warfare. So it seems plausible that religious participation in public life does not necessarily lead to disunity and sectarian strife, but may actually promote solidarity. Of course, the value of civil religion and religion in general, comes under attack in every generation by those secularists who do not consider it to be an unqualified good and perhaps even a great evil. And some secularists worry that they will lose their political voice if religious points of view are encouraged to participate, although the barrage of recent anti-religious polemics makes this outcome seem unlikely. Nevertheless, in a democracy we must learn to live with multiple voices, sometimes voices with which we stridently disagree; this is true of religious citizens also. A robust democracy does not implore the agency of the state to suppress such voices, but rather tries to find a way to achieve unity pragmatically while ensuring that all responsible voices get a fair hearing. I say "all responsible voices" because, as argued above, there are some voices, those of bigots, racists, etc. that should be disallowed if not by state action as in the case of anti-incitement laws, then by social disapproval and marginalization.[299] There is nothing in my proposed revisions to standard liberal theory that would give license to such abuse.

---

[299] I do not mention hate-speech laws in this context, because I find their implementation problematic from the standpoint of free speech. Ironically, they are most often defended by secularists when abused by religionists who are offended when their views are criticized. Hate-speech laws are part of the problem because they encourage non-discursive religious attitudes. If one criticizes your sacred beliefs, the appropriate response is to offer a counter-argument, not charge him with hate speech as if religion enjoys special privilege, i.e. is sacred, in the sense that other beliefs are not. It is unclear, however, whether Habermas agrees. Although he thinks that sacredness is disqualified from public deliberation, he makes heavy use of speech act theory, which is a major impetus for the rationale behind hate-speech legislation. I will briefly address Habermas's appropriation of speech act theory in the next chapter.

Finally, there is the 'Pandora's Box' objection that, given what I say, anything claiming to be religious will expect to be taken seriously. I have already noted that restraints on religious practice continue to be operative under my proposal. But what about those religious beliefs that fall outside the purview of 'civil religion?' In other words, those fringe beliefs that are regarded as irrational by the majority of citizens, both religious and secular. Bear in mind, however, as noted above in response to Bohman and Rehg, that I have not abandoned the notion of reasons that are publicly accessible; I simply deny that they should be identified with exclusively secular reasons. We are not suddenly left without epistemological criteria because we acknowledge the empirical given that not all people find the same premises persuasive. As I argued, we can still pragmatically build as wide a consensus as possible which sometimes requires translation, sometimes immanent critique, and at other times religious premises. But by definition, publicly accessible premises will have wide rhetorical appeal, and the 'fringe' by definition does not. So we should not be overly worried, in my judgment, about the influence of marginal beliefs to which few subscribe. Recall that under my proposal they would still need to offer an argument in order to be taken seriously and even then their premises would be unlikely to find wide support. The Pandora's Box objection assumes that anything merely claiming to be religious will automatically be given a hearing and that is emphatically not what I propose. On my view, no additional respect (or disrespect) attaches to a claim simply by virtue of its being labeled 'religious'. So the objection is irrelevant. But even if it were relevant, there are already legal criteria in many democracies for defining religion in practice; for the purposes of determining whether a particular group qualifies for tax exemption on the basis of religion, the state effectively defines 'religion'. Although the potential for arbitrary discrimination exists, there is a practical necessity for state agencies to determine what religions should be publicly recognized and which should not. While I have no expertise in this area, it seems to me that we already have mechanisms for determining which religions should and should not have public standing, which should assuage fears about opening Pandora's Box.

Therefore, we have good reason to conclude that the above pragmatic revisions to contemporary liberal theory are, on balance, an improvement. Moreover, they are, in my judgment an improvement over Habermas's admittedly noble efforts to balance burdens among both religious and secular citizens. Because we stand to lose none of the protections that state neutrality affords secularists and religious minorities and stand to gain increased political participation for religious citizens, we have good reason to conclude that the aforementioned pragmatic revisions to contemporary liberal theory are, on balance, an improvement. Moreover, they are, in my judgment an improvement over Habermas's admittedly noble efforts to balance burdens among both religious and secular citizens.

In this chapter, I have attempted to demonstrate that the idealized liberal position as articulated by Rawls and Habermas is more restrictive than the liberalism that is actually instantiated in working democracies. Although Habermas is more open than Rawls to seeing religious concepts as having cognitive content as opposed to merely posing as promissory notes for such content, he arguably still places undue epistemic constraints on religious citizens in the public sphere. With Wolterstorff, I have argued that the liberal position is not justified in imposing these epistemic constraints insofar as religious arguments do not break the restraints on content established by the law of the land. I also argue, like Wolterstorff, that the liberal emphasis on consensus is overwrought. The kind of consensus aimed at by liberal theorists is probably not a live option in working democracies. If one defines the success of democratic discourse as the achievement of such consensus, then the project is doomed to fail. However, we don't need to agree on a common basis prior to debate. It suffices for pragmatic purposes that a majority agree on some concrete proposal, policy, or law. The public sphere is not an endlessly discursive, consensus-building domain; practically speaking, the debate comes to an end through the democratic process of voting. I take seriously Wolterstorff's insight that some liberal theorists seem to be uncomfortable with the politics of multiple identities. In this way, liberalism is not unlike communitarianism; the liberal theorist is trying to create the ideal type of community – an ideal speech situation, one might say – in which rational consensus is achieved. However, like Wolterstorff, I suspect that such consensus is very difficult if not impossible to achieve on the issues that matter most deeply. I am not opposed to consensus in principle; if it happens, all well and good. But I remain skeptical that the idealized version of consensus promoted in liberal theory is necessary for the smooth functioning of a democracy.

The implications of the foregoing critique for religious arguments are clear. I have argued that religious arguments are not a special case that must be singled out as particularly problematic for democratic discourse. Granted, dogmatism is problematic, but insofar as we are dealing with religious *arguments* the fact that their premises are controversial does not immediately exclude them from public debate. There are, in fact, many controversial premises in many arguments, both religious and secular, in the public sphere. In other words, we disagree about what premises are reasonable and it is unlikely that we shall discover non-tautological premises that command universal assent in the near future. As such, a person who appeals to the Bible for support of a premise in a political argument is in principle no more idiosyncratic than a person who appeals to Marx. In a robust democracy, there are bound to be controversial premises. Thus, I have argued that it is useful to dispense with talk about 'public' versus 'private' reasons and to instead talk about universally accepted premises and controversial premises. Once one does so, one can easily see that the issue of religion in the context of liberal theory is a red-herring. Of course, the religious citizen may, for pragmatic reasons, translate the premises of her argument to make them more persuasive to her secular interlocutors. But we must bear in mind that it is the particularities of the discursive context that make some reasons more 'publicly accessible' than others; they are not so simply by virtue of their being secular, or by being acceptable to all rational people in some abstract sense.

I have also argued that Habermas's qualification of the translation requirement at the informal level can be extended to the formal level without damaging the legitimacy of the laws for all citizens. There is an insight behind Habermas's ITP, but one can preserve that insight – that each citizen must in principle be able to understand the justification of the law – by ensuring that legislation is written in as neutral a language as possible with respect to comprehensive worldviews. But 'neutral' in this context does not necessarily mean secular. Just as one would not cite the Bible as justification for some law, one would not cite Marx either. However, nothing should bar citizens, or their official representatives, from citing the Bible or Marx when debating *prospective* laws in a democracy. I have argued that my proposed revision to Habermas's ITP does everything he wants it to with respect to preserving democratic legitimacy, while relaxing the translation requirement at the formal level as well as the informal level. Again, translation may be useful for pragmatic purposes in such contexts, but we need not construe it as a formal requirement.

Although my approach is indebted to pragmatism, the question remains: do pragmatists object to allowing religious arguments into the public sphere? At first blush, the writings of Richard Rorty on this question don't inspire much confidence in my efforts to use pragmatism to argue for the inclusion of religious arguments in public. Fortunately, pragmatism as a style of philosophy is not amenable to monolithic interpretations. Nonetheless, Rorty being the primary proponent of pragmatism in the latter half of the twentieth century deserves to be taken seriously. In the next chapter, I will take up Rorty's concerns over religion's public accessibility in relation to his debates on related matters with Habermas, Wolterstorff, and Stout. Specifically, I will suggest that Rorty's defense of the public/private schema rests on something very much like Habermas's translation requirement. As a pragmatist, it's a bit strange that Rorty cites Rawls and Habermas as model epistemologists on the issue of religion in the public sphere. In response to criticisms from Wolterstorff and Stout, which we shall examine, Rorty has reconsidered his position. I will also consider alternative pragmatist accounts of religion in public, such as Stout's method of immanent critique, in order to see whether or not pragmatism can provide other resources more sympathetic to the project of defending the legitimacy of religious reasons and arguments in the public sphere.

Chapter 4
Religion as an Abnormal Conversation Starter: Considering Pragmatist Alternatives to Rorty

My critique of Habermas in the foregoing chapter rests on considerations that stem from the pragmatist tradition broadly conceived. One can use pragmatism to question the 'common basis' on which liberal theorists justify the exclusion of religion from the public sphere. However, this is a somewhat indirect consequence of the application of pragmatism to political theory. Do pragmatists themselves see their view as offering resources to the religionist who seeks to cast political arguments in a religious idiom? Because pragmatism is far from monolithic, I suspect it depends on which pragmatist one asks. In this chapter, I will look at two representatives of pragmatism: Richard Rorty and Jeffrey Stout. Although neither thinker identifies himself as religious, Rorty is much less sympathetic to the prospect of religious arguments in public than Stout.

In the proceeding section, I highlight some of the epistemic differences between Habermas and Rorty. While Habermas does draw on a certain strain of pragmatism in constructing his 'formal pragmatics', he wants to hold on to the concept of context-independent truth and its importance for the modern political project. A consequence of this view is his insistence that rhetoric, or perlocutionary speech acts, are disallowed. Rorty, by contrast, abandons the notion of context-independent truth and is, consequently, more comfortable with employing rhetoric for political purposes. On the surface, Rorty's pragmatism seems to offer some comfort to the religionist who wants to employ religious arguments in public. However, Rorty finds religious rhetoric to be in bad taste and cites Rawls and Habermas as model epistemologists on the issue.

Especially telling is Rorty's essay "Religion as Conversation-stopper". In this essay, he argues that religion should be excluded from the public sphere. He does so by defending the well-worn public/private distinction; religion belongs to the latter. However, a careful analysis of Rorty's distinction shows that he is using the term 'private' to mean essentially 'not shared by the public at large'. In other words, Rorty appears to be endorsing the standard liberal model. However, we have already looked at some problems with the notion of 'publicly shared' or 'premises held in common'. Moreover, pragmatism itself questions the notion of an ideal consensus. Rorty, however, may be using 'shared in common', or 'public', to mean 'actually shared' rather than 'ideally shared'. But this view is also problematic; if we had to limit our political arguments to premises actually held in common, no argument could get off the ground. So the pragmatist knows that there is actual public disagreement about premises in political arguments, and presumably not all of these disagreements are in bad taste, even if some function as conversation-stoppers. After all, the public is not an endlessly discursive arena; conversation stopping always occurs as a result of one of our most cherished democratic practices, namely voting. It is difficult, then, to see why public disagreement over religion is in 'bad taste' if public disagreement in general is not.

However, Rorty, in light of criticism from the likes of Wolterstorff and Stout, has reconsidered some of his more unguarded statements with respect to religion. He suspects that his disagreement with religious critics like Wolterstorff hang on empirical, rather than strictly philosophical, considerations. Religionists simply underestimate the harm that is caused by their forcing their religious views on the general public, particularly vulnerable minorities. As such, religionists ought to find another language to express their political point of view, one that has less potential for abuse. This recommendation sounds like a version of the translation requirement. Rorty is quick to note, however, that he can think of no principle that would commit religious believers to changing their rhetorical strategy. So, for example, when Christians cite Leviticus 18:22 in opposition to gay rights, Rorty cannot invoke a philosophical principle to stop them from doing so. Nevertheless, he thinks they should stop invoking such rhetoric, and hopes that the rhetorical strategies favored by secularists will continue to marginalize religious voices. In this chapter, I explore Rorty's argument to see if it contains any lessons for politically engaged religious citizens, and offer an analysis of his recommendation that religious citizens switch rhetorical strategies with an eye to its pragmatic advantages and disadvantages.

In providing this analysis, I also explore alternative rhetorical strategies, such as Jeffrey Stout's 'immanent critique'. While I suggest that Stout's 'immanent critique' is a promising tack to pursue, I am aware that it is not without critics. Below, I examine how Habermas might evaluate Stout's proposal, and how Stout's affirmation of religious tradition in the course of critique may not satisfy the critical theorist's demands. In order to clarify these issues, I discuss the differences between 'critique' as understood by a pragmatist like Stout and as understood by a critical theorist like Habermas. Important in this context is the relation of 'critique' to 'tradition' and whether democracy itself is to be understood as a substantive tradition. Stout and Habermas appear to disagree on this issue, but I still see 'immanent critique' as a pragmatically viable option within democracies. While Stout is sympathetic to religious language informing public debate, he offers a rigorous critique of more conservative traditions within Christianity. Moreover, for him, it remains to be seen whether or not Christian language is the best vehicle to express our shared commitments to democratic principles.

I conclude the chapter by assessing whether or not pragmatism, as expressed by two prominent spokespersons for the movement, is compatible with the project of a public place for religion. But first, I turn to discussing the matter of Habermas's differences with Rorty with respect to the place of rhetoric and context-independent truth in political discourse.

The Three 'R's': Reason, Rhetoric, and Reeducation

My critique throughout the foregoing chapters of Habermas's insistence on a common basis for publicly accessible, or secular, reasons is largely inspired by pragmatist considerations concerning the scope of argumentation and justification. Among the most prominent of Habermas's pragmatist critics is Richard Rorty. Interestingly, although he differs with Habermas on whether or not there is a distinction between truth and justification, he is mainly in agreement when it comes to the discursive bankruptcy of religion in public debate. However, Rorty's criticism of religion in the public sphere is based on pragmatic considerations rather than any attempt to define an idealized common basis for rational deliberation. Thus, when Rorty talks about premises held in common, he refers to those that are held in common in practice rather than in principle. As such, he makes a good foil for my argument in the last chapter that seeks to expand the scope of religious arguments along pragmatic lines. Before we get to these concrete issues, however, it is helpful to establish the background of the debate between Habermas and Rorty over truth and justification. This will enable us to see more clearly how a pragmatist can criticize the ideal of a common basis, but nevertheless advocate a shrinking of religion from the public sphere.

Since his early work on the public sphere, Habermas has attempted to rigorously delineate the means by which we assess the validity of arguments, the process whereby opinion is transformed into knowledge. In the first volume of TCA, Habermas takes up theories of argumentation or the question: "What makes some arguments stronger or weaker than other arguments?"[300] He takes up three aspects of argumentation: "Rhetoric is concerned with argumentation as *process*, dialectic with the pragmatic *procedures* of argumentation, and logic with its *products* .... The fundamental intuition connected with argumentation can best be characterized from the process perspective by the intention of convincing a *universal audience* and gaining general assent for an utterance."[301] This approach is heavily indebted to Peirce's pragmatism, later defended and fleshed out by Putnam. Earlier, Habermas says that in order to enter argumentation, participants must presuppose "that the structure of their communication excludes all force ... except the force of the better argument."[302] Later, Habermas makes it clear that this criterion also excludes subtle rhetorical force. All of these considerations are included in what Habermas refers to as an "ideal speech situation." [303] In summary, the three purposes of argumentation are to 1) convince a universal audience; 2) to resolve disputes about hypothetical validity claims in rationally motivated agreement; 3) to ground or redeem a validity claim via reason. Although these levels can be separated in abstraction, in practice they always occur together.

    Habermas distances himself from earlier theories of rational action, such as Weber's, which consider only teleological action capable of rationalization. This model deals only with strategic action, or action oriented to success; Habermas wants to develop a model oriented to reaching understanding, or communicative action. He looks for resources in speech act theory in order to accomplish this task. He claims that the difference between strategic and communicative action is structural rather than psychological. He considers "reaching understanding" (hereafter RU) to be distinct "from merely de facto accord."[304] RU occurs when the propositional content of validity claims is differentiated and all participants understand and accept the validity of the claims. This differs from 'collective like-mindedness' which can be influenced by other factors, such as rhetoric. An implication for democracy is that solidarity in

---

[300]   Jürgen Habermas, *The Theory of Communicative Action, vol. 1: Reason and the Rationalization of Society*, 24.
[301]   Habermas, 26.
[302]   Habermas, 25.
[303]   Habermas, 25.
[304]   Habermas, 287.

society must result from rationally motivated agreement as opposed to a mere *modus vivendi*. Already, the bar for RU is set high because agreement rests on common conviction which cannot be coerced or influenced by instrumental or strategic action. Also, upon my reading, agreement is not necessarily equivalent to consensus. The agreement of which Habermas speaks seems to be a very thin, formal (as opposed to content-full) agreement; a procedural agreement. Another interesting point is that Habermas seems to want to be both normative and descriptive here: we should aim for this type of normative understanding (*Einverständnis*) but it is also the case that "language with an orientation to reaching understanding is the *original mode* of language use."[305] He turns to Austin's speech act theory to substantiate this claim and to differentiate actions oriented to success and actions oriented to RU.

Very briefly, Austin distinguishes three speech acts: locutionary, illocutionary, and perlocutionary. These "can be characterized in the following catchphrases: to say *something*, to act *in* saying something, to bring about something *through* acting in saying something."[306] Glossing over much of Austin's speech act theory and Habermas's analysis of it, we can say that perlocutionary acts, oriented as they are to teleological action, cannot be part of RU. For Habermas, the meaning of what is said is constitutive of illocutionary acts, whereas the intentions of the agent are constitutive for teleological actions. Perlocutions lend themselves to manipulation, to the kind of strategic action that Habermas thinks precludes RU. This account echoes, in a more sophisticated way, the debate between logic and rhetoric in ancient Athens. Habermas seems to want to banish would-be sophists from exercising any influence on public consensus through their 'distorted communication.' In some respects, this is a worthy goal, but I think it attributes disingenuous intentions to actors without sufficient justification. Human beings do have goals and intentions – this is the descriptive side – and these do not necessarily rely upon distorted communication. If I submit a paper that is below par and the professor asks for a rewrite, she is trying to get me to act, to persuade me that it is in my interests to do a rewrite. Is this a perlocutionary act? Perhaps, but is it distorted communication? Not necessarily. Notice that it does not suffice to simply acknowledge the rationality of my professor's position; she is trying to get me to take action, not merely say, "Yes, I understand your criticisms, but I like my paper

---

[305] Habermas, 288, italics in original.
[306] Habermas, 289.

the way it is." Now, perhaps this example is not entirely apt, but it shows what I take to be an unrealistic standard in Habermas's model, especially if it purports to be descriptive as well as normative – rather than emphasizing rhetoric, dialectic, or logic at the expense of each other.

In my judgment, this raises four problems with Habermas's appropriation of Austin. Firstly, he has to attribute intentions to everybody. This is a very Kantian move, but it seems to belie his claim that the distinction between communicative and strategic action is not psychological. Once one starts imputing intentions, it becomes at least partly psychological, although there may be structural elements as well. Indeed, in his debate with Gadamer, Habermas invokes psychoanalysis as an example of the "depth hermeneutics" necessary for rooting out distorted communication.[307] Is this move fully within the linguistic turn or does it reveal a latent return to phenomenology? This is not a rhetorical question, but one which deserves careful attention, although I leave it to other scholars to pursue the implications.

Secondly this model may well fail to motivate action, as in my above example. I think Habermas is again echoing Kant, and saying that the rationality of the claim alone should be enough to motivate, or oblige, action. Perhaps, ideally, but this does not always happen and if Habermas is making, and I believe he is, empirical as well as normative claims – the demarcation of which is not always clear – this may be a serious shortcoming.

Thirdly, human beings do have intentions and goals, and it is well nigh impossible to completely separate ourselves from them. Habermas implicitly recognizes this when he admits that illocutionary acts may have perlocutionary effects, or elements not intended by the speaker. In that case, do we not fully enter into psychologism and find ourselves in the unenviable position of having to psychoanalyze and root out the intentions, sometimes unbeknownst to the speakers, behind their actions? Perhaps this critique is overwrought, but it is at least potentially problematic. As the maxim goes, "ought implies can." In my judgment, Habermas has set the bar for RU too high; we cannot, by his own admission, dissociate ourselves from our goal-oriented action in the world.

---

[307] See Habermas, "The Hermeneutical Claim to Universality," in *Contemporary Hermeneutics: Hermeneutics as Method, Philosophy, and Critique*, ed. Josef Bleicher (London: Routledge and Kegan Paul, 1980), 181 – 211.

Finally, the type of agreement he aims for is too thin. Throughout TCA, Habermas tenaciously adheres to the form/content distinction. He is reticent to say anything substantive about how much agreement we can reasonably expect among rational agents. Rational people often disagree on matters of great import and there are rational arguments on either side of many debates. This is why rhetoric is employed in the public sphere sometimes subtly, oftentimes overtly. I share Habermas's (and Plato's) frustration with some of these tactics, but see it as a necessary evil in a democracy. What kind of substantive consensus – as opposed to mere accord – does Habermas think rational people can achieve on the basis of formal argumentation alone? Habermas acknowledges that not all fields of inquiry are captured by the propositional content of formal argumentation. In this situation, in which conventional procedures are applied in different fields, often requiring a high degree of specialization – expert cultures to use another Habermasian term – which reasons count as publicly accessible? Does the public exercise of reason, for the purposes of political praxis, not also include the consensus building power of rhetoric? Or is the consensus achieved by rhetoric illusory?

Richard Rorty takes up these questions in criticism of Habermas. Although both employ elements and methods from the broadly pragmatist tradition, they differ with respect to justificatory practices. More precisely, both agree on an anti-foundationalist understanding of justification, but disagree with respect to the implications of this view for establishing intersubjective validity. Both thinkers also hold that the notion of publicly accessible reasons only comes to the fore with the linguistic turn – within modernity the epistemological turn's presuppositions about the knowing subject could not allow the potential latent in communicative rationality to completely unfold. The pragmatist would put the same point differently: the isolated subject promoted truth as correspondence, which resulted in skepticism, rather than construing truth as convincing the widest possible audience. However, the contextualist implications of this position – that we cannot distinguish between truth and justification – is rejected by Habermas and embraced by Rorty.[308] For Habermas, "Reaching

---

[308] According to Maeve Cooke, Habermas "wishes to develop a pragmatic account of meaning that avoids what he sees as the main weaknesses of pragmatic accounts: the tendency to reduce validity to the conventional validity of given forms of life. He thus aims at developing a pragmatic account that holds on to an idea of validity that potentially transcends all accepted agreements in definitions or judgments. The idea that we understand an utterance when we know what makes it acceptable is intended as an

understanding cannot function unless the participants refer to a single objective world, thereby stabilizing intersubjectively the shared public space with which everything that is merely subjective can be contrasted."[309] Habermas is not defending representationalism, but making an attempt to rescue our realist intuitions about the world: "What is at stake is not the correct representation of reality but everyday practices that cannot fall apart. The contextualist unease betrays a worry about the smooth functioning of language games and practices."[310] However, this contextualist unease does not trouble Rorty: he is more than willing to treat everyday realism as an illusion and "wants to combat this illusion by rhetorical means and pleas for *reeducation*. We ought to get used to replacing the desire for objectivity with the desire for solidarity and, with William James, to understanding 'truth' as no more than that in which it is good for 'us' – the liberal members of Western culture or Western societies – to believe."[311] Rorty likewise challenges the notion of reaching agreement in an ideal speech situation:

> I cannot see what 'idealized rational acceptability' can mean except 'acceptability to an ideal community.' Nor can I see, given that no such community is going to have a God's eye view, that this ideal community can be anything more than us as we should like to be. Nor can I see what 'us' can mean here except: us educated, sophisticated, tolerant, wet liberals, the people who are always willing to hear the other side, to think out all their implications, etc.[312]

Habermas objects by pointing out that the notion of an ideal community need not presuppose a 'thick' conception of one's own culture, but rather is meant to include the formal, procedural practices that are universal to all argumentation. Habermas's formalism does not presuppose a correct picture of the world or specify what the content of our beliefs should be. Thus rhetoric, the attempt to persuade people, by changing the language and 'common sense' assumptions

---

attempt to make room for some notion of context-transcendent validity ('truth') within a pragmatic framework." *Language and Reason: A Study of Habermas's Pragmatics* (Cambridge, MA: The MIT Press, 1994), 97.

[309] Habermas, "Richard Rorty's Pragmatic Turn," in *Truth: Engagements Across Philosophical Traditions* ed. José Medina and David Wood (Wiley-Blackwell, 2005), 114.
[310] Habermas, 114.
[311] Habermas, 115.
[312] Quoted in Habermas, 119.

inherited from Greek metaphysics and monotheism, as Rorty advocates, is too content-full for Habermas's formal pragmatics. Rhetoric, in this capacity, is off limits. But Rorty does effectively problematize the notion of ideal publicly acceptable reasons or ideal rational acceptability. Again, it is debatable whether the 'force of rational motivation' or 'rationally motivated binding' (*Bildung*) is powerful enough to motivate action or build consensus. Thus, Rorty thinks that a thicker conception of culture is necessary for fostering solidarity. Formal argumentation alone is not sufficient: one must supplement one's arguments with substantive and affective elements from the liberal tradition. Hence, Rorty employs a distinction between arguing and educating. The latter, often more effective than the former, consists of narrative and literature and other means of engendering sympathy. Many of the great civil rights movements have employed such means effectively in addition to offering compelling arguments. The civil rights movement, as we have noted, did not shy away from specifically religious forms of rhetoric. Therefore, could not Rorty's appreciation of narrative and rhetoric allow some space for religious language in the accomplishment of political goals?

On the surface, Rorty does not offer any comfort to the religious believer who wants to utilize the semantic power of her tradition in the public sphere. On the contrary, Rorty defends the distinction between the public and the private sphere – religion belongs to the latter.[313] When introduced into public discourse, religious arguments – or rhetoric for that matter – act only as conversation stoppers. One could certainly criticize Rorty for a certain inconsistency here. After all, religious forms of argument often play precisely the rhetorical role Rorty advocates, despite the fact that they do not always 'reeducate' in the direction of the liberal values Rorty wants to defend. But sometimes they do. Moreover, they frequently appeal to narrative (for example, how often was the story of the Exodus used by American abolitionists and civil rights leaders?[314]), an appeal which often widens the scope of solidarity more effectively than rational argument alone. However, before advancing the charge of inconsistency, let us look more closely at Rorty's reasons for eyeing public appeals to religion with suspicion.

---

[313] For a critique, see Hendrik Hart, "The Consequences of Liberalism: Ideological Domination in Rorty's Public/Private Split," in *Towards and Ethics of Community*, ed. James H. Olthuis (Wilfred Laurier Press, 2000), 37 – 50.
[314] See Eddie S. Glaude, *Exodus!: Religion, Race, and Nation in Early Nineteenth-century Black America* (University of Chicago Press, 2000).

Is Religion a Conversation Stopper?

Perhaps a natural place to begin is Rorty's essay "Religion As Conversation-stopper." In what follows, I want to revisit in greater detail some of the material alluded to in my introductory comments in the first chapter. It should be noted, however, that this essay is hardly Rorty's most philosophically careful work – in fact at times it appears quite reckless – and he has publicly backed away from some of the hasty generalizations he makes while still defending a secular core. Nevertheless, it is an important essay insofar as it clearly articulates common secularist attitudes toward religion in public and seeks to link them to their epistemological roots in the Enlightenment and American pragmatism. Interestingly, although Rorty contrasts these two streams in epistemology elsewhere, he sees them as united on the practical question of the place of religion within a wider polity.

As I mentioned in chapter one, Rorty's essay is mainly directed against Stephen Carter's book *The Culture of Disbelief: How American Law and Politics Trivialize Religious Devotion*. However, Rorty introduces his essay with a few cursory remarks that are quite revealing. Throughout the essay, Rorty defends the public/private dualism but begins by introducing a parallel distinction between the "typical intellectual" and the "typical nonintellectual."[315] Moreover, the typical intellectual, we are told, "does not find religion what James called 'a live, forced and momentous option'. She thinks of religion as, at its best, Whitehead's 'what we do with our solitude', rather than something people do together in churches."[316] I am curious to know what Rorty thinks people are doing together in churches, but I let that pass. More germane to the point is the fact that Rorty imbues this distinction with a lot of normative weight. The intellectual is unlikely to find religion a live option, presumably due to her education, whereas the nonintellectual simply lacks the epistemological acumen to see that religion simply is, and should remain, a private matter. One would be hard pressed to find a clearer statement of the textbook secularization thesis I have been criticizing throughout this volume. So Rorty's assessment is far from a neutral description of the facts. But even stripped of its normative, and frankly, smug baggage, it is not an accurate description of the facts. There are some, if not many, intellectuals who do consider religion a live option and are not lacking in

---

[315] Richard Rorty, "Religion As Conversation- stopper," in *Philosophy and Social Hope* (Penguin, 2000), 169.
[316] Rorty, 169.

philosophical sophistication. Moreover, I suspect that those who follow Rorty's line, whether intellectuals or not, do so for reasons other than purely philosophical ones, as he tacitly admits later.

For example, he complains that Carter wants to bring religious considerations into public debate and says his hypothetical intellectual "is bound to be puzzled or annoyed"[317] by Carter's book. I fail to see how annoyance is strictly speaking relevant in assessing an argument. To paraphrase something Rorty says later in his essay 'we didn't ask about your private feelings; we were discussing arguments'. Nevertheless, Rorty is annoyed by Carter's effort to dissolve, in Rorty's view, the "happy, Jeffersonian compromise that the Enlightenment reached with the religious. This compromise consists in privatizing religion – keeping it out of what Carter calls 'the public square', making it seem bad taste to bring religion into discussion of public policy."[318] But one must wonder if 'bad taste' is all Rorty finds objectionable in religious language in public. Is it merely a sense of decorum that he wants to maintain, or is something more normative at stake, as in the case of Habermas and Rawls, whom he cites in support? I would think that a pragmatist would not want to police the public sphere, ridding it of anything that could be deemed bad taste, but would rather want to foster a domain of free expression and robust discourse even if it must be rough and ready at times, as in a democracy it must. Wolterstorff agrees: "Rorty's comments about the role of religion in the democratic polity breathe a very different spirit from that of his comments on every other topic .... What Rorty praises in those other passages is imagination, openness, re-description, self-creation; here, the talk is all about *limits*. Religion is to *limit* itself to the private; the conversation is to be *limited* to premises held in common."[319] Here, Rorty seems close to a contractarian position. Stout agrees, but comments, correctly, that Rorty does not theorize about universally valid principles; when he speaks of premises held in common, he means those that are in fact held in common in a given society, not an idealized one. If this is the case, I wonder, with Stout, why Rawls and Habermas are cited as superior epistemologists.[320] Regardless, Rorty's pragmatism in this context is at best unclear, at worst inconsistent. These difficulties are exacerbated when Rorty

---

[317] Rorty, 169.
[318] Rorty, 169.
[319] Nicholas Wolterstorff, "An Engagement with Rorty," *Journal of Religious Ethics*, 31.1 (2003): 134.
[320] Jeffrey Stout, *Democracy and Tradition* (Princeton University Press, 2005), 86.

says that he and fellow atheists do their best to "enforce" the Jeffersonian compromise. Although his primary tool for doing so may be social pressure rather than social contract, the notion of enforcement implies a normative rule to be enforced. This is why I think Stout is too quick to contrast contractarian or "moralistic" restraints on religious language in public with Rorty's "pragmatic" restraints.[321] Social pressure usually contains a heavy dose of moralism.

Case in point, he then goes on to catalogue the indignities and injustices that atheists must endure in American society: they are unlikely to be elected to public office without pretending to believe in God and secular conscientious objectors go to prison, unlike those who object on religious grounds. He concludes, "Such facts suggest to us (atheists) that the claims of religion need, if anything, to be pushed back still further, and that religious believers have no business asking for more public respect than they now receive."[322] But in my view, this statement misconstrues the real issue. Indeed, for my argument, respect in this context is irrelevant. I do not think that some arguments should be afforded more respect simply by virtue of being religious; they must vie for respect critically and dialectically like all other arguments. But to say that religious arguments should not be afforded more respect than other arguments is not to say that they ought to be excluded from the dialectical process at the outset. Rorty gets it right, although without realizing it, when he says "moral decisions that are to be enforced by a pluralist and democratic state's monopoly on violence are best made by public discussion in which voices claiming to be God's, or reason's, or science's are put on a par with everybody else's."[323] Putting voices that claim to be God's on a par with other voices, is not tantamount to excluding voices that claim to be God's, as Rorty is wont to do. So he should drop the old canard about religious voices getting more respect than they deserve in liberal democracies. Arguably, in recent years, the pendulum has swung the other way, as Rorty's own condescending tone toward the 'nonintellectual' implies.

Carter argues that "the legal culture that guards the public square still seems most comfortable thinking of religion as a hobby, something done in privacy, something that mature, public-spirited adults do not use as the basis for

---

[321] Stout, 85.
[322] Rorty, 169.
[323] Rorty, 172.

politics."324 Rorty correctly notes that "Carter's inference from privatization to trivialization is invalid unless supplemented with the premise that the nonpolitical is always trivial. But this premise seems false."325 He suggests that there are many things that are private, such as our family and love lives that are non-political, but are obviously not trivial. I grant Rorty this point. However, his thesis is complicated when he includes pursuits such as poetry, which may be private, but may also express sentiments that have political implications. He says, "the poems we atheists write, like the prayers our religious friends raise, are private, nonpolitical and nontrivial."326 While this may be true in some cases, it is not necessarily true in every case. After all, poetry and other forms of literature, as effective forms of rhetoric, can often broaden the sympathies of its audience and allow them to experience vicariously the plight of the disadvantaged.327 In such a way, good literature can have political entailments as can good prayers or sermons. Rorty seems to be referring here to poems that never see a wide audience, those that are only shared with intimates. But limiting the scope in this way seems ad hoc, serving only to make Rorty's point. But his argument is further complicated when he includes reading poetry as a private, and thus nonpolitical, pursuit. Is he still referring to poetry that has not been published, poetry intended only for intimates? If so, this is again ad hoc. If not, who is to say that it cannot function rhetorically toward some political end? Certainly not Rorty, since he defends this contention in another context.328 However, he provides a clue to his rationale when he says, "The search for private perfection, pursued by theists and atheists alike, is neither trivial nor, in a pluralistic democracy, relevant to public policy."329

As other scholars have noted, Rorty's appeal to the classical liberal distinction between the public and private appears, at least on the surface, like a tired move.330 However, Rorty's rationale for maintaining this modern distinction is not particularly modern at all. He believes that the public/private schema

---

324   Rorty, 170.
325   Rorty, 170.
326   Rorty, 170.
327   Richard Rorty, *Contingency, Irony, and Solidarity*, 141.
328   See especially the chapters on Nabokov and Orwell in *Contingency, Irony and Solidarity*.
329   Rorty, "Religion As Conversation-stopper," 170.
330   Ronald A. Kuipers, "Singular Interruptions: Rortian Liberalism and the Ethics of Deconstruction," in *Knowing Other-wise: Philosophy at the threshold of spirituality*, ed. James H. Olthuis (New York: Fordham University Press, 1997), 111.

must be maintained lest we slip back into the classical onto-theological project in Western philosophy.[331] Our private, idiosyncratic attempts at self-actualization and our public responsibility to ameliorate the suffering of others are often at odds. Attempts to reconcile both in theory are precisely the sorts of metaphysical projects pragmatists reject. The fact is there is no grand meta-narrative, no master vocabulary that can completely reconcile the conflicts between our public and private concerns. Theory may be able to offer coping strategies for us to deal with some of these conflicts, but more often than not, it is unhelpful. Literature provides a more helpful tool for helping us reconcile both public and private concerns, and it is by this means that the 'ironist' gains awareness of different vocabularies and narratives. Literature, in a piecemeal fashion, does the job that metaphysics used to do; provide a basis for solidarity. However, this observation is not a guarantee that such reconciliation between public and private will be total; again, most of the time, there is a conflict between my public utilitarian calculus and my private will to power. Rorty recognizes this as a necessary consequence of the failure of metaphysics and resultant secularization. As he acknowledges: "For a few such people – Christians (and others) for whom the search for private perfection coincides with living for others – the two sorts of questions come together. For most such, they do not."[332] I would agree with Ronald Kuipers when he says, commenting on this passage, that "Rorty paints a somewhat tragic picture of atheist society here, a society whose individual members are so selfish in their private pursuits that reconciling them with shared public concerns becomes the job of two different vocabularies. Surely, however, many atheists would be unhappy with this picture."[333] Nevertheless, Rorty is suspicious of any metaphysical or teleological justifications for solidarity. Hence, multiple vocabularies, both useful within in their own context, are necessary. As Kuipers explains:

> Simply put, Rorty is trying to describe a kind of society where public and private pursuits are no longer in conflict, not because they find synthesis under a common metaphysical rubric, but simply because they can operate side by side, like different tools for different purposes. Rorty puts

---

[331] In *Contingency, Irony and Solidarity* Rorty accuses Habermas of this tendency: "Habermas assumes that the task of philosophy is to supply some social glue which will replace religious belief, and to see Enlightenment talk of 'universality' and 'rationality' as the best candidate for this glue" 83.
[332] Rorty, 143.
[333] Kuipers, 113.

as much stock in what liberal democracies have been able to achieve for individual freedom as he does in how they have helped maximize human solidarity and minimize public cruelty. It is by no means evident that he values one more highly that the other.[334]

Therefore, Rorty values the private ironist as offering valuable tools within the private domain. In this regard, he acknowledges the power of poetry and other literature. But he apparently judges it less useful when it comes to the equally important public task of building a just society. Nevertheless, I still detect a tension here between these considerations and his conception of rhetoric as reeducation.

But let us return to the problematic public/private distinction in reference to religion. Rorty's comments regarding religion are usually quite critical. For example, when he says it would be best if religious institutions would "wither away" because they create "unnecessary human misery"[335] it is quite easy to get the impression that Rorty thinks we would all be better off without religion, at least in its institutionalized forms. And, in broad strokes, this is what he believes, although with a few caveats. To his credit, he is realistic enough not to expect that religion in every manifestation will disappear, however, he hopes that institutionalized religion will do so; in other words, he hopes that the privatization of religion begun in the modern period and embodied in the 'Jeffersonian compromise' will be someday total. So religion must be privatized, which is not to say trivialized. To restate, "The main reason religion needs to be privatized is that, in political discussion with those outside the relevant religious community, it is a conversation-stopper."[336] However, there are several problems with Rorty's employment of the public/private distinction in this context. One could, of course, question the utility of the distinction itself as does Wolterstorff. "I find the public/private dualism both obscure and ideologically loaded; I myself try to avoid placing any weight on it. I am surprised to see Rorty, implacable enemy of dualisms, placing so much weight on this one."[337] But even granting the distinction for the moment, Rorty's

---

[334] Kuipers, 114.
[335] Rorty, "Religion in the Public Square: A Reconsideration," *Journal of Religious Ethics*, 31.1 (2003), 142.
[336] Rorty, "Religion As Conversation-stopper," 171.
[337] Wolterstorff, 131.

appeal to it does not do the work he wants it to. Firstly, although religious reasons may stop conversation in some contexts, it is by no means clear that they have a monopoly on doing so. Rorty acknowledges that the conversation has to stop somewhere. Indeed, he acknowledges that his appeal to Darwinian, pragmatic, antirealist reasons begs all the important questions as do his opponents' appeals to Platonic, idealist, and realist reasons.[338] Moreover, the reason these appeals stop conversation has nothing to do with being statements about private life. Rather, it has to do with the nature of argumentation; at some point we all return to what Rorty elsewhere calls 'final vocabularies.'[339] He even finds some common ground with Carter on this issue:

> The best parts of his (Carter's) very thoughtful, and often persuasive book, are those in which he points up the inconsistency of our behavior, and the hypocrisy involved in saying that believers somehow have no right to base their political views on their religious faith, whereas we atheists have every right to base ours on Enlightenment philosophy. The claim that in doing so we are appealing to reason, whereas the religious are being irrational is hokum. Carter is quite right to debunk it.[340]

If this analysis is correct, then it is difficult to avoid stopping conversation at some point and this is so, by Rorty's own logic, because of the final vocabularies we all appeal to at the end of the day, not simply because one side invokes 'private' reasons whereas the other has a monopoly on 'public' reason. By his own admission, Rorty is quite pessimistic about the dialogical process, claiming that the best interlocutors can do is to restate their positions over and over, although, as Wolterstorff notes, this appears in tension with his hope for universal intersubjective agreement.[341] But perhaps we can do more than state our positions *ad infinitum*; perhaps we can engage in immanent critique, as Stout advocates, even if we do appeal to final vocabularies in the last resort. But this observation brings us back to the point that religion does not uniquely act as a conversation-stopper. I think this point is sufficiently clear.

Secondly, Rorty's equates religious reasons with private ones although the examples he uses are quite unfortunate for his case and ultimately show

---

338   Rorty, *Philosophy and Social Hope*, xxxii.
339   Rorty, *Contingency, Irony, and Solidarity*, 73.
340   Rorty, "Religion As Conversation-stopper," 170.
341   Wolterstorff, 129 – 30.

dissimilarity between religious reasons and the 'private' reasons he cites. To review, Carter's appeal to the will of God when discussing the issues of abortion and pornography stops conversation, by his own admission. Rorty thinks this is because an appeal to one's private religious beliefs is out of place in political discourse. "The same goes" he says, "for telling the group, 'I would never have an abortion' or 'Reading pornography is about the only pleasure I get out of life these days.' In these examples, as in Carter's, the ensuing silence masks the group's inclination to say, 'So what? We weren't discussing your private life; we were discussing public policy. Don't bother us with matters that are not our concern."[342] But it seems clear that these cases are not analogous. As Wolterstorff queries in response, "So in what ways does King's offering a religious reason in favor of outlawing segregation resemble revealing that one's only pleasure nowadays comes from reading pornography, so that both are comments about one's private life?"[343] The question is clearly rhetorical. This serves to confirm Wolterstorff's suspicion about Rorty's use of the public/private distinction:

> So far as I can make out, Rorty's reference to privacy is really a throw-away reference; it's not doing any real work. A good example of my point about the uselessness in such discussions about the public/private dualism! My surmise is that the problem Rorty sees with offering religious reasons for political positions is not that such reasons are "private" in any clear sense of that term, but that they are not shared by the citizenry in general.[344]

We are again back to the problem of common basis, which I repudiated in the last chapter, and which Rorty himself rejects at least in its idealized versions. As mentioned above, 'public reasons' need not imply that they must be universally acceptable by all rational persons; indeed, it could not, otherwise we would be forced to conclude that none of the reasons to which we commonly appeal in political discourse are public reasons. Of course, this problem is only exacerbated if we take a pragmatic tack and only consider premises that are actually held in common, rather than an idealized common basis. We would be left with precious few such premises indeed. Again, some translation of religious

---

[342] Rorty, 171.
[343] Wolterstorff, 132.
[344] Wolterstorff, 132.

premises may be pragmatically necessary to keep the conversation going, but that is not to say that religious premises always automatically stop conversation in its tracks.

Rorty has a point, however, that faith-claims stop conversation. To review Stout's distinction, if I make a faith-claim, I do not accept the responsibility of demonstrating my epistemic entitlement to the claim.[345] Clearly, such claims tend to terminate the exchange of reasons. But as we saw in the last chapter, not all religious statements are faith-claims. Many religious persons are prepared to offer reasons for their beliefs. Rorty implicitly seems to recognize this, but nevertheless urges religious citizens to drop reference to the religious sources of their beliefs with regard to particular social issues. Again in criticism of Carter, who urges liberalism to 'develop a politics that accepts whatever form of dialogue a member of the public offers'[346] Rorty responds:

> What is a specifically religious 'form of dialogue', except perhaps a dialogue in which some members cite religious sources for their beliefs? What could a specifically religious argument be, except an argument whose premises are accepted by some people because they believe that these premises express the will of God? I may accept those same premises for purely secular reasons – for example, reasons having to do with maximizing human happiness. Does that make my argument a non-religious one? Even if it is exactly the argument made by my religious fellow citizen? Surely the fact that one of us gets his premises in church and the other in the library is, and should be, of no interest to our audience in the public square.[347]

My inclination is to say if such a translation of religious to secular premises can be made and consensus thus achieved, then all well and good. In the situation Rorty describes, in which we already have consensus, it is of relatively little interest how we each justify our premises. But such a situation seems to me to be ideal, and a pragmatist such as Rorty presumably knows that his hypothetical scenario avoids all of the thorny issues of translation and justification which I

---

[345] Stout, 87.
[346] Cited in Rorty, 172.
[347] Rorty, 172.

have been addressing thus far.[348] The problem is precisely that we disagree about the truth of premises, at least when it comes to the most contentious issues facing pluralistic democracies, and are thus pressed to give further justifications for them. What recourse do we have, whether we are secular or religious, but to appeal to our final vocabularies? Thus it is not a matter of simply "dropping reference to the source of the premises of the arguments"[349] as Rorty admonishes. As we saw in the last chapter in Wolterstorff's response to Audi, if having secular arguments for beliefs based on religious sources were this easy, religious citizens would almost always automatically have such secular arguments.[350] (If Carter is opposed to abortion because God says abortion is wrong, then he is *ipso facto* opposed to abortion because abortion is wrong.) But these do not necessarily function for the religious person as adequate, independent secular rationales or motivations for political action. Unlike Audi, however, Rorty is pragmatic enough not to expect peoples' religious beliefs to have no influence on their political convictions, but thinks they should simply drop the references to the true source of their religious convictions. This might be advisable, despite being disingenuous, when the desired consensus has already been achieved as in Rorty's hypothetical scenario. But it becomes practically impossible to obscure the source of one's premises when the argument is more contentious. For example, if Carter is arguing that abortion is wrong, not because it is against the will of God, but because the fetus is a person and thus has a right to life, the contention that the fetus is a person could in principle have either a secular or religious justification. If both parties to the discussion agree with the premise, it scarcely matters if one accepts it on religious grounds and the other on secular ones. There is no practical reason to

---

[348] G. Elijah Dann, commenting on Rorty, also takes a rather naïve view of what is involved in translation: [I]f religious believers wish to discuss, in the public square, their opposition to abortion, they must first translate their claim into a language suitable for discussion in the public square – the common language of democracy." *After Rorty: The Possibilities for Ethics and Religious Belief* (London: Continuum, 2006), 64.

[349] Rorty, 173.

[350] Dann evidently thinks it *is* this easy: "Some may be dubious about the possibility of translating religious concepts into secular terms, especially on the topic of abortion. This is largely the fault of the Pro-Life advocates who repeatedly have made their public opposition to abortion on the basis of religious platitudes. It is nevertheless possible to make the translation by speaking of 'human dignity' instead of the 'sacredness of life.' Whereas speaking of the sacredness of life carries a religious assumption, human dignity does not" 64. Above and in what follows, I attempt to problematize this simplistic solution.

get into the reasons behind the premises if agreement has already been reached. Of course, secular liberals like Rorty disagree with that premise and thus force a discussion of the sources of belief behind the premise. This much seems obvious. Now it seems practically impossible for Carter to follow Rorty's advice and simply drop reference to the source of his beliefs and limit himself to premises held in common. He has no recourse but to make reference to 'comprehensive' (in Rawls's sense) evidence that will not likely convince Rorty and the conversation may well end there, unless one of them can find a way to get inside the other's way of thinking. But that alone does not prove that religious sources of belief are in 'bad taste' when introduced into the discussion even if it happens that the two parties continue to disagree. Is it always in bad taste to end up openly disagreeing with someone? This is surely not what Rorty is claiming. Of course the avenue of immanent critique, Stout's option 3 from the last chapter, is still open and it is surprising that Rorty would not pursue it before saying 'so what?' and giving up on the conversation. But even if Rorty and Carter end their discussion in disagreement, why is this outcome so bad? What is wrong with Rorty simply declaring that he disagrees with Carter? As Wolterstorff observes, "He, Rorty, does after all disagree with Carter. He does not believe that it's against the will of God to legalize abortion. What's so bad about saying that, and thus winding up disagreeing with Carter in public?"[351] As Wolterstorff also notes, there is a familiar mechanism for reaching a practical decision after our political discussion ends in disagreement, as it inevitably does: voting. It is ironic that a pragmatist like Rorty overlooks this very pragmatic feature of politics in democracies, namely that since conversation-stopping is inevitable, there is a venerable process for overcoming such an impasse. To quote Wolterstorff again: "Conversation-stopping is not some appalling evil perpetrated upon an otherwise endlessly-talkative public by religious people. Stopped conversation is an all-pervasive feature of political debate in a democracy; and voting is a procedure for arriving at a decision of the body when conversation has stopped."[352]

Rorty's Reconsideration

However, Rorty has since qualified his views on religion in the public sphere, so lest I seem unfair to him, I will now take up some of his more philosophically and rhetorically cautious reflections on the subject. His 'reconsideration' of his

---

[351] Wolterstorff, 136.
[352] Wolterstorff, 136.

earlier essay comes in response to, by his own estimation, impressive criticisms from Stout and Wolterstorff.[353] In my view, his more chastened comments amount to defending a more modest version of the secularization thesis than that suggested by his earlier treatment of the subject. Indeed, it is a more defensible version than that of Weber, for example, from which Habermas has distanced himself. However, it might still be a stronger statement of it than Habermas would be willing to endorse in light of his more recent writings, although nothing substantial rests on that suspicion.

Rorty begins "back-pedaling" by making a distinction between religion at the parish level and ecclesiastical institutions. The former, which, in Rorty's view, provides pastoral care and meaning to peoples' lives, is not, or at least should not be, the immediate target of secularists. Rather ecclesiastical institutions which claim to speak with divine authority and seek to impose orthodoxy on the wider public through abuse of their tax exempt status are the real menace to liberal democracy. Rorty provides some examples of who he has in mind, namely the usual suspects, "Catholic bishops, the Mormon General Authorities, the televangelists."[354] These institutionally supported religious authorities are what Rorty, and like-minded secularists, hope will eventually wither away. He recognizes that, if his hopes are realized, such hierarchical religious bodies will be sorely missed by religious believers in the short-term. The feeling of belonging to something greater than oneself, which religious institutions once provided, will be gone. But, Rorty hopes, religious believers can compensate for that loss by working in common cause with secular citizens for the advancement of humanity as a whole despite the fact that increasing social justice and economic equality will weaken religion's role; it will no longer be needed to keep the masses in check by threatening eternal punishment or excusing poverty by promising otherworldly rewards. Thus religion's role will be reduced to providing pastoral care to those who still find solace in faith. As Rorty informs us, "Religion will, in this secularist utopia, be pruned back to the parish level."[355]

He concedes that "the social ideals that we secular humanists champion are often cast in religious terms. But we hope that they will eventually cease to

---

[353] Rorty, "A Reconsideration," 141.
[354] Rorty, 141.
[355] Rorty, 142.

be so stated."[356] His reasons are two-fold. Firstly, couching social ideals in a religious idiom gives succor to those ecclesiastical institutions that use such language as a vehicle for their bigotry. Secondly, the cause of leftist politics, including economic equality, is "strengthened just insofar as belief in a providential deity who will provide pie in the sky is weakened."[357] It is explicitly not the case for Rorty that religious belief in this context is intrinsically irrational or wrong-headed. He shares the ethics of belief of William James and agrees with Wolterstorff about the vacuity of epistemological foundationalism. In a bold statement, Rorty says "I view the struggle between utilitarians and homophobic Christian fundamentalists as no more a struggle between reason and unreason than is the Catholic-Protestant struggle in Northern Ireland."[358] So the rationality of religious belief is not on trial; rather Rorty finds religious belief, especially above the parish level, as inexpedient given the goals he wishes to achieve. This is not to say that religion has always been inexpedient. But he thinks "that the occasional Gustavo Guttierez or Martin Luther King does not compensate for the ubiquitous Joseph Ratzingers and Jerry Falwells."[359] Thus, he thinks it best to treat religion as a ladder up which our ancestors climbed, but which should now be cast aside.

Although retaining the language of 'secularist utopia' – with possible irony – this is a more modest articulation of the secularization thesis and one that is, in my judgment, more defensible on both normative and empirical grounds. It does not forecast the disappearance of religion *per se*, but simply envisions it as something other than what it has been historically. In my view Rorty does not go far enough, at least in this context, toward creatively envisioning what else religion might become, besides the threatening bastions of orthodoxy to which he objects. Since he still tacitly clings to the public/private distinction, he fails to imagine that religion might become something more, might find another voice, evolve in a positive way rather than merely getting 'pruned back' to the private domain. This failure of imagination is surprising, however, since he envisions a positive public role for religion in an imaginative essay called "Looking Backwards from the Year 2096." Written as a retrospective of twenty-first century American political history by a Hispanic female Jesuit and an Asian-Jewish American, it diagnoses what Rorty sees as the egregious social ills

---

[356] Rorty, 142.
[357] Rorty, 142.
[358] Rorty, 144.
[359] Rorty, 142.

of our time and prophetically intones where they might lead if left unchecked. The article chronicles a period of economic collapse, civil unrest, and martial law from 2014 – 44 called the Dark Years. This crisis comes about due to a breakdown of solidarity among the citizenry who are divided along economic and racial lines. The liberal rights discourse with its inherent individualism could not restore solidarity and hence social order. Therefore, a new political vocabulary had to replace it:

> Here, in the late twenty-first century, as talk of fraternity and unselfishness has replaced talk of rights, American political discourse has come to be dominated by quotations from Scripture and literature, rather than from political theorists or social scientists. Fraternity, like friendship, was not a concept that either philosophers or lawyers knew how to handle. They could formulate principles of justice, equality and liberty, and invoke these principles when weighing hard moral or legal issues. But how to formulate a 'principle of fraternity'? Fraternity is an inclination of the heart, one that produces a sense of shame at having much when others have little. It is not the sort of thing that anybody can have a theory about or that people can be argued into having.[360]

The means of restoring solidarity includes the rhetorical power of both religious and secular literature. However, religion has an even more robust role in Rorty's parable. In 2044, a coalition of churches and trade unions, The Democratic Vistas Party, topple the military dictatorship of the Dark Years and still hold Congress in 2096. The social gospel is rediscovered and sermons focus on improving the plight of others instead of individual salvation. Although reducing religion to either of these roles, in my judgment, is problematic, Rorty's essay at least shows his capacity to imagine how religion might offer society something other than pie in the sky and why it might not be advisable to prune religion back too far. Rorty's vision in "2096" is hardly the secularist utopia he envisions in his "Reconsideration." However, the fact that he has made peace with some form of religion being around for awhile, does not entail that he has retreated from the *Kulturkampf* or plans to wage it with any less fervor.

---

[360] Rorty, "Looking Backwards from the Year 2096," in *Philosophy and Social Hope*, 248.

Rorty then takes up some of Wolterstorff's criticisms. Rorty is convinced that the religious believer should not be prohibited by law or custom from bringing his favorite texts into political discussion, any more than the secularist should be prohibited. For example, Wolterstorff's citing of Psalm 72 in support of redistributionist policies is just as legitimate as Rorty's citation of J.S. Mill in support of the same measures. As Rorty acknowledges:

> The fact that Psalm 72 belongs to a set of Scriptures claimed by various ecclesiastical organizations which I regard as politically dangerous is not a good reason to hinder Wolterstorff from citing this Psalm, any more than the fact that many people regard Mill's utilitarianism as morally dangerous is a good reason to stop me citing *On Liberty*. Neither law nor custom should stop either of us from bringing our favorite texts with us into the public square."[361]

However, it becomes more complicated when religious believers cite Scripture, not in favor of redistribution of wealth, but in opposition to gay rights, for example. On this issue, Rorty does have a problem with citing religious texts. Citing Leviticus 18:22, for example, as the final word on same-sex marriage, should be off limits. According to Rorty: "Here I cannot help feeling that, though the law should not forbid someone from citing such texts in support of a political position, custom *should* forbid it. Citing such passages should be deemed not just in bad taste, but as heartlessly cruel, as reckless persecution, as incitement to violence."[362] Interestingly, he confesses here what I suspected above: that his exclusion of religious expression from political debate rests on more than just bad taste; there is a normative core to his distaste toward religion. However, although there is a normative core, he is still unwilling to enforce it via the social contract. He speaks a different language here than that of Jeffersonian compromise and clarifies his position vis-à-vis Rawls that remained fuzzy in "Religion as Conversation-stopper." Nevertheless, although not a contractarian, he feels that custom should forbid using religion to justify odious political opinions, such as criminalizing homosexuality. In Rorty's view, religious homophobes should be treated with the same contempt reserved for anti-Semites and white supremacists. Though legislation was instrumental in improving the plight of Jews and African Americans, and likely will play a

---

361   Rorty, "A Reconsideration," 143.
362   Rorty, 143.

substantial role in securing gay rights, Rorty recognizes, correctly, that the marginalization of anti-Semites and white supremacists from mainstream American society was accomplished without prohibiting freedom of speech.

This brings us to a seeming inconsistency in Rorty's position. Why is it permissible to cite Scripture in support of liberal policies Rorty would espouse, but not in favor of those he would not? At this point, Rorty is candid: he would like to have a principle which would disallow appeals to Lev. 18:22 but allow appeals to Psalm 72. Unfortunately, he does not. Again, the problem for Rorty is not principally a philosophical problem, but a practical one. The debate between fundamentalists and secularists cannot be framed, as some secularists affirm, as a battle between rationality and irrationality. For Rorty, the vacuity of epistemological foundationalism is clear. His epistemic stance leads him to believe that his disagreement with religious critics, like Wolterstorff, is primarily empirical rather than philosophical. He simply thinks that Wolterstorff underestimates the danger to democracy posed by ecclesiastical institutions.

As we saw above, Wolterstorff concedes that there was a certain rationale in the seventeenth century, in the context of religious wars, to limit the expression of religion in the public sphere. But he believes that democracy in America, with a rich history of religious tolerance behind her, is mature enough to readmit religion into public debate, arguing that "liberalism's myopic preoccupation with religious wars is outdated."[363] For Rorty, speaking also for persecuted minorities, the difference between the centuries is negligible. He finds parallels between European Jews in the seventeenth century and American homosexuals in ours. Although the church did not explicitly make war on Jews, it encouraged anti-Semitism through its teaching, with pogroms as the result. In much the same way, when American Christians declare that homosexuality is an abomination hated by God, gay-bashing is likely to result. As Rorty summarizes, "Nowadays, the problem within most countries in which Christianity is still the majority religion is not the possibility of religious war, but the sort of everyday peacetime sadism that uses religion to excuse cruelty."[364]

For the sake of brevity, I must leave to one side the empirical and historical issues that divide Rorty and Wolterstorff which amount to the perennial question of whether religion is, on balance, a force for good or ill. In

---

[363] Quoted in Rorty, 145.
[364] Rorty, 145.

my judgment, Rorty is too quick to claim that philosophical issues take a back seat to empirical matters in this context.

He dismisses philosophical considerations by way of a professed agreement with Wolterstorff against Audi's notion that religious citizens must have secular reasons for political decisions that are both motivationally sufficient and epistemologically adequate. Rorty confesses that he does not find these terms very useful and furthermore thinks we lack the criteria for determining their presence.[365] But he seems to want to put the same point in different language. One can detect a residual point from 'Religion as Conversation-stopper': that religious people, despite the secularist's failure to hold them to a principle, really should try to find another way of expressing themselves publicly.

For example, in his discussion of gay rights *vis-à-vis* Christianity, he comments, "They (gays and lesbians) are struck by the fact that religious reasons are now pretty much the *only* reasons brought forward in favor of treating them with contempt."[366] His emphasis on 'only' here leads one to believe that he thinks that either religious reasons are not 'real' reasons or that religious citizens should really try to find a secular way of stating their position. Given what he says earlier about reason and unreason being beside the point in such debates, I think Rorty is implicitly stating the latter position. Furthermore, he goes on to say that "Audi is not *entirely* wrong when he says that 'the concept of a liberal democracy' forbids certain moves being made in the course of political discussion."[367] Again, I think that Rorty wants to make substantially the same claim as Audi on a practical level, but thinks that Audi's principle of motivational sufficiency and epistemological adequacy is dubious. But saying that religious people should really find another language to express their views, or that custom should forbid certain religious appeals, puts the same requirements on religious people, in practice, that Audi wants to impose in principle. Thus, the issue of translation comes to the fore again. One of the differences between Rorty and Audi is that the former is realistic enough not to pretend that religious people will have secular reasons sufficient to motivate them to act even in the absence of their religious convictions. It may be the case, for Rorty, that it would be sound strategy on a pragmatic level for religious citizens to play the language game of the wider polity. But his moralizing on gay rights leads one to believe that his

---

[365] Rorty, 144.
[366] Rorty, 146, italics in original.
[367] Rorty, 147, italics in original.

desire that religious citizens stop invoking Scripture on this issue goes deeper than hoping Christians will adopt a different rhetorical strategy. Certainly it would be beneficial if Christians who, say, oppose same-sex marriage did indeed adopt a different strategy than quoting Lev 18:22. Despite Rorty's hyperbole, I think most have. But besides robbing gay-bashing thugs of justification for their actions, which is no small victory, translating the argument into a different moral rubric will probably not move the argument along much further.

For example, the Christian argument, as derived from Romans 1, rather than Lev 18:22 – space does not permit a careful exegetical or hermeneutical examination of these passages – against homosexual practice takes the form of a natural law argument. This argument, hardly unique to Paul, also circulated among ancient pagan moralists. It is asserted that homosexuality goes 'against nature', or humanity's telos. My point is not to defend this argument, but merely to point out that it's not specific to a particular religion, or even theism, so far as I can tell, despite the historical fact that natural law theory as inherited from Aristotle and the Stoics was thought to be particularly amenable to Christian moral theology. In any case, we have here an example of an argument, albeit contentious, rather than a *mere* appeal to authority.

From what Rorty says, it is difficult to tell whether or not this natural law argument would be allowable or not in democratic discussion. He claims, along with Stout, that what should be discouraged in a democracy are mere appeals to authority, or faith-claims. "It is one thing" he argues, "to explain how a given political stance is bound up with one's religious belief, and another to think that it is enough, when defending a political view, simply to cite authority, scriptural or otherwise."[368] Likewise, Rorty thinks he would not be properly arguing with his interlocutors if he simply quoted J.S. Mill at them. So Rorty's problem with most religious language in public is that it simply appeals to authority. Citing Lev 18:22 is an appeal to authority, and I would agree with Rorty that those who simply cite it as a divine command which brooks no argument do invoke a faith-claim that is likely to be a conversation-stopper. Put in a different moral rubric, however, like that of natural law, one can at least see some discursive potential, although in my view, it will be short-lived. A utilitarian like Rorty is not going be convinced by an argument from natural law, and vice versa, so consensus will not likely be achieved in this way. (I see Stout as more helpful in his willingness to go

---

[368] Rorty, 147.

quite a long way with his religious interlocutor's argument.)[369] His attempts to forestall invoking conversation-stoppers ultimately fail.

In short, convincing religious citizens to simply switch moral rubrics is not an effective solution to building practical consensus on such issues. Presumably, Rorty would not see the debate between utilitarianism and natural law theory as a battle between reason and unreason any more than the debate between utilitarianism and divine command theory would be. He simply hopes that the dominant language of public morality will continue to be couched in utilitarian terms, and is committed to waging that rhetorical battle. But in that case, it seems inconsequential which moral rubric religious persons choose to give expression to their convictions. What is the point of translation besides, perhaps, improving the decorum of the conversation? To answer this question, I think one must part company with Rorty and side with Habermas. In my view, there is more discursive potential between arguments that have been couched in a moral language that does not merely appeal to authority because of the objective nature of language and argument. What Rorty is grasping, correctly, is that citing Lev 18:22 in the way it's commonly used, is not an argument. It's a different speech act, such as a threat. To threaten homosexuals with stoning or hellfire should be disallowed in civil political discourse. Politicians and moral philosophers are right to dismiss it. Sustaining this position logically, however, requires a more robust Habermasian view of the objectivity achieved by language. Therefore, I think Rorty is inconsistent in saying that ideological conflicts have nothing more to do with rationality than the struggle between Irish Catholics and Protestants. If that is the case, we lack any clear solution to achieving a workable consensus on contentious issues. On Rorty's view, so far as I can discern, there is no discursive point to translation. The conversation might be elevated, but it's not clear it will move forward in pragmatically relevant ways.

Although I find Habermas's translation requirement too stringent, there is a discursive point to it: interlocutors are supposed to agree to the secularized statements for rationally compelling reasons. Like the pragmatists, however, I am skeptical that such an achieved consensus can be reached. Moreover, translation as Habermas understands it lacks utility once certain pragmatic assumptions are made, i.e. anti-foundationalism. For this reason, I think Rorty is inconsistent in expecting translation from his religious interlocutors in the

---

[369] See Jeffrey Stout, "How Charity Transcends the Culture Wars: Eugene Rogers and Others on Same-Sex Marriage," *Journal of Religious Ethics*, 31.2 (2003): 169 – 180.

absence of any principle that would establish secular language as rationally normative. Habermas is at least consistent, but I think Rorty is right in regarding any attempt to formulate such a principle as highly dubious. But we still need a discursive avenue to keep the conversation going, and if neither of our protagonists can offer a pragmatically viable solution, where else should we look? We have already looked at Stout's correctives to Rorty. I would like now to turn to his differences with Habermas before considering his more positive suggestions for fruitful dialogue between religious and secular interlocutors in a democracy. We will then consider some criticisms of Stout's approach.

Immanent Critique and Translation

On the matter of translation, Stout does not engage Habermas directly, but from what he does say, we can glean some information about the differences and convergences of their respective approaches. Stout draws attention to differences between the two over the 'secularization thesis'. Habermas's disciple, Seyla Benhabib, criticizes Stout for not grounding his account of secularization in a social theory like Habermas's.[370] Stout, however, is suspicious of Habermas's assumptions, *via* Weber, about the effects of rationalization on religious worldviews.[371] Stout's conception of secularization is much more modest: "What becomes secularized, according to my model, is a set of discursive presuppositions, not necessarily the worldview or state of consciousness of participants in the relevant form of discourse."[372]

Given my research, these comments apply more readily to Habermas's early articulation of secularization. Now that he has distanced himself from the most ambitious elements of Weber's social theory, he might also be persuaded to accept that what has been secularized are the 'discursive presuppositions' of democratic societies. However, the two thinkers would place different normative weight on that phrase. For Stout, a pragmatist, discursive presuppositions are secularized because it does not often advance one's rhetorical purposes to appeal to particular theological presuppositions. But sometimes it does. As he says in response to Rorty's claim that religion is 'essentially' a conversation-stopper, "I

---

[370] See Seyla Benhabib, *Situating the Self: Gender, Community, and Postmodernism in Contemporary Ethics* (New York: Routledge, 1992), 147. Cited in Stout, *Democracy and Tradition*, 175.
[371] Stout, *Democracy and Tradition*, 175.
[372] Stout, 175.

would have thought the pragmatist line should be that religion is not *essentially* anything, that the conversational utility of employing religious premises in political arguments depends on the situation."[373] So our secular discursive presuppositions are normative in a dialectical, Hegelian sense that is open, as we saw before, to novel expressions. By contrast, for Habermas, the secularity of our discursive presuppositions is normative in the Kantian sense, that is to say, their normativity comes from their being 'transcendental' or "already being presupposed by anyone who wishes to offer reasons to other people."[374] For this reason, translation, for Habermas, is incumbent on any rational party to the discussion. Stout implicitly rejects translation in favor of immanent critique, because he rejects the Kantian assumptions that undergird it. Notwithstanding these philosophical differences, which are significant, I want to explore the potential for practical convergence between the two thinkers.

I want to look now in greater depth at Stout's avenue of immanent critique – the method of reasoning with one's interlocutors from premises they might find convincing, thereby taking seriously their distinctive point of view[375] – and consider whether this option is all Habermas really needs in order to overcome some of the tensions of translation. It is also worth raising the question, as we did in regard to translation, whether immanent criticism is easier for some people than others. For example, can a secularist engage in immanent criticism without insincerity? Stout seems to think that one can, but there are serious questions to be raised here. As Kuipers points out:

> In putting forward his argument for the importance and efficacy of immanent criticism, however, Stout appears to ignore one of its most important implications. This implication has to do with the fact that, in order to work at all, immanent criticism must affirm more than it questions. That is, in questioning one aspect of a traditional perspective by appealing to others, the immanent critic must affirm a significant portion of the traditional source of meaning that motivates the interlocutor's problematic stand.[376]

---

[373] Stout, 86, italics in original.
[374] Stout, 175.
[375] Stout, 73.
[376] Ronald A. Kuipers, "Stout's Democracy without Secularism: But is it a Tradition?" *Contemporary Pragmatism*, 3.1 (June, 2006): 94.

He goes on to observe that Stout does precisely this in response to the new traditionalists' rejection of secular liberalism. Stout's understanding of the Christian tradition allows him to deftly draw out implications within Christianity that are friendly to his own liberal views. There are two problematic entailments here from a Habermasian perspective: first, accommodating traditionalism to the extent that Stout does, rather than offering critique, gives his interlocutors no reason to question their assumptions; second, it invites the charge of manipulation through rhetoric since Stout ultimately rejects the views he adopts for the purposes of immanent critique. Despite these hypothetical Habermasian criticisms, what Stout is proposing is, in many respects, the mirror image of what Habermas expects religious citizens to do via translation. We will have occasion to return to this point, but I want to further press the question of whether Stout can authentically affirm more than he questions in religious points of view without being manipulative.

The suspicion that immanent critique is just another rhetorical trick is voiced by even a sympathetic commentator like Kuipers. Although he thinks Stout genuinely appreciates the insights of the Christian tradition he no longer accepts, one is still tempted to think that Stout either does not fully reject them or that his secularism is in some sense parasitic on them. Through a detailed account of Stout's migration from Christianity to 'Emersonian perfectionism', Kuipers situates him as an "alienated theologian"[377] or a "post-institutional Christian who pushes at its boundaries harder than most, but who does so with a desire to ensure that its best insights are not lost to the suffocation of dogmatic habituation."[378] From what Stout says about his religious odyssey and his persistent interest in religious ethics, I would concur that he is in a good position to engage the Christian tradition in a way that takes it seriously, while questioning the worst of its "dogmatic habituation." In his published work, for example, Stout is willing to go quite a long way with those he calls the new traditionalists, much further than most secular liberals would be willing to travel. But although Stout may be in a position to engage in immanent critique authentically, it does not follow that everyone who engages in public discussion is so well situated. As we saw with respect to translation, not all citizens may be equally equipped to engage in it.

---

[377] Kuipers, 95.
[378] Kuipers, 97.

This applies also to intellectuals. For example, could Habermas, as an atheist, engage in immanent critique legitimately? Or does doing so apply only to those who find religious rationales genuinely compelling? Despite Habermas's appeal to the semantic potential of religious language, is immanent criticism really a live option for him? Or does the semantic potential only become actual when it is translated into a secular idiom? Habermas, as we have seen, implicitly rejects immanent criticism for philosophical (and perhaps practical?) reasons and opts instead for translation of religious semantic potential into a universal secular language. For him, translation, even at the informal level, is a one-way street. Immanent criticism attempts to make it a two-way street, not because of any obligation on the part of secular citizens to translate their arguments, but for reasons of facilitating 'abnormal conversations' at precisely those points where we have reached an impasse due to differences in worldviews. Thus the Habermasian objections to immanent criticism, namely that it fails to properly critique the tradition it engages and that it risks insincerity apply equally to the burden of translation adopted by religious persons. The Habermasian fails, in my judgment, to consider that traditional perspectives might offer a critique of secularism that might have force for secular interlocutors. And clearly, religious persons, although capable of translation, are not going to see secular reasons as rationally binding for them in the same sense a secularist would. So unless something like Audi's principle of motivational and epistemological sufficiency can be met – and we have seen reasons to doubt that it can – then the religious citizen runs the risk of rhetorical manipulation when offering translations. The advantage that immanent criticism has over translation, as Stout construes it, is that it is a thoroughly pragmatic enterprise that does not appeal to an epistemic 'transcendental' high ground on which we must all be expected to agree.

In my judgment, Habermas implicitly rejects immanent critique as a live option because he subscribes to a subtraction story of secularization. For him, religious people, in order to participate in the secular language game, merely have to drop their particular 'discursive presuppositions', whereas secularists would have to strain to affirm theological presuppositions they would otherwise reject. Stout overcomes this problem with both his more modest model of secularization (towards which Habermas is now moving) and his thick conception of democracy as a tradition embodying a number of substantive virtues rather than simply being a set of formal rules of engagement for persons of differing worldviews. Whether democracy, as a tradition, is as thick a concept as Stout claims is an open question, but one need not accept his claim to pose the following question: In order to appreciate the semantic potential of religious points of view, does not Habermas have to be willing to travel as far as Stout with the presuppositions of his religious interlocutor? To put this question differently, is Habermas unable to affirm in religious worldviews more than he questions rendering him incapable of feeling the force of the semantic potential of religious discourse despite his efforts to do so, or is it simply the case that he, as a secularist, is in a bad position to articulate these semantic potentials and incapable of engaging in immanent criticism?

Of course, it is difficult to separate these questions in practice. There may be those who simply cannot appreciate religious insights because they find the religious worldviews that house them to be inherently implausible or the institutions that promote them to be odious. Some secularists simply lack the background in religious ways of thinking to make effective immanent critics. But Habermas is not excused that easily, since he thinks secularists should aid translation and that democratic discussion at its best is arduous. It is perhaps true that Habermas lacks the acculturation that makes Stout so adept at immanent criticism, although the former has dialogued with many of Europe's most influential theologians over the course of his career.[379] More important than his ability to articulate religious insights (which is considerable as we saw in relation to his comments on biotechnology) is the priority he gives to critique – which in his social theory is the fundamental engine of democratic discourse and the solvent of various forms of oppression – at the expense of tradition. This difference is evident in his exchange with Gadamer, to which I briefly alluded at the beginning of this chapter, but it is relevant in discussing the differences between him and Stout. In other words, Habermas is unable, primarily for *a priori* philosophical reasons, to affirm more than he questions in whatever tradition he engages, whereas Stout, despite placing a high value on democratic questioning, does seem able to affirm enough of his religious interlocutor's position to provide some discursive potential. One is tempted to speculate that Habermas would not regard Stout's immanent critique as authentic critique. And to be sure, 'critique' will have different resonances for the pragmatist, especially in America, than it will for the critical theorist in largely post-Christian Europe. Moreover, the utility of corrosive, as opposed to more sympathetic, criticism will vary from context to context. What Stout has attempted to do, whether

---

[379] See Jürgen Habermas and Joseph Ratzinger, *The Dialectics of Secularization: On Reason and Religion*, ed. Florian Schuller and trans. Brian McNeil, C.R.V. (San Francisco: Ignatius Press, 2006).

successfully or not, is to affirm the importance of critique while retaining the substantive contributions of tradition.

He does so by treating democratic questioning itself as a substantive tradition. Again, this claim is open to question. No doubt Stout has a narrative to tell about democracy, particularly in America, which, in his estimation, draws much of its intellectual and even spiritual content from Emerson, Thoreau, Whitman, and Dewey. In his view, this inheritance is enough to constitute a tradition. However, Kuipers, who is generally sympathetic to Stout, thinks that he fails to make the case. He says, "While I agree with Stout that the practice of democratic questioning can be a valuable tool in preventing such [traditionalist] enervation and ensuring the contemporary relevance of living traditions, this is not the same as saying that such a practice by itself characterizes the *content* of an independent tradition, or that it describes a tradition at all."[380] He goes on to quote a reviewer of Stout's book who claims one can only consider democratic questioning a tradition if one makes the assumption that "a practice that recognizes no authority or mediation, and in which self-formation relies entirely on 'employing one's own standards of worth' is properly called a tradition."[381] If these critics are right, and Stout's narrative fails, it would seem that we are left with only a formal commitment to democratic questioning which looks very much like Habermas's and the standard liberal model's.

But I may have overstated the stakes. Perhaps even if Stout cannot convince us that democracy is yet another tradition, his strategy of immanent critique might well have utility in democratic debate. I am inclined to think that is the case. After all, Stout tells us that he resists embedding his pragmatic recommendations in a robust social theory or account of secularization. Despite the tensions between this minimalism on the one hand, and the claim that democracy itself is a substantive tradition on the other, we are free to accept or reject his account of democracy's content while still finding the practice of immanent critique quite useful. Then it becomes less a theoretical matter and more a matter of developing certain skills, such as learning about traditions different from one's own and developing a reflexivity about one's own epistemic stance and finally being able to articulate religious perspectives in a manner that adherents could plausibly recognize as their own.

---

[380] Kuipers, 97.
[381] Quoted in Kuipers, 97.

But even Stout, who is more sympathetic to religion in public life than most secular philosophers, is ambiguous regarding the long-term utility of stating political virtues in the language of the monotheistic traditions. Although he rejects robust versions of the secularization thesis, he seems to want to find a language – perhaps "Emersonian perfectionism" – that differs from, and may eventually replace, monotheism as a 'spiritual option' to borrow Taylor's phrase. As much as Stout extols, for example, King's contribution to American political discourse and admires the power of the language in which he framed it, Stout remains ambivalent. For example, speaking of both Jesus and King as "persons of ethical interest," Stout says: "Nowadays things have become more complicated, because I have learned more about these figures of virtue than their hagiographers and publicists wanted me to know. Now that I am less innocent of the complexities, I am no less moved by love and justice, no less cognizant of the place of such traits in a virtuous character, and no less able to put these concepts to work discursively than I used to be."[382] In this passage, we hear Stout's commitment to immanent critique. However, now that he has lost his adolescent faith, exemplifying such virtues as love and justice "requires a different, less doctrinal, more improvisational kind of explication."[383] Although no explicit contradiction exists between this statement and the practical project of immanent critique, his statements leave open the possibility that this less doctrinal, more improvisational explication of virtue might be better accomplished using a different language than that of, say, Christianity. It might be the case for Stout, as for Rorty, that "the social ideals that we secular humanists champion are often cast in religious terms. But we hope that they will eventually cease to be so stated."[384]

This suggestion that monotheism may not be the best vehicle for what Stout wants to say about virtue in public life comes up in an insightful interview by Kuipers.[385] When asked to explain "Emersonian perfectionism" Stout conveys that it ties together various strands of religious thought, some of which Christians declare heretical, such as the rejection of original sin. For this reason, Stout says, "It is easy to see why Emersonianism, despite the strongly religious content of its principal themes, rapidly moved outside the churches and in that

---

[382] Stout, 173.
[383] Stout, 173.
[384] Rorty, 142.
[385] Ronald A. Kuipers, "Excellence and the Emersonian Perfectionist: An Interview with Jeffrey Stout, part 1," http://www.theotherjournal.com/article.php?id=864.

sense became secular."[386] Nevertheless, he wants to preserve the notion of sacred value and thinks that religion can help protect it.

Stout's notion of the sacred is very close to that of the 'sublime.' He says, "Piety toward nature, because it perfects and expresses a sense of dependence, mainly connects with the sublime, which, as Edmund Burke pointed out, is deeply related to danger and precariousness. It's horrendous to respond to the intrinsic beauty, sublimity, and wondrousness of nature by spoiling it or reducing it to something that has merely instrumental value for us. This has more to do with the sacred than with piety *per se*."[387] Here Stout taps into a tradition that Taylor discusses as a move toward secularization.[388]

The concept of the 'sublime' arguably emerges from the seventeenth century attempts on the part of religious believers to combat deism. As the post-Newtonian universe revealed its secrets, apologists crafted arguments that stressed the providential design of God. Design, as such, was not necessarily disputed; the deists lauded the Creator's technical prowess, but they questioned the details of the biblical account and the notion that nature is contrived exclusively for human benefit. Against the anthropocentrism of apologists who insisted on a world specially crafted for humanity, some thinkers broke the mould, arguing that the awe-inspiring and genuinely dangerous power of nature served another purpose. One such thinker was Thomas Burnet, mentioned briefly in the second chapter. In agreement with the deists with respect to nature's indifference to human comfort, he nevertheless believed that he could salvage the biblical account. He interpreted the world that science had uncovered as a ruinous creation punctuated by divine judgments, the latest of which was the Genesis flood. Nevertheless, even such a ruinous creation can arouse in us appropriate religious feeling:

> The greatest objects of Nature, are methinks, the most pleasing to behold ... there is nothing that I look upon with more pleasure that the wide Sea and the Mountains of the Earth. There is something august and stately in the Air of these things, that inspires the mind with great thoughts and passions; We do naturally, upon such occasions, think of God and his greatness; and whatsoever hath but a shadow and appearance of

---

[386] Kuipers.
[387] Kuipers.
[388] Charles Taylor, *A Secular Age* (Belknap Press of Harvard University Press, 2007), 322 - 51.

> INFINITE, as all great things have that are too big for our comprehension, they fill and overbear the mind with their Excess, and cast it into a pleasing kind of stupor and admiration.[389]

Without using the word, Burnet is preparing the way for the sublime as a major aesthetic category of the eighteenth century. Kant's reflections on the sublimity of nature and also the religious feeling it occasions are prefigured here. The fear characteristic of a mythological age is transcribed into an aesthetic key in a disenchanted world. The fear evoked by nature is now aesthetically pleasing. Joseph Addison, for example, remarks of the Alps that they "fill the mind with an agreeable kind of horror."[390] I mention these historical precedents because it is instructive to note in this connection that Burnet prototypically suggests at least two quintessentially modern themes: 'the sublime' and 'the state of nature'. In this respect, Kant's parallel between our antagonism toward nature and the antagonism that exists among free persons in the state is not accidental. However, in the former case we are reminded of our limitations by nature's raw power whereas in the latter, we are kept in our place by the authority of positive law. Stout draws together the connection between the sacred/sublime and politics when he comments, "The concepts of the horrendous and the sacred are linked. Something is sacred if it is worthy of reverence. We express reverence positively in certain forms of celebration and express it negatively in certain forms of protection or prohibition. Anything the violation or destruction of which would be horrendous is sacred."[391] Here the notion of the sacred, of which the sublime is a secularized version, is connected not only with the 'horrendousness' of nature but also protection and prohibition, presumably enforced by the state.

In this regard, Stout's reference to Burke is telling, since he is perhaps the first to articulate an explicit connection between the sublime and the political order. Burke holds that terror and pain, below the appropriate threshold and at a distance, can invoke in us feelings of awe and respect. Through such feelings of appropriate dread we experience a delight that cannot be found in mere pleasure. According to Burke, we should experience similar healthy dread in the face of political power. Like other British moral theorists, Burke attaches great significance to the passions and quite naturally makes the transition from the

---

[389] Quoted in Taylor, 334.
[390] Quoted in Taylor, 337.
[391] Kuipers.

sensations that produce feelings of the sublime to those that produce appropriate respect for authority. Stout would likely repudiate Burke's appeal to the sublime as justifying a hierarchical social order, but he does suggest a connection between the sublime and the sacred, the value of which should be upheld politically: "One reason for holding onto the notion of sacred value nowadays is that advanced capitalism tends to reduce everything, including the natural environment and human beings, to objects of merely instrumental value. Religious, democratic, and artistic practices, at their best, help us counter that tendency. Virtuous religion perfects our disposition to celebrate and protect sacred value."[392]

Although Stout speaks of religion as playing a role, his notion of the sacred, if the above analysis is correct, is already secularized. This analysis is further reinforced a little further along. When reflecting on whether there is an appropriate object of reverence that is not natural or social, perhaps God, Stout reveals: "My worry about monotheism is that it appears to conflate ideals and powers. The monotheistic assumption is that there must be one object that can serve as the ultimate reference point for all of the positive religious attitudes."[393] Stout does not believe in God, but wants to create a space for sacred value. But this leads to my speculation above that perhaps, for him, a language other than that of monotheism would be better suited to this task. I see Stout as pursuing one of the proliferations of spiritual options available in 'a secular age'. He continues: "Maybe this is what people are trying to say when they respond to pollsters by saying they are spiritual but not religious. They sense that some things are worthy of reverence, that some things are worthy of awe, and that some things are worthy of piety, but organized religion tends to come with big, unifying pictures that are hard to believe."[394]

Stout regards these big, unifying pictures as "ossified poetry."[395] The tendency toward ossification is inherent in all cultural formations, but especially evident in religion with its scriptures and creedal formulations. Stout delineates the disadvantages of ossification: "Influential scriptures and traditions present horrors as divinely authorized. They promulgate taboos and conceptions of the sacred that made sense only in the context of patriarchal tribes struggling for

---

[392] Kuipers.
[393] Kuipers.
[394] Kuipers.
[395] Stout, *Democracy and Tradition*, 41.

survival in an ancient war of all against all. They drape a sacred canopy over myriad forms of domination. They promote cruelty. Ossification tends to freeze all of the bad stuff, as well as the good stuff, in place."[396] However, this rejection of ossified poetry does not necessarily lead to a rejection of sacred value. Quite the contrary: "I think of myself as someone whose life is centered in trying to respond appropriately to sacred value and to horrendous assaults on it. I consider my vocation to ascend into excellence and to help others do the same. You decide whether that makes me religious." [397]

Ironically, Kuipers had already done so in an article on Stout's pragmatic approach to religion in public:

> [N]o one can doubt that modern democratic questioning has had a profound effect on the current shape of religious traditions, including the increased freedom and discursive responsibility their adherents have come to enjoy. Stout considers both himself and the rest of us to be beneficiaries of this shift, which he credits for allowing him personally to carry forward important religious values while at the same time jettisoning soul-insulting lies. From the other side, Stout's ability to engage in effective immanent criticism of the Christian tradition shows him to be less alienated from its store of meanings than he perhaps considers himself to be, as he deftly puts these to work in criticizing what he thinks are some distortions of Christianity in the views of his religious opponents.[398]

In regard to the question of whether or not Stout is religious, Kuipers offers the following:

> In light of the foregoing, one is tempted to characterize Stout not as a secular democrat, but as a post-institutional Christian who pushes at its boundaries harder than most, but who does so with a desire to ensure that its best insights are not lost to the suffocation of dogmatic habituation. Even if this characterization of Stout (or am I implicitly using a too-loose definition of Christianity?) goes too far, Christians and members of other traditions can still be grateful to him for providing

---

[396] Kuipers.
[397] Kuipers.
[398] Kuipers, "Stout's Democracy without Secularism: But is it a Tradition?" 97.

them with a valuable service in mounting a persuasive argument for the responsibility of members of different religious traditions to habituate themselves more democratically so as to avoid the enervation that results when a tradition succumbs to dogmatic stasis.[399]

In addition, Stout's contribution, whether it is 'religious' or not, avoids Rorty's assumption that religious discourse cannot be publicly accessible in the way secular discourse can. Thinking of the religious and secular as absolutes instead of shifting poles on a continuum of public accessibility or utility is something that Stout's analysis helps us to overcome. Thus, Stout's account of the discursive power of religion, despite his own unbelief, shows that religion is not essentially a conversation-stopper. I have self-consciously focused on religious argumentation, but a case could be made, and Stout implies, that perhaps broader rhetorical means could also be employed, provided that the interlocutors remain willing to engage in democratic questioning, offering fresh perspectives that articulate to a wider polity what many of us, whether secular or religious, mean by 'sacred value.'

To summarize, in this chapter I have argued that nothing in the tradition of American pragmatism disqualifies religious contributions to public debate. We have seen that Rorty's charge that religion is a conversation-stopper only applies to faith-claims that rest uncritically on authority. But such claims do not exhaust religious contributions to public discourse. We have also seen that Rorty has reconsidered his initial sentiments toward religion in public. He now recognizes that the "Jeffersonian compromise" he once defended is untenable. He offers no principle whereby religion should be excluded from the public sphere and has dropped reference to Rawls and Habermas as model epistemologists on this matter. However, he believes that custom and habit should prohibit certain appeals to religion when discussing issues such as gay rights. He still wants to press religious citizens to find another way of expressing their arguments, a secular way. I have argued that such a call for translation, in the absence of any robust notion of rationality, has little discursive point and is, ironically, not the most pragmatic tack to pursue. I then argued, with caveat, that Stout's approach of immanent critique is the more promising discursive avenue for the kinds of 'abnormal conversations' that we are bound to have in a pluralistic democracy. I

---

[399] Kuipers, 97.

also think it represents an improvement over Habermas's translation requirement. I therefore conclude that pragmatism can be an ally of the thesis that religious citizens should be able to contribute to public debate in the language of their tradition.

In the final chapter, I will explore ways in which religious language may still be publicly permissible and even useful. As mentioned, Habermas is sensitive to the ways in which the monopoly of scientific expert cultures has the potential to erode our self-understanding as autonomous agents. New research in biogenetics and neurology have given renewed impetus to the old philosophical debate over freedom and determinism by offering empirical evidence with which philosophers must grapple. This issue, among others generated by pushing the frontiers of biotechnology, leads Habermas to recognize that naturalistic challenges to our self-understanding threaten not only religious worldviews, but also the traditional bases of our political and legal frameworks in the West. Again, Habermas has hinted that we may need to salvage the semantic potential of religious language to meet these challenges, particularly to human autonomy.

Although Habermas stops short of ascribing transcendence to humanity – perhaps due to its 'otherworldly' connotations – I argue that his political vision can be read as anticipating transcendence of a kind. In order to elucidate this point, however, it will be necessary to examine what 'transcendence' might mean under the conditions of secularization. Again, I will draw upon Taylor's analysis of the phenomenology of secularization as well as the insights of Jürgen Moltmann. Through an articulation of transcendence for the modern age, I shall endeavor to create a space in which religion can be seen as providing a redemptive critique of our current political organization in much the same way that Habermas sees the ideal speech situation as the end of our antagonistic politics and the beginning of intersubjective agreement. I will argue that Habermas, in the tradition of his predecessors in critical theory, has offered a secular eschatology that can be usefully described as redemptive and 'transcendent'. If this is a worthy goal of secular political theory, then I suggest it is also a legitimate goal for religious citizens to pursue. This interpretation allows us to imagine a positive role for religious engagement, rather than the dogmatic role against which Habermas cautions. If I am successful, Habermas should have no objection to religious citizens engaging in such redemptive critique in political contexts.

Chapter 5
Freedom and Future Transcendence:
Beyond *Kulturkampf* to Redemptive Critique

In this final chapter, I will attempt to extend the argument of the preceding chapters to the effect that Habermas, despite his concern with procedural matters, makes many substantive assumptions of his own. For example, Habermas's political philosophy depends upon the assumption that persons are autonomous, rational agents. However, he is also acutely aware that the reigning materialistic paradigm, with its deterministic picture of the world, undermines the political notion of responsible agency. Thus, Habermas is concerned to reconcile the modern, scientific image of the person with the phenomenological experience of ourselves as rational agents, an experience upon which liberal political theory is based. In order to do so, Habermas opts for a non-reductive naturalism. However, the reconciliation he seeks remains promissory. As such, I argue that his commitment to autonomy functions for him as a substantive rather than procedural commitment—arguably a fiduciary commitment.

However, Habermas is reticent to say more about his substantive commitments because he is wary of encroaching upon metaphysics. Attempts to explain aspects of the human person, such as freedom, over and against the materialist view run the risk of becoming metaphysically overdetermined. Nonetheless, some, like William J. Meyer, argue that Habermas cannot consistently avoid metaphysics; the post-metaphysical stance is untenable. Moreover, Meyer's position entails that religion cannot be post-metaphysical in the way Habermas thinks it must in the modern world. After surveying these arguments, however, I conclude that stressing 'metaphysics' plays into the hands of the subtraction story. I argue that conceiving of religion metaphysically, i.e. in terms of beliefs about what lies beyond the immanent frame, allows one to exclude religion from the public sphere. On this view, the presence of religion in the public sphere is seen as the presence of idiosyncratic beliefs rather than the presence of religious citizens whose participation and arguments have value.

Nevertheless, it is true that Western religions represent an 'open' interpretation of the immanent frame; religion is open to the transcendent in a way that secularism is not. However, is it possible to conceive of transcendence without the metaphysical overdetermination about which Habermas cautions? In hopes of answering this question, I follow Taylor in sketching a phenomenological account of the experience of transcendence under the conditions of secularization. Several interesting features emerge. Far from overdetermination, transcendence is expressed by moderns in terms of 'ontological indeterminacy'. There is a sense in which human beings experience certain 'boundary conditions', but the immanence of the modern worldview makes it more difficult to interpret these along dogmatic religious lines. Instead, they are interpreted using a 'subtler language' that communicates the feeling of the transcendence in ontologically indeterminate ways. I believe that Habermas is gesturing toward this account in his talk of the semantic power still latent within religious language. I also suggest a way in which Habermas's own political philosophy can be interpreted as looking forward to a future 'transcendence' in which the ideal speech situation breaks into our immanent antagonistic politics and thereby offers redemption of a sort. Perhaps this is analogous to the kind of redemptive critique of modernity that religion might provide. If so, there is a role for religious language quite unlike the dogmatic habituation that Habermas criticizes.

Finally, I make some practical suggestions about how religion might play this different role in the future and how politics might remain open to insights from this quarter. I reiterate my point that one can maintain that which is distinctive about modern liberalism without adopting ideological secularism. The formal secularity of the political sphere is a valuable aspect of liberalism. However, it can be affirmed without naive secularism on the part of citizens. In confronting the challenges of globalization, I suggest that the global citizen should not be naively secular. Rather the global citizen must understand religious points of view and stand ready to engage in translation and immanent critique as needed.

Soft Naturalism and Substantive Commitments

Throughout the preceding argument, I have endeavored to demonstrate that the allegedly procedural secular assumptions upon which Habermas thinks we must base public arguments entail substantive commitments and thus a thicker conception of the world and our place in it than he is prepared to admit. Therefore, it becomes arbitrary to disallow appeals to religious premises on the basis of their substantive commitments. However, this argument can be pressed further. It may be the case, as Habermas claims, that secularism entails fewer, or minimal, assumptions about humanity and the world by comparison with religious worldviews, although I would not necessarily concede this point. It may be the case also that the reductionism implied by a secular outlook is more easily justifiable, although I would not concede that either. It may even be the case that – and I do not concede this for a moment – that secularism is simply a matter of subtraction of certain metaphysical beliefs, a process of negation rather than affirmation. If these dubious theses turn out to be true, it does not follow that secularism, generalized as a worldview, can sustain our self-understanding as rational, autonomous agents. In fact, Habermas is increasingly recognizing the conflict between a totalizing secularist outlook and the substantive, rather than merely procedural, claims about the human subject he must espouse in order to speak meaningfully about rational agency. In other words, secularism, in some of its manifestations, may indeed be thinner than some or most religious outlooks, but such reductionism erodes much more than religious beliefs; it also undermines the political and legal culture of modernity. The image of the self as an autonomous, rational agent which has functioned so pivotally in political theory since the seventeenth century is, I would argue, a substantive assumption about humanity, not merely a procedural one. To be sure, reconciling our everyday self-understanding with a scientific understanding of ourselves as subject to mechanistic laws has been a preoccupation of modern philosophy, but Habermas remains optimistic that such reconciliation can be accomplished; he does not for a moment suggest that our self-understanding is simply a political fiction. Rather he thinks that it belongs to a true picture of the world. Insofar as it does, it functions for him as a substantive assumption, a part of his philosophical anthropology and not merely a methodological consideration.

I have frequently referenced Habermas's reservations about the over-generalization of a secular worldview in the direction of a scientism that robs the individual of any real agency. Here is yet another example of his misgivings:

> In our everyday dealings, we focus on others whom we address as a second person .... The awareness of authorship implying accountability is the core of our self-understanding, disclosed only to the perspective of a participant, but eluding revisionary scientific description. The scientistic belief in a science which will one day not only supplement, but replace the self-understanding of actors as persons by an objectivating self-description is not science, but bad philosophy. No science will relieve common sense, even if scientifically informed, of the task of forming a

judgment, for instance, on how we should deal with prepersonal human life under descriptions of molecular biology that make genetic interventions possible.[400]

I take it as uncontroversial that Habermas views with suspicion any reductionist metaphysics and to this extent makes substantive assumptions of his own that may be secular but nevertheless fall under the rubric of an 'addition story' – hence his efforts to articulate a position "between naturalism and religion." However, my point is that substantive issues inform and underlie any procedural consensus we can achieve. Insofar as we can make progress here pragmatically, we do so because most parties to the discussion have not adopted the subtraction story to its logical extent. But such voices do exist, which makes a defense of our substantive, normative self-understanding necessary. Habermas has recently realized this and has tried to elucidate a non-reductionist naturalism that preserves human autonomy.

In an essay called "Freedom and Determinism" he advocates what he calls "nonscientistic or 'soft' naturalism."[401] By this he means a naturalism that does not simply reduce our thoughts and actions to neurophysiology, thereby making responsible agency an illusion. Habermas wants to avoid the conclusion that our thinking and acting in the world can be explained entirely in terms of non-rational, causal factors, completely excluding the rational motivation upon which communicative action depends. "In everyday life" he says, "we cannot avoid provisionally attributing responsible authorship for our actions to one another."[402] But he also realizes that scientific accounts of the world which describe phenomena in the language of scientific expert cultures often do clash with common sense. Thus, the folk psychology by which we attribute responsible agency to each other may simply be another casualty of scientific progress. However, on the basis of the above block quote, Habermas is unwilling to accept this conclusion. Indeed, when he speaks of science never relieving common sense with respect to our first person experience, and when he further characterizes the sought-after idealized science that will provide third person

---

[400] Jürgen Habermas, "Faith and Knowledge," in *The Frankfurt School on Religion: Key Writings by the Major Thinkers*, ed. Eduardo Mendieta (Routledge, 2004), 331 - 32.
[401] Jürgen Habermas, "Freedom and Determinism," in *Between Naturalism and Religion: Philosophical Essays* (Polity, 2008), 151 - 80.
[402] Habermas, 152.

descriptions of all mental phenomena as "not science, but bad philosophy," he betrays a fiduciary commitment to human autonomy. Therefore, it seems plausible to say that he has at least one substantive assumption upon which his philosophy depends. In order to more fully defend this claim, I want to look more closely at how Habermas develops his critique of 'hard' materialism.

If reductionist, materialistic accounts of human behavior are true, this would seem to leave no room for the kind of rational motivation Habermas defends as necessary for grounding justified action. But he remains skeptical that such thoroughgoing materialism is a necessary assumption even for a methodological atheist like himself. He asks, "But is determinism a scientifically founded thesis, or is it merely a component of a naturalistic worldview based on a speculative interpretation of scientific knowledge? I would like to continue the debate over freedom and determinism as a dispute concerning the *right way* to naturalize the mind."[403] Here he intimates that a metaphysically over-determined naturalism is the wrong way to approach this debate. He further states that "reality is not exhausted by the totality of scientific statements that count as true according to current empirical scientific standards."[404] Nevertheless, he does not think that the dualism that exists between our experienced self-awareness as agents and the data of empirical research should be ontologized into a dualism between mind and nature. He still seeks a naturalistic account of how these two aspects of our experience hold together. In his view, the task is to reconcile what Kant has taught us about the transcendental conditions of knowledge, including freedom, and what Darwin has taught us about natural evolution.[405] Although the details of Habermas's strategy for accomplishing such reconciliation are beyond the scope of this chapter, I want to pursue his line of argument further for the purposes of showing that autonomy functions for him as a substantive rather than merely procedural assumption.

He considers broadly compatibilist alternatives to the freedom and determinism polarity. It is plausible to think of all decisions as conditioned, not necessarily by causes, but by reasons. "If an act of 'free decision' implies that the actor 'binds' her will 'through reasons', then the openness of the decision does

---

[403] Habermas, 152.
[404] Habermas, 153.
[405] Habermas, 153.

not preclude its being *rationally* conditioned."[406] Although it remains difficult to explain how, upon a purely materialist view, reasons do not reduce to causes, a standard compatibilist response is available: the opposite of 'free' is not 'caused' but 'coerced'. We are free to the extent that our will is free from non-rational constraint. Such a response fits well with Habermas's understanding of political freedom which is by no means libertarian, but rather 'epistemically demanding'. He summarizes:

> The forceless force of the better argument that motivates us to take a "yes" or "no" position must be distinguished from the causal constraint of an imposed restriction that compels us to perform actions we do not want to perform: "If we experience a failure of agency, then it is because we fail to influence our will and doing as thinking and judging subjects. Freedom in this sense is not only compatible with conditionality …; it requires conditionality and would be unthinkable without it."[407]

These last lines quote Swiss philosopher Peter Bieri who further writes, "Reflection on the alternatives is on the whole an occurrence that will ultimately bind me and my history to a specific will …. I know that and it doesn't bother me."[408] Habermas worries that such compatibilism collapses into determinism: "However, it would certainly bother me if my decision were determined by a neural event in which I was no longer involved as a person who takes a position; for then it would no longer be *my* decision."[409] Furthermore, he cautions: "The correct concept of conditioned freedom does not lend support to the overhasty ontological monism that declares reasons and causes are two aspects of a single phenomenon."[410] Therefore, just as dualism between mind and nature must not be ontologized, neither then should monism. However, the third way Habermas seeks remains elusive throughout the essay.[411]

---

[406] Habermas, 156.
[407] Habermas, 157.
[408] Quoted in Habermas, 158.
[409] Habermas, 158.
[410] Habermas, 158.
[411] Rorty, for example, does not see a problem here: "it is trivially the case that no phenomenal property can be a physical one. But why should this *epistemic* distinction reflect an *ontological* distinction?" *Philosophy and the Mirror of Nature, Thirtieth Anniversary Edition* (Princeton University Press, 2009), 29.

Habermas wants to affirm both our phenomenological self-understanding as autonomous, rational thinking, judging, and acting agents and also the self-contained naturalistic picture of the world revealed by experimental science. These are, of course, difficult to hold in tension. However, it is not my purpose here to force Habermas to take a position on either the dualist or monist pole of the debate. Nor do I seek to defend a metaphysically over-determined dualistic view. Although such a perspective has its defenders, many of them motivated by religion, dualism between the mind, supposedly of like-substance with God, and the body, subject to mechanistic laws, is not necessary to a religious worldview. Indeed, such a perspective tends to reinforce the rigid demarcation between the transcendent and the 'immanent frame' that gives rise to secularism. Therefore, I take Habermas seriously when he cautions against the over-determination of any particular metaphysical view. But regardless of how post-metaphysical we are in our thinking, we run up against the limits of our procedural apparatus and must make some more substantive assumptions. My purpose here is to show that human autonomy functions as such a substantive assumption for Habermas, even though he presently lacks a language that bridges the gap between the two language games of phenomenological awareness and empirical data. In speaking about these respective language games, he maintains that we must, for the moment, hold both of them in tension, but he also betrays the limits of procedural assumptions and the longing for a more substantive grounding of his intuitions: "Granted this is an epistemic dualism [between the explanatory perspectives of subject and object] only in a methodological, not an ontological sense. However, it is not yet clear how it can be squared with a monistic conception of the universe that would satisfy our need for a coherent picture of the world."[412] Nevertheless, he is quite candid that materialism poses serious problems for the defender of the efficacy of reasons, over physical causes, in motivating our action. Therefore, his trust in our shared experience as rational, responsible agents who decide and come to consensus autonomously is presently based on a substantive, fiduciary commitment. Again, here we run up against the limits of merely procedural assumptions and uncover the role that more substantive commitments play in the formation of our worldviews, whether religious or secular. For Habermas, the explanatory dualism that we encounter "must not be conjured up out of transcendental thin air. It must have *emerged* in the course of an evolutionary learning process …. On this assumption, the continuity of a natural history that we can conceive at least *on an analogy*

---

[412] Habermas, 162.

with Darwinian evolution, though we cannot form a theoretically satisfying concept of it, can ensure the unity of a universe to which human beings belong as natural creatures."[413] The confidence that it cannot be grounded transcendentally and that it must have emerged via an evolutionary process expresses a profoundly substantive, rather than merely procedural, understanding of secularism as closed from any porously transcendent space; indeed such a buffered view of the world is bound to suffer the excesses of the subtraction story. Of course, the problem for Habermas is that any appeal to transcendence is metaphysically over-determined. While I am sympathetic to Habermas's postmetaphysical stance, it is worth asking at this juncture whether it can be plausibly maintained. Thus far, I have been operating in a postmetaphysical mode, choosing adjectives like 'substantive,' 'heavy,' 'light,' 'thick,' and 'thin' to express what I take to be the latent fiduciary commitments embedded in both religious and secular worldviews. However, there are surely those who think Habermas should drop his agnostic, postmetaphysical stance, and be more explicit about where his commitments lie.

Is Postmetaphysical Thinking Untenable?

One writer who thinks that Habermas is forced by his own logic to abandon his postmetaphysical stance is William J. Meyer.[414] He does a good job summarizing Habermas's early view on religion, namely that religious mythology and metaphysics are insufficiently reflexive on their own first principles. They thus preserve a sacred core that is immune to rational criticism. By contrast, the type of rationality that develops with modernity is free to criticize all foundational assumptions. In Meyer's words: "Put simply, Habermas believes that modern communicative rationality, unlike mythologies and metaphysical worldviews, enables one to examine validity claims free from dogmatic constraints."[415] In addition, "[b]ecause religious and metaphysical worldviews limited the claims that were subject to rational criticism, they served an ideological function."[416] Although Meyer acknowledges that Habermas has moved with respect to religion, his incredulity toward metaphysics remains intact. I would concur with

---

[413] Habermas, 166.
[414] William J. Meyer, "Private Faith or Public Religion? An Assessment of Habermas's Changing View of Religion," *The Journal of Religion* 75. 3 (1995): 371 – 391.
[415] Meyer, 373.
[416] Meyer, 374.

this assessment; regardless of how much room Habermas has made for religion, it must remain postmetaphysical. Meyer thinks that given Habermas's movement on the issue, his postmetaphysical position has become untenable.

As we have discussed, Habermas has acknowledged that religion may have semantic contents that, at least presently, resist translation into the language of communicative rationality. From passages like those we have already considered, Meyer draws the conclusion, "it is evident that Habermas now views religion more tolerably, if not favorably, insofar as it is able to provide resources to help human beings come to grips with the shattering experiences that crash in on the profane character of everyday life. Religion, he suggests, in spite of its nonrational content, still offers something that eluded the differentiated character of modern communicative reason and culture."[417] Meyer interprets Habermas as claiming that religion is useful here in an existential sense, as a source of private meaning. Such religious language does not rise to the level of making public, cognitive claims. However, theological language tries to rise to this level by making a fourth kind of validity claim (in addition to science, morality and law, and art). Habermas recognizes this, but insists that in the wake of the death of metaphysics such a validity claim cannot be fully realized. Meyer summarizes: "Because metaphysics is dead, Habermas reasons, theology cannot publicly or rationally justify its truth claims and, therefore, should stick to the dogmatic task of interpreting and explaining the religious experiences and practices distinctive to its own culturally specific form of life."[418] Arguably, Habermas has moved closer to a public role for religion in the fifteen years since Meyer wrote his piece. However, in his judgment one cannot uphold religion's public role, i.e. its public validity claims, without metaphysics. If Meyer is right, we must conclude that Habermas's postmetphysical stance is still wrongheaded as it stands.

According to Meyer, Habermas has two main objections to metaphysics: 1) since metaphysics makes claims about totality, it necessarily homogenizes the differentiated spheres achieved by modernity; 2) metaphysical claims cannot be rationally justified. Meyer argues that Habermas is mistaken on both counts. On the first point, Meyer claims: "The cognitive claims of religion and metaphysics can speak coherently of totality inclusive of diversity (i.e. without collapsing differentiation) because the religious dimension or horizon emerges at the limits

---

[417] Meyer, 376.
[418] Meyer, 378.

of our common human experience – as found in everyday life and in the various cultural spheres (science, morality and law, and art)."[419] When we reach the limits of these discourses, it is legitimate, argues Meyer, to invoke religious or metaphysical accounts. For example, he asks us to consider the question "Why be moral?" which is not a question that can be answered within the moral discourse itself. "[A]n answer to this type of limit question must come from some underlying evaluation of the whole of reality – some fundamental affirmation of the worthwhileness of existence or some basic affirmation of order and value."[420] For Habermas, however, this question "does not arise meaningfully for communicatively socialized individuals."[421] For Meyer, this response simply presupposes an affirmation of life's meaningfulness – in other words, an answer to the 'limit question' about the totality. In addition, Meyer believes that Habermas uses a double standard in evaluating totality claims: "Habermas suggests that our fundamental evaluations of totality are intuitive, prereflexive, and private, as opposed to cognitive, reflexive, and public."[422] He quotes Habermas as follows: "This background [i.e., the lifeworld], which is presupposed in communicative action, constitutes a totality that is implicit and comes along prereflexively – one that crumbles the moment it is thematized; it remains a totality only in the form of implicit, intuitively presupposed background knowledge."[423] Meyer concludes:

> It is interesting to note that Habermas, who places so much value and importance on reflexivity as one of the gains of modernity, strongly denies the need for it when it comes to evaluations of totality. We all operate with some evaluation of the whole, he suggests, but this evaluation must remain implicit and prereflexive, for "it crumbles the moment it is thematized." Of course, the reason why he thinks it crumbles and the reason why he downplays the importance of reflexivity is because he denies the possibility of metaphysics, which is to say, he believes that all evaluations of totality are culturally specific.[424]

---

[419] Meyer, 381.
[420] Meyer, 382.
[421] Quoted in Meyer, 382.
[422] Meyer, 383.
[423] Habermas, *Postmetaphysical Thinking: Philosophical Essays*, trans. William Mark Hohengarten (Cambridge, MA: MIT Press, 1992), 51. Quoted in Meyer, 383.
[424] Meyer, 383.

Furthermore, Meyer alleges an inconsistency between Habermas's concession that religion can be existentially efficacious and his claim that under postmetaphysical conditions it cannot address the whole of reality. For what else could the existential efficacy of religion mean, Meyer asks, if not that religion provides answers to those existential questions that arise in life's "boundary situations" – "such as illness, guilt, anxiety, or the recognition of one's own mortality"[425] – situations upon which our rationally differentiated discourses offer no consolation? But if it is the case, as Habermas suggests, that religion does address such existential questions, then he must presuppose that religion provides an overarching context in which such questions can be rendered meaningful – as he admits they cannot from the standpoint of communicative rationality. "In other words," says Meyer, "Habermas's current affirmation of the existential usefulness or necessity of religion, suggestively points, it seems to me, to the limits and weaknesses of his own postmetaphysical view."[426] He elaborates: "insofar as one gives existential meaning to human experience, one implicitly affirms or claims that this meaning is adequate because it is true or authentic (i.e., because it is in conformity with the way things really are). Hence, Habermas's affirmation of the existential usefulness of religion implicitly points to the importance of metaphysics and the metaphysical question."[427] Habermas, of course, may deny that he is using 'existential' to point to anything other than the private comfort religion provides, however, Meyer argues that the power of religious language to provide such solace comes from truth-claims that take themselves to be universal and comprehensive, not merely private: "to ignore this [comprehensive character] is to eviscerate them, to do them the disservice of making them other than what they take themselves to be."[428]

Meyer then moves to Habermas's second objection to metaphysics, namely that metaphysical assertions about totality cannot be rationally justified in public discourse as can the claims of science, for example. Habermas "is convinced that the question of metaphysics has been put to rest and that a postmetaphysical understanding of existence is sufficient."[429] Meyer thinks that Habermas simply misunderstands the nature of metaphysical claims. Meyer thinks there is a form of validation appropriate to metaphysical claims:

---

[425] Meyer, 384.
[426] Meyer, 384.
[427] Meyer, 384.
[428] Meyer, 385.
[429] Meyer, 387.

> [V]alid metaphysical assertions refer to those characteristics or aspects of existence that are logically necessary, as opposed to those aspects that are merely logically contingent. Therefore, since valid metaphysical claims refer to those traits that are logically necessary, they are validated by showing that their denials are self-contradictory (i.e. by showing that their absence is logically inconceivable). Hence, metaphysical claims are self-validating because they cannot be denied without contradiction.[430]

When Habermas takes an agnostic stance – e.g. 'we can't know the truth of totality claims' – he is nonetheless making a totality claim. In making such a claim, Meyer alleges, Habermas is contradicting himself by making the very sort of claim he says cannot be validated: "In sum, negative claims about totality are, nonetheless, claims about totality that require their own distinct kind of validation. Hence, Habermas's denial of metaphysics is self-contradictory because it requires a metaphysical form of validation. In short, his denial presupposes what it explicitly denies."[431]

Postmetaphysical Responses to Meyer

There is much to unpack in Meyer's criticisms. Firstly, his point that claims about totality do not necessarily homogenize difference is well taken. However, his execution of this point leaves much to be desired. In elucidating the "limits" or the "boundary situations" of our everyday experience and rational discourses, I believe he chooses a rather unfortunate example. Although the question 'why be moral?' is not itself a moral question, and cannot be answered in that universe of discourse, upon a pragmatist interpretation it is simply wrongheaded. The question as it stands, devoid of context, suggests the person asking it is a sociopath who simply does not intuitively grasp the fact that we are social animals who live in communities that must take a certain shape. I suspect this is why Habermas says that the question "does not arise meaningfully for communicatively socialized individuals."[432] An immanent basis for morality is adequate for pragmatic purposes. Whether or not we have, as it were, ontologically prior reasons for being moral is an open question; whether or not

---

[430] Meyer, 387 – 88.
[431] Meyer, 389.
[432] Quoted in Meyer, 382.

we need them in order to be moral is less debatable. In my judgment, a negative answer to the question as to whether we need such ontologically prior reasons is justified by the empirical fact that we live in largely successful pluralistic societies that do not presuppose an answer to the ontological question. To be sure, we do not moralize in a vacuum; morality comes packaged in very culturally specific ways and some of those ways include obligations that go beyond the community, to God, for example. However, even – perhaps especially – morality that comes religiously packaged must justify itself discursively. Meyer seems to assume that Habermas, by failing to consider "limit questions" like 'why be moral?' and relate them to a totality claim, can only ground them subjectively and intuitively, rather than intersubjectively and communicatively. In fairness, Habermas leaves himself open to this charge when he says that "[w]e acquire our moral intuitions in our parents' home not in school."[433] This suggests that our acquisition of morality is prereflective and Meyer pounces on the opportunity to point out the inconsistency. Of course, our acquisition of morality is largely prereflective when we are children, but presumably it should not be when we are adults. In any case, reflection on the totality of Habermas's corpus does not lead one to the false dichotomy that Meyer erects between metaphysical grounding and subjective intuition. After all, justifying our claims intersubjectively is a major theme for Habermas.

Secondly, I am not persuaded by Meyer's allegation that Habermas is inconsistent in affirming the existential meaningfulness of religion and denying the metaphysical ground to which it points. Simply put, I can see no contradiction, implicit or otherwise, between affirming religion as a source of private meaning, even if this meaning gains its purchase in part from totality claims that are taken as true by its adherents, and not recognizing the validity of those totality claims. Habermas's point is surely that these claims cannot in fact be legitimated discursively and are thus not public claims. Of course, Meyer disagrees with this assertion, which brings us to our next point.

Thirdly, I appreciate the suggestion that Habermas has not exhausted all that philosophers have meant by 'metaphysics': according to Marc P. Lalonde, "By 'metaphysics' Habermas intends the tradition of philosophical idealism extending from Plato to Hegel, or from Iona to Jena as Franz Rosenzweig neatly

---

[433] Quoted in Meyer, 382.

put it."⁴³⁴ For Meyer, Habermas has in mind only the pre-modern conception of metaphysics criticized by Kant. Metaphysics before Kant took for granted the idea of a necessary being, a being whose existence could not be logically denied. However, Kant argued that all existential statements are synthetic – existence is not a predicate – and statements about a necessary being were mistaken; existential statements are always logically contingent and thus can be denied without contradiction. Meyer recognizes this Kantian critique:

> By calling for renewed attention to the metaphysical enterprise, I am not calling for a return to classical metaphysics or the premodern worldview that Habermas rightly dismisses. The classical metaphysical concept of a completely necessary being – one that is immutable and necessary in all respects – has indeed been shown by Kant and others to be incoherent. Rather I am suggesting that there is a coherent alternative, namely, neoclassical process metaphysics.⁴³⁵

Meyer contends that process metaphysicians such as Franklin Gamwell and Charles Hartshorne have convincingly shown that one can identify logically necessary existential claims.⁴³⁶ If this is so, I wonder why Meyer credits Kant with demonstrating the incoherence of classical metaphysics, since he disagrees with him precisely on the crucial question of whether there are any existential statements that can be denied without self-contradiction. It seems to me that either Kant is right in claiming that existential statements are always contingent, and thus Meyer's claim that metaphysical claims are valid insofar as their denials are contradictory is false, or Kant is wrong and existential statements can be necessarily true, in which case he has failed to demonstrate the incoherence of classical metaphysics. Introducing process theology really only muddies the waters here. In describing process metaphysics as a "coherent alternative" he says: "On its dipolar account, the divine reality must be, in differing respects, both contingent and necessary, changing and unchanging, temporal and eternal, relative and absolute, etc. It is this process alternative that Habermas has, thus far, failed to address adequately."⁴³⁷ But why would Habermas need to address

---

434   Marc P. Lalonde, *Critical Theology and the Challenge of Jürgen Habermas* (New York: Peter Lang Publishing, 1999), 30.
435   Meyer, 389.
436   Meyer, n. 50, 390.
437   Meyer, 389.

this view if process metaphysics concedes the thrust of Kant's critique? Moreover, the alternative Meyer proposes does not seem *prima facie* coherent, nor does it do much to combat Habermas's (or Kant's) claim that the underlying structure of reality is unknowable. How would we know what aspects of the divine reality are necessary or contingent etc. and what practical difference would it make?

To be fair, there are post-Kantian efforts to re-define metaphysics, but Meyer, in my view, fails to press Habermas on this point because either Kant's critique of metaphysics is sound or it is not, and Meyer's waffling on this point leaves Habermas with no obligation to critique a position that is so ill-defined. Moreover, if Meyer means something different by 'metaphysics' than what Kant and Habermas do, which he does, having conceded the incoherence of classical metaphysics, then it is simply not relevant to Habermas's critique. Process theology is not Habermas's target, nor is process theology the standard understanding of "metaphysics," the connotations of which are still largely classical and pre-Kantian. For these reasons, I think it is best to dispense with the terminology of metaphysics rather than try to redefine it. In my judgment, "metaphysics" places God over and against the world, sealing transcendence off from the world in deistic fashion. Presumably, process theology would want to avoid this preconception too. However, simply because I advocate leaving behind the language of metaphysics, does not mean I think that Habermas's "postmetaphysical" stance necessarily imposes the kind of limits on religious language that he thinks it does. I would want to tease out space for the language of transcendence within a postmetaphysical context. I will have more to say about this later.

With respect to arguing for the legitimacy of religious perspectives in public, which I want to defend along with Meyer, I do not think that pressing the metaphysical question is the best strategic move for accomplishing this goal. Although I have hinted at some of the reasons for this assessment already, let me say a few more words about it because I believe it cuts to the heart of the issue between secularists and religionists. As I have mentioned, the connotations of "metaphysics" in the modern world tend to reinforce the secularism of the immanent frame that Taylor talks about.[438] The world is experienced as buffered from any inbreaking of the transcendent. There is a rigid, as opposed to porous,

---

[438] Charles Taylor, *A Secular Age* (Belknap Press of Harvard University Press, 2007), 539 - 93.

boundary between sacred and secular. This conception leads first to a deistic interpretation of God, and in time allows modernity to dispense with the divine altogether. It also buttresses the notion one finds in Habermas that religious perspectives have "heavier metaphysical baggage"[439] than do secular perspectives. Modernity construes religion as mainly a set of beliefs about reality, beliefs which cannot be affirmed according to the standards of evidence found in science, for example. Secularists tend to think of religious people primarily as having beliefs that are not ratified by the evidence. That is, in addition to believing that there are chairs, flowers, and atoms, religious people also believe in God, as though God were one more item in the inventory of reality, and a superfluous one at that. The secularist sees himself as simply lacking this belief. But this is to give an account entirely from the perspective of the subtraction story that Taylor criticizes.

    Moreover, such a story makes the task of marginalizing religion from the public sphere easy because it sees the presence of religion there as the presence of idiosyncratic beliefs rather than the presence of religious persons who may have good arguments. Of course, religious people often do little to discourage this secular perception of them, but invoking the language of metaphysics, in my judgment, only exacerbates the problem. Rather than speaking of metaphysical beliefs, I find it a useful strategy to speak about the premises we use in arguments. If we concede that the premises we use to construct political arguments are non-trivial – that is, do not express a tautology – then it becomes clear that we all, regardless of religious commitment, appeal to premises that are not held in common. Once we realize this, the exception made for religious premises in these contexts is seen for the red herring that it is. The difference is not between idiosyncratic beliefs and ordinary ones, but between premises that are universally accepted and those that are not. In my view, the former category is simply an empty domain, so we are all engaged in appealing to controversial premises and we should not expect universal assent on the basis of an idealized rationality. I think one can make this crucial point without appealing to metaphysics.

    A consequence of showing that religious and secular interlocutors are in the same position with respect to their premises is that secularists might become aware of their own substantive commitments. They may be forced to

---

[439] Habermas, "Religious Tolerance as Pacemaker for Cultural Rights," in Between *Naturalism and Religion*, 263.

countenance the fact that their assumptions are not simply methodological, but deeply substantive. I argued above that Habermas's commitment to human autonomy functions for him as a substantive, rather than merely procedural, commitment. And secularists no doubt have many such substantive commitments. They certainly have a philosophical anthropology – the fundamental unit of humanity is the individual who is by nature free and autonomous – as we saw in the case of Habermas. Taylor is quite right to point out that the modern, secular perspective came to ascendency, not because the ancient, religious view fell away, but because of the positive attractions of the new worldview. Even someone like Weber, in telling the secularization narrative, leaves the reader with the distinct impression that moderns did not abandon religious ways of thinking so much as reinterpret them against the success of science and technology. For Weber, the anxieties of the human condition remain the same: our fragility and fear in the face of nature, and our desire to propitiate and control these forces. But the object(s) of our trust has shifted. Therefore, even on the standard Weberian telling of the secularization story, secularism can be seen for what it is: a substantive story that seeks to provide better answers to religious questions. I would argue that it is, in fact, an immanent religion. Of course, this claim opens me to the charge that this is an overly broad stipulative re-definition of religion. However, I believe such a criticism is also indebted to a metaphysical understanding of religion. In other words, it implies that in order to be called "religious" a position must have "metaphysical" beliefs, i.e. beliefs about what is "outside" the immanent order that science observes. Again, such an approach is wrongheaded. Giving any kind of essentialist definition of religion is a fool's errand and to suggest that religion is necessarily "metaphysical" in some sense is to beg the question at hand. In such contexts, it might be advisable to dispense with the term "religion" too, because it too often prejudices the parties to the discussion in one direction or another and forecloses on the possibility of articulating a new way of recognizing our deeply substantive commitments. Although generally good on this point, I think that even Taylor missteps in adopting Bruce's definition of religion, even though it is more generous than most.[440] Better to use language like that of

---

[440] Taylor, 429: "Actions, beliefs, and institutions predicated upon the assumption of the existence of either supernatural entities with powers of agency, or impersonal powers or processes possessed of moral purpose, which have the capacity to set the conditions of, or to intervene in, human affairs."

"anticipatory confidence"[441] which stays away from metaphysics and endeavors to articulate a phenomenological description in which everyone can recognize themselves as adopting some substantive "spin"[442] on issues of ultimate concern. Nevertheless, it is important to differentiate an open spin from a closed spin. Although both exercise anticipatory confidence, the former is open to transcendence whereas the latter is not. I now want to return to the task alluded to above: articulating what transcendence might mean within a postmetaphysical context in which many people, due to the aura of the obvious that surrounds the closed spin, have difficulty imagining reality in other than purely immanent terms.

Transcendence Today

One of the difficulties is defining transcendence in a way that is not metaphysically over-determined in the way that Habermas, and many other moderns, suspect is untenable under such secular conditions as the explanatory power and technical success of natural science, and the autonomy and universality of secular morality and law. Therefore, I want to continue to offer a phenomenological account of the possible experience of transcendence under conditions of secularization. As for definitions, I find Jürgen Moltmann's particularly helpful in its simplicity:

> We generally use the word 'transcendence' for whatever exceeds the immanence that is present and open to our experience – for whatever goes further, into what is beyond immanence …. Conversely, there is no concept of immanence which does not imply an understanding of transcendence …. There is no dichotomy between immanence and transcendence. There is only a distinction and a relationship in the experience of 'the boundary.'[443]

He suggests that secularization, including the closed universe and the rise of atheism as a live option in the Western world, has not necessarily eliminated

---

[441] Taylor, 551.
[442] Taylor, 551.
[443] Jürgen Moltmann, "The Future as a New Paradigm of Transcendence," in *The Future of Creation: Collected Essays* (Fortress Press, 2007), 1.

transcendence, but merely changed how we experience the boundary between immanence and transcendence:

> We are merely being faced with transformations of transcendence and transformations in the boundary experience of immanence. The experience of transcendence, the experience of the boundary and religion in the general sense of the word are just as relevant today as they ever were. It is just that we no longer find them in the places where they used to be.[444]

In a very general way, Moltmann is making a point that Taylor and others have made at greater length: on the one hand, secularization does not bring an end to religion because religion continues to speak to an irreducible aspect of humanity's phenomenological experience, but on the other hand secularization does make it more difficult to experience this *qua* religious. Rather, the thrust of secularization is to subsume all experience under the immanent frame. In this respect, it historically shifts the boundary conditions for the experience of anything extra-immanent. It is now more difficult for modern people than for their forebears to find the margins of the immanent frame. In order to delve deeper into this historical shifting of these boundary conditions, we must again turn to Taylor's exhaustive analysis.

In the last chapter of Taylor's *A Secular Age*, he tries to articulate what he, and others, find attractive about the "open spin" orientation to the "immanent frame." Here, he wants to describe phenomenologically a sense of "fullness"[445] that could be appreciated by moderns regardless of religious belief or lack thereof. Although he admits that his "full-disclosure ... seems to have polluted the entire book for some people,"[446] he does much more than speak in a confessional mode. As I read him, he is striving, sometimes at the margins of language, to articulate a paradigm of the transcendent that makes sense to modern people. He speculates that we moderns have difficulty imagining our way outside the "internal economy of the immanent theory"[447] in which our

---

[444] Moltmann, 5.
[445] Taylor, 729.
[446] Ronald A. Kuipers, "An Interview with Charles Taylor," in *'God Is Dead' and I Don't Feel So Good Myself: Theological Engagements With the New Atheism*, Andrew David, Christopher J. Keller, and Jon Stanley, eds. (Cascade Books, 2010), 122.
[447] Taylor, 731.

selves have become "buffered" against any extra-physical or extra-mental effects or agency. Unlike our ancestors, who experienced the visible world as only a fraction of the totality, many of us moderns have difficulty imagining what it would be like to experience anything else. For this reason, Taylor is particularly interested in the experiences of modern 'converts' from immanent to transcendent perspectives. Whereas earlier generations of converts to, say, Christianity – as in Taylor's examples – lived within a more porous paradigm, where the transcendent was only thinly veiled,

> [b]y contrast, these moderns are all breaking beyond systems which their opponents see as totalities in a new sense; they are systems of immanent order which can be explained and accounted for in their own terms. That is what the modern idea of the "natural," counterposed to the "supernatural" means. It is possible, even tempting to make a claim on behalf of this, that there is no need whatever to go beyond it to understand our world.[448]

What is attractive about the naturalist worldview is its neat and tidy, self-contained picture of reality; everything is rendered predictable at least in principle. Thus, any inbreaking of the transcendent into this picture upsets this predictable paradigm. For Taylor, the "rage for order"[449] is one of the main motivations for keeping the immanent frame intact and, conversely, the reason many moderns have difficulty making any conceptual room for the transcendent. In addition, because of the self-contained nature of the immanent view, moderns have difficulty experiencing the 'boundary' between immanent and transcendent; everything abides within our scientific purview. Therefore, part of the challenge for those, like Taylor, who see open perspectives as live options, is to articulate what such a boundary might look like to the children of modernity. However, the language we use within the immanent frame makes this project difficult:

> The terms in which the paradigm shift can be made are suspect, and difficult to credit; they either belong to outlooks which can be discredited as "premodern" (e.g. God, evil, agape); or else one has to have recourse to a new "subtler language," whose terms on their own don't have generally accepted referents, but which can point us beyond ordinary, "immanent"

---

[448] Taylor, 732.
[449] Taylor, 63.

realities. Indeed, what may have to be challenged here is the very distinction between nature/supernature itself.[450]

At the risk of oversimplification, one might think of this distinction as conceiving of the immanent/transcendent boundary along a vertical axis, which has now largely been abandoned by moderns. Perhaps the boundary should be conceptualized along a horizontal axis, as it were, within time and history. Although in my judgment, there is mileage in this suggestion, there are also challenges to such 'horizontal' thinking within our modern social imaginary. Of course, earlier generations had both a 'vertical' and 'horizontal' boundary, although doubtless expressed in richer metaphorical language. In addition to the boundary between heaven and earth they also keenly felt the boundary between this age and the age to come. However, through the course of modernization, even this latter distinction has been weakened.

In the medieval period, as Taylor notes, the distinction between the current age and the eschaton was more deeply engrained in the social imaginary and functioned as a boundary between the immanent and the transcendent. For example, assumptions about the homogeneity of time, in which any future is seen as an extension of the immanent order, were not part of the general background assumptions of the era.[451] Rather, they saw the future as continuity and discontinuity, the latter being largely hidden until the transcendent breaks into history at the Parousia. For Taylor, the flattening out of time and history began long before modern secularism became a cultural competitor to Christianity. Rather, the religious and ethical attitudes that led to the Reformation played a major role in bringing it about. In his estimation, the medieval church largely took it for granted that "the full demands of Christian life would never be met, outside of isolated pockets of sanctity, in history, but only ... at the end of time."[452] However, the "thrust of Reform was to make a Church in which everyone should show the same degree of personal commitment and devotion which had hitherto been the stance of a dedicated elite." Furthermore, "this couldn't help but bring about a definition of the demands of Christian faith closer into line with what is attainable in this world, with what can be realized in history. The distance between the ultimate City of God and the properly

---

450   Taylor, 732.
451   See Taylor, 195 – 96 for a discussion of 'homogenous' and 'profane' time.
452   Taylor, 735.

Christian-conforming earthly city has to be reduced."[453] The conflation of the two orders, for Taylor, inevitably invites deism and then an impersonal natural order in which God is rendered superfluous. Therefore, the boundary between transcendence and immanence is obscured on both the vertical and horizontal axes.

Despite these shifts in the boundary conditions, Taylor thinks it is still possible for moderns to experience such a boundary and relate to it. Indeed, many people, even in the secularized West, whether or not they profess any particular faith, have a phenomenological sense of something 'beyond' mundane experience although they may express it in ontologically indeterminate ways. This indeterminacy is a crucial component of the secularization story for Taylor, and one that is often neglected in narratives that speak of secularization only in terms of disenchantment and rationalization. For example, Romanticism stresses neither of these aspects of the story – and actually reacts against them – despite the fact that it moves away from traditional metaphysics and institutionalized religiosity. It is suspicious of the language in which we traditionally cast what we might call transcendent experiences and thus develops what Taylor calls a "subtler language":

> What is crucial to the new "subtler" languages of post-Romantic poets, as I argued in an earlier chapter, was that they permit a kind of suspension or indeterminacy of ontological commitments …. The language can be taken in more than one sense, ranging from the fullest ontological commitment to the transcendent to the most subjective, human-, even language-centred.[454]

Of course, there is a chance that such an inward focus can contribute to the immanent picture since those experiences which would have been ascribed to forces beyond us in traditional religious accounts now retreat into the inner depths of our psyche. However, according to Taylor, such subjectivism is not a necessary outcome: "Reflexive awareness can bring about subjectivism, and a collapse of transcendence, but doesn't need to."[455] As such, one is tempted to say that these subtler languages allow us to harvest the semantic potential of

---

[453] Taylor, 736.
[454] Taylor, 757.
[455] Taylor, 757.

religious language while maintaining a post-metaphysical stance regarding the ontological truth or falsity of religious worldviews.

Although this indeterminacy seems to be similar to the post-metaphysical position Habermas takes, one must be cautious in ascribing these post-romantic views to him without qualification. For example, although he has moved toward a more favorable position with respect to religious language, he still insists that it be translated into language that can be vindicated rationally and discursively. It remains unclear whether the "subtler languages" Taylor speaks of, with their "ontological indeterminacy" are capable of such translation. Moreover, Habermas is no friend of Romanticism. One thinks of his critique of Adorno's and Horkheimer's *Dialectic of Enlightenment* in which he accuses them of retreating into non-discursive aestheticism and jettisoning the potential for communicative rationality already latent in the Enlightenment.[456] Although his interpretation of the relevant passage is suspect, as other scholars have pointed out,[457] Habermas is suspicious of anything resembling aestheticism or Romanticism, which he regards as an escape into the ineffable. For Habermas, the value of art is its capacity to expand communicative discourse. His disciple, Albrecht Wellmer, continues in this vein and criticizes Adorno specifically for positing a radical disconnect between the pathologies of modernity and a promised utopia achieved by an aesthetic reconciliation to nature.[458] Again, this reading of Adorno is highly problematic on its own terms; however, it serves to make the point that Habermas resists any aesthetic articulation of what I have been calling the boundary. He sees his predecessors in critical theory as essentially placing the boundary at the ineffability of aesthetic experience and he rejects this move as non-discursive and non-communicative. Thus any "subtle" language would have to demonstrate itself capable of communicative redemption; as such, its "indeterminacy" must give way to the more determinate terminologies of secular science, law, and (critical) art.

However, even Habermas is not immune to experiences of the boundary. If I read him correctly, he feels acutely the attraction of transcendent orientations to the "immanent frame," despite having reservations about the ontologies in

---

[456] Jürgen Habermas, *The Theory of Communicative Action, Vol. 1*, trans. Thomas McCarthy (Boston: Beacon Press, 1984), 384.
[457] Lambert Zuidervaart, *Social Philosophy after Adorno* (New York: Cambridge University Press, 2007), 114 – 15.
[458] Albrecht Wellmer, "Adorno, Modernity, and the Sublime" in *The Actuality of Adorno*, ed. Max Pensky (Albany: State University of New York Press, 1997), 112 – 134.

which many of these are embedded. His recent stance between naturalism and religion marks a middle path between scientific reductionism on the one hand and the ontologizing of our phenomenal experience on the other. In this respect, he is speaking a "subtler language" than either of these discourses. Despite the polarizing voices on either side of the debate, this indeterminate centre may well be the majority experience under contemporary secularism. Certainly Taylor makes such a case. In a review of *A Secular Age*, Vittorio Hösle captures the dynamism of our contemporary experience of the boundary:

> Modern science indeed offers an immanent framework, but one that is open to various interpretations. It is a peculiarity of our time that we are subjected to influences from opposing directions, seek out a middle path between orthodoxy and atheism (deism being the first of these), and try to make ontological sense of the phenomenal experiences of freedom, of the moral law and of beauty.[459]

Although modern people may remain indeterminate in their ontological commitments, or be suspicious of traditional articulations of transcendence, these phenomenal experiences can still function as boundary conditions for them. I agree with Taylor on this score: it is the plethora of loosely 'spiritual options' regarding these experiences, rather than the wholesale adoption of a naturalistic worldview, that motivates contemporary secularization. Habermas's methodological atheism notwithstanding, he does not advocate the overdetermination of a naturalistic worldview which would reduce our phenomenal experiences to brain chemistry, as we have seen. Nevertheless, these experiences alone do not exhaust potential boundary conditions.[460]

Death as a Boundary Condition

Even for moderns – perhaps especially for them – death functions as the ultimate boundary condition. Religion is most conspicuous when we are coming to terms with death, even in public contexts where the presence of religion would otherwise be unwelcome. This fact has, more or less, remained constant

---

[459] Vittorio Hösle, "Review Essay: A Metaphysical History of Atheism," *Symposium*, 14. 1 (Spring, 2001): 54.
[460] Karl Jaspers, *Way to Wisdom: An Introduction to Philosophy*, trans. Ralph Manheim (New Haven, CT: Yale University Press, 1954), 19.

throughout the secularization process. This is not to say that attitudes toward death have not changed under conditions of secularization – they certainly have – but it is to say that despite a decline in religious belief and practice, death still functions as a unique boundary condition and one about which religion is still expected to have something to say. Nevertheless, I should say more about the changing attitudes simply to highlight the resiliency of religious thought in spite of them.

For example, one might think of death as the ultimate negation of human flourishing, one that must be avoided at all costs, usually through the technocracy of modern science and medicine. This is a common contemporary view, shared by both the religious and the secular. Taylor identifies it with the position of modern humanism which roughly emerges during the Enlightenment. However, such humanism has its critics, as Taylor explains:

> Against this, there have developed a whole range of views in the post-Enlightenment world, which while remaining atheist, or at least ambivalent and unclear about transcendence, have seen in death, at least the moment of death, or the standpoint of death, a privileged position, one at which the meaning, the point of life becomes clear, or can be more closely attained than in the fullness of life.[461]

He goes on to mention thinkers such as Heidegger, Camus, and Beckett, and concludes that "[s]trangely, many things reminiscent of the religious tradition emerge in these and other writers, while it is also in some cases clear that they mean to reject religion, at least as it has been understood."[462] Thus, there is in these thinkers an implicit critique of the kind of humanism that considers any understanding of death as a boundary to be a form of 'otherworldly' thinking that distracts us from maximizing human flourishing in this world. Related to this attitude is the notion that longing for anything beyond the boundary is infantile wish fulfillment. Ironically, this condemnation of wish fulfillment seldom discourages the humanist from trying to avoid the inevitability of death or failing that, as indeed he must, ignore it.

This latter strategy often involves eschewing the traditional rites of passage associated with death. To quote Taylor again, "Sometimes the dying will

---

[461] Taylor, 320.
[462] Taylor, 321.

ask that their loved ones make no fuss over them, hold no ceremony, just cremate them and move on; as though they were doing the bereaved a favour in colluding in their aversion to death."[463] However, most people feel that this is inadequate. The bereaved feel the need to "struggle to hold on to the meaning they have built with the deceased, while (unavoidably) letting go of the person. This is what funeral rites have always meant to do, whatever other goals they have served."[464] Even atheists feel the need to eulogize and 'live on' in some sense even if it is a weaker substitute for the traditional religious sense. One sees this for example in the arch-atheist Richard Dawkins's eulogy for colleague William Hamilton who wished upon his death "to be laid out on the forest floor in the Amazon jungle and interred by burying beetles as food for their larvae. Later in their children, reared with care by horned parents out of fist-sized balls moulded from my flesh, I will escape. No worm for me, or sordid fly: rearranged and multiple, I will at last buzz from the soil … out into the Brazilian wilderness beneath the stars."[465] Regardless of the fact that no consciousness is preserved on this materialist account, one detects a longing for transcendence; even for the materialist, death acts as a boundary through which one realizes new possibilities. Nevertheless, the surrogate immortality of being transformed into beetles is probably not going to appeal to most people as much as traditional conceptions of what lies beyond. For Taylor: "even people who otherwise don't practice have recourse to religious funerals; perhaps because here at least is a language which fits with the need for eternity, even if you're not sure you believe all that."[466] In a recently published dialogue with four Jesuit academics, Habermas reflects on precisely this issue. As Stanley Fish comments in his *New York Times* review:

> Habermas begins his initial contribution to the conversation by recalling the funeral of a friend who in life "rejected any profession of faith," and yet indicated before his death that he wanted his memorial service to take place at St. Peter's Church in Zurich. Habermas decides that his friend "had sensed the awkwardness of non-religious burial practices and, by his choice of place, publicly declared that the enlightened modern age has failed to find a suitable replacement for a religious way of coping with the final rite de passage." The point can be sharpened: in the context

---

[463]   Taylor, 723.
[464]   Taylor, 722.
[465]   Quoted in Taylor, 606.
[466]   Taylor, 723.

of full-bodied secularism, there would seem to be nothing to pass on to, and therefore no reason for anything like a funeral.[467]

Habermas echoes here in a more personal register what he has said elsewhere: "religion, which has largely been deprived of its worldview functions, is still indispensable in ordinary life for normalizing intercourse with the extraordinary."[468] This "intercourse with the extraordinary" I take to be akin to what I have, following Karl Jaspers, been calling 'boundary conditions'. Furthermore, he says: "On the premises of postmetaphysical thought, philosophy cannot provide a substitute for the consolation whereby religion invests unavoidable suffering and unrecompensed justice, the contingencies of need, loneliness, sickness, and death, with new significance and teaches us to bear them."[469] In other words, religion invests these events with meaning, and perhaps allows us to see our lives as more porous, open to extra-mundane insight. This is perhaps especially true of death: "A need for meaning, a desire for eternity, can press us against the boundaries of the human domain. But death in another way can offer a way to escape the confinement of this domain, to breathe the air beyond."[470] This impulse is not specific to an explicitly religious point of view either, as Taylor shows. Rather, it attempts to capture a sense of fullness that all moderns can recognize as permeating their experience.

The sense of meaning that we have touched upon is closely bound up with the theme of hope. Ironically, in recent years Habermas has been moving closer to his predecessors in the Frankfurt School insofar as his Enlightenment optimism has waned. Adorno, for example, presciently reflected on how the death of metaphysics has disrupted our equanimity toward our own individual deaths: "In the socialized society, however, in the inescapably dense web of immanence, death is felt exclusively as external and strange. Men have lost the illusion that it is commensurable with their lives. They cannot absorb the fact that they must die."[471] Moreover, as Adorno also reminds us, the meaning of our

---

[467] Stanley Fish, "Does Reason Know What It Is Missing?" http://opinionator.blogs.nytimes.com/2010/04/12/does-reason-know-what-it-is-missing/?emc=etal.
[468] Quoted in Meyer, 376.
[469] Quoted in Meyer, 376.
[470] Taylor, 723.
[471] Theodor Adorno, "Meditations on Metaphysics," in *The Frankfurt School on Religion,* 181.

individual deaths is inseparable from the meaning of history: "Death and history, particularly the collective history of the individual category, form a constellation."[472]   After the horrors of the twentieth century, particularly the death camps, the critical theorists are pessimistic that any meaning to history or hope for the future can be salvaged. Habermas also questions his earlier optimism in the adequacy of secular reason and, in conversation with his predecessors, recognizes the semantic power of the religious traditions that have been lost:

> When sin was converted to culpability, and the breaking of divine commands to an offense against human laws, something was lost. The wish for forgiveness is still bound up with the unsentimental wish to undo the harm inflicted on others. What is even more disconcerting is the irreversibility of past sufferings – the injustice inflicted on innocent people who were abused, debased, and murdered, reaching far beyond any extent of reparation within human power. The loss of hope for resurrection is keenly felt as a void. Horkheimer's justified skepticism – "The slaughtered are really slaughtered" – with which he countered Benjamin's emphatic, or rather excessive, hope for the anamnestic power of reparation inherent in human remembrance, is far from denying the helpless impulse to change what cannot be changed any more.[473]

At this point, one might question how far 'ontological indeterminacy' can take us toward coming to terms with suffering and death. Taylor, having reflected on various secular strategies for wringing some meaning out of death, such as the "eternity" of "the clan, the tribe, the society, the way of life"[474] concludes that these all fall short of a genuinely theological response: "And of course, this eternity can't preserve those who are really forgotten, or those who haven't left their mark, or those who have been damned, excluded. There is no general resurrection in this 'eternity' of grateful posterity. This is what exercised Benjamin, the unfilled need to rescue those who were trampled by history."[475] Also in conversation with the Frankfurt School, no less a theologian than Benedict XVI, in his encyclical *Spe Salvi* (Saved by Hope), questions whether

---

472   Adorno, 182.
473   Habermas, "Faith and Knowledge," in *The Frankfurt School on Religion*, 333.
474   Taylor, 721.
475   Taylor, 722.

theological language can be separated from the ontology in which it is traditionally at home:

> Max Horkheimer and Theodor W. Adorno were equally critical of theism and atheism. Horkheimer radically excluded the possibility of ever finding a this-worldly substitute for God, while at the same time he rejected the image of a good and just God .... Adorno also firmly upheld this total rejection of images, which naturally meant the exclusion of any "image" of a loving God. On the other hand, he also constantly emphasized this "negative" dialectic and asserted that justice – true justice – would require a world "where not only present suffering would be wiped out, but also that which is irrevocably past would be undone." This would mean, however – to express it with more positive and hence, for him, inadequate symbols – that there can be no justice without a resurrection of the dead. Yet this would have to involve "the resurrection of the flesh, something that is totally foreign to idealism and the realm of Absolute spirit."[476]

For Benedict, any meaningful interpretation of history is anchored to an eschatological hope in the future. But modern people, who are not innocent of the philosophical critique of religion, will be hard-pressed to fully embrace the ontological categories in which this eschatology is expressed. Nevertheless, for moderns, whether secular or religious, the future and the promise (or threat) it entails functions as a boundary condition, the possibility for the inbreaking of something new into our experience. This is readily seen in the many modern utopian narratives of progress that have emerged since the Enlightenment, which function as secular eschatologies. The critique of these narratives can perhaps open up some space to see the future as 'a paradigm of transcendence' as Jürgen Moltmann has suggested.[477] I want to return now to develop the concept of transcendence along a horizontal axis. I hope to use Moltmann, in conversation with the critical theorists, to craft a language of the transcendent that Habermas would recognize as offering a legitimate critique of the pathological narratives of modernity. If successful, this in turn will also

---

[476] Benedict XVI, *Spe Salvi*, section 42 http://www.vatican.va/holy_father/benedict_xvi/encyclicals/documents/hf_ben-xvi_enc_20071130_spe-salvi_en.html
[477] Moltmann, 1 – 14.

articulate a public role for religious language that moves beyond the *Kulturkampf* and has genuine critical and redemptive significance.

The Future as Possibility

As mentioned, the early Frankfurt School did not share Habermas's optimism about the progress inherent in the Enlightenment. For Adorno, the myth of progress was shattered in the twentieth century, first in the death camps of Auschwitz and second in the 'progress' that culminated in humanity's capacity to destroy itself.[478] Thus, we can only speak of progress in any meaningful sense if we can avoid unmitigated disaster, if humanity has a future. An 'established' humanity can no longer be taken for granted: the non-existence of humanity is a real possibility. Unlike previous generations, we have the power to actualize this possibility. We can destroy ourselves not only atomically, but also biologically, chemically, demographically, ecologically, and this only brings us to the letter 'E'. Therefore, the future only has meaning if we can avoid annihilation. For the critical theorists, "progress obtains legitimation in the doctrine that the idea of the happiness of unborn generations – without which one cannot speak of progress – inalienably includes the idea of redemption."[479] Adorno goes on to say that "the aspect of redemption, no matter how secularized, cannot be removed from the concept of progress."[480] If this is the case, we need to explore how the future might be redeemed from the pathological secular myth of progress.

For Adorno, a major theme in the progress narrative of modernity is the domination of nature. Progress is motivated by coming to terms with fear, specifically the fear of nature's power over us. Despite achieving various means to exercise control over nature, technological progress has not delivered on its promised liberation. Rather, it has served to increase humanity's alienation from both the natural and social world. According to Moltmann, the modern man is far from liberated:

> But instead he is surrounded by an ever denser web of his own works – social institutions, political organizations, giant industrial firms – like a new quasi-nature. The natural cosmos, which man sees through and

---

[478] Theodor Adorno, "Progress" in *How Can One Live after Auschwitz*, ed. Rolf Tiedemann (Stanford, CA: Stanford University Press, 2002), 141.
[479] Adorno, 128.
[480] Adorno, 132.

dominates more and more, is being replaced by a new cosmos of his own objectifications; and this cosmos is increasingly harder to see through, and harder still to dominate and control …. They are taking on autonomous form, are running away from him, acquiring power over him.[481]

The longing for freedom and emancipation promised, but not delivered, by secularism is once again opening up possibilities for experiencing the boundary. Many moderns have seen through the myth of freedom supposedly achieved by the endless exploitation of material resources and domination of nature. In addition to the natural disasters exacerbated by this strategy, we are also faced with social and political disasters. Contrary to Habermas's early optimism for the emancipation of rationalization, "now the creations dominate their creators, and rationalized conditions exercise irrational dictatorship over people. This is the new 'boundary' at which people reach out for transcendence. It is a transcendence of an existing system. It is therefore directed to 'the future.'"[482] Thus, any sense of hope for the future cannot simply be conceptualized as an expansion of the immanent order of things, those events and processes within our immediate horizon of experience. Rather, it must transcend the limitations of such experience. Therefore, hope oriented toward the future must look for an 'age to come' and this expectation functions as a boundary condition for the experience of the transcendent. To further quote Moltmann:

> If the 'boundary' of present immanence is experienced in the fact that man is alienated from his world and that this world is alienated from man, transcendence will be experienced at the point where critical perspectives open up for our present conflicts, where new possibilities emerge for a meaningful incarnation of man, and new potentialities for a humanization of his alienated conditions – in short, where a future of reconciliation and alteration wins the upper hand over this situation.[483]

Interestingly, Habermas also wants to realize this future through the ideal speech situation. He wants to form the relevant 'incarnation' of humanity in a

---

[481] Moltmann, 5.
[482] Moltmann, 9.
[483] Moltmann, 9 – 10.

harmonious community of communicative individuals which transcends the currently antagonistic public sphere and culminates in perfect rational consensus. However, as Adorno, and Kant before him, have noted, the engine of progress in modernity is conflict. And this is not only the case in political contexts, but such conflict is ontologized, it goes all the way down, as it were, to the way the world fundamentally is. Habermas realizes that his ideal speech situation stands in tension with the reductionism typical of naturalism which holds the struggle for survival to be the driving force behind evolutionary progress. He states the problem as follows:

> If reasons and the logical processing of reasons do not play any causal role from a neurobiological point of view, it becomes mysterious from the perspective of the theory of evolution why nature allows itself the luxury of a "space of reasons" (Wilfrid Sellars) at all. Reasons do not swim about like globules of fat on the soup of consciousness. On the contrary, judging and acting are always associated with good reasons for the subjects concerned. If the process of "giving and asking for reasons" had to be dismissed as an epiphenomenon, there would not be much left of the biological functions of the self-understanding of subjects capable of speech and action. Why do we have to demand justifications from each other? What purpose is served by having a whole superstructure of agencies of socialization that drill into children causally superfluous habits of this sort?[484]

Here, Habermas recognizes that if this scenario is the last word, if reductionism is true on an ontologically fundamental level, then this has grave implications for a theory of communicative action that aims at being normative. Although Habermas wants to resist such reductionism, the question remains whether his methodological atheism has the resources to do so. If the pathology to be overcome by communicative action, namely antagonism and conflict, is the driving force of the entire evolutionary process, including the origination of illusory "reasons," then how can such an epiphenomenon eradicate the cause? Ironically, Habermas falls prey to a criticism he levels at *Dialectic of Enlightenment*. In TCA, he charges Adorno and Horkheimer with claiming that reification is fundamental to human consciousness, rather than arising with the

---

[484] Habermas, "Freedom and Determinism," 163 – 64.

advent of capitalism as in orthodox Marxism. A consequence of this idea is that reason is fundamentally instrumental. In order to undo the pathologies wrought by instrumental reason they "have to rely on a reason that is before reason (which was from the beginning instrumental)."[485] In other words, if reason is part of the problem, how can reason possibly provide a solution? However, Habermas faces an even greater difficulty. If reason is only an epiphenomenon of causes, and these causes are driven by the pathology of instrumentality, namely the struggle for survival, how can reason eradicate the pathology? How does Habermas find a "reason that is before reason" from within a naturalistic ontology? He realizes that he must abandon such reductionism, opting for "soft naturalism" instead.

Thus the kind of reconciliation Habermas hopes for cannot be achieved by simply projecting the failed promise of modernity coupled with an antagonistic ontology into the future. The fact that he does not suggest that we do so and, in fact, suggests we should not, is perhaps evidence that he realizes the futility of envisioning the future exclusively along an 'immanent' axis. To do so would be to perpetuate the pathologies of modernity and to close the future off to possibilities rather than open it. However, to think of the future as a horizon of hope and possibility, as Habermas does, is precisely to conceive of it transcendently, as a 'boundary'. It is also to conceive of it eschatologically rather than teleologically. In my judgment, Habermas's critique of religion is valid insofar as it rightly criticizes the overly determinate teleology inherent in many theologies.   To elaborate, teleology, as its etymology suggests, implies a determinative end, purpose, or goal. Religious thinking that claims to know in no uncertain terms what that end is, is bound to preserve a sacred core that is identified with the plan of God and therefore claim that this core is immune from rational criticism.   Ironically, as Adorno notes, it colludes with secularism because such theology also has a very immanent perspective on the current world; the conflict – expressed not only in the culture war but also in actual, bloody conflict – is necessary to bring about God's plan, culminating in the 'end of the world.'[486] We are not, then, merely speaking here of 'end' in the sense of telos, but also in the sense of terminus. Upon this model, the inbreaking of transcendence is not imagined unless it is thematized metaphysically; as radical discontinuity with the world of space and time. Such a determinative teleology is

---

[485]   Habermas, *The Theory of Communicative Action*, vol. 1, trans. Thomas McCarthy (Boston: Beacon Press, 1984), 382.
[486]   Adorno, 131.

closed, as is the immanent order, to the future as a horizon of hope, the boundary through which we transcend the present historical moment of conflict. Therefore, I would conclude that what often passes for eschatology in Christian theology is more accurately described as a form of teleology. True eschatology opens future possibilities rather than determining them. Faith in such contexts is, as Kuipers puts it, "the art of the possible."[487]

The realization of a novel future seems to be the thrust of what Habermas wants to achieve through the ideal of rational consensus. However, under the current conditions of secularism, with its insistence upon the immanent frame and the ontology of antagonism that it presupposes, such an achievement does not have the philosophical space in which to grow. I would suggest that Habermas does view the future transcendently, although he does not use that language, insofar as he envisions a transformation of current political systems, an end to the contest of ideologies, and the triumph of rational consensus. Unfortunately, as I have argued in earlier chapters, his strategy of trying to establish secular criteria for political discourse closes the possibility for dialogue at precisely those points where we should be opening it. Granted, religious language can be problematic, but at its best it facilitates abnormal conversations that bring us closer to the ideal that Habermas upholds: reaching genuine understanding, rather than unending ideological battles. But the use of religious language is not confined to facilitating abnormal dialogues. There are other appropriate ways it can inform our politics.

First, I should address some misconceptions that might arise given what I have been saying about the future as transcendence. Some might be inclined to think that investing the future with eschatological potential could only encourage political quietism. From the perspective of the earliest Christian traditions, contrary to their later Platonic interpretations, this conclusion could not be more wrongheaded. Christian expectation for the future, if it is to be understood at all, must be conceived as an inaugurated eschatology. In other words, there is tension between the novelty already begun and its completion yet to come. Moreover, due to this tension, Christian eschatology is collaborative: humanity has a role in bringing it about. Therefore, conceiving of the boundary

---

[487] Ronald A. Kuipers, "Faith as the Art of the Possible: Invigorating Religious Tradition in an Amnesiac Society," in *'God Is Dead' and I Don't Feel So Good Myself*, 145 - 56.

eschatologically does not imply that there is no work to be done in the present age, as it were, to the contrary.

Secondly, openness to future transcendence does not imply a static future, the end of history in which political organization itself is transcended. Again, the eschatological vision I am proposing is not about closure. Quite the contrary, it is about opening previously foreclosed possibilities. This task cannot be projected completely into the future – which, remember, only functions as a boundary – but must begin in the present. To repeat, inaugurated eschatology means that there is work to do in the present which contributes to the inbreaking of novelty in the future. However, in speaking about the present and the future rather artificially, as discrete moments, there is a danger that we will neglect the past. This, in large measure, is what modernism does in its eschewing of religious tradition and in so doing not only fails to be self-conscious of its own history, but fails to appropriate any insights such traditions might have to offer. Kuipers writes persuasively about this 'amnesiac' element in modern culture through engagement with Paul Ricoeur:

> For Ricoeur, the condition of "being-affected-by-a-past" forms a pair with the futural intending of a "horizon of expectation." That is, our hopes and expectations relative to the future inform and thus have repercussions on our reinterpretations of the past. One major repercussive effect, he suggests, is to open up "forgotten possibilities, aborted potentialities, repressed endeavors in the supposedly closed past." The same effect occurs in the opposite direction: through our attempt to interpret a textual tradition inherited from a distant past we create a space in which to subject our present reality to critical scrutiny, and thus, imagine a better future.[488]

Thus, there is a robust role for redemptive critique within an eschatological framework. Consequently, an important task for religion *qua* religion within broadly secular systems of political organization is to critique the surprisingly uncritical, and often pathological, progress narrative that still predominates much of our political discourse in the West. Moreover, this is a task that Habermas, even if not fully endorsing, should at least recognize as a legitimate, critical contribution to public debate. However, the task of religion is not purely

---

[488] Kuipers, 153.

negative. As Habermas says of the theology he witnessed during his student days: "With an undogmatic understanding of transcendence and faith, this engagement took seriously this-worldly goals of human dignity and social emancipation. It joined in a multivoiced arena with other forces pressing for radical democratization."[489] Therefore, the religious critique of modernity is also, importantly, a redemptive exercise: it offers a new construal of progress, a way of imagining the future otherwise.   Working out this novel vision of a transcendently-oriented future in practical terms will require a great deal more work and reflection, but I have endeavored throughout this project to gesture toward some of the ways religious and secular interlocutors can make room for conversations that push 'the boundary', as it were, of our mundane, and often moribund, public discourse. Now, I want to continue in this vein by addressing some of the challenges put to the kind of post-secular democracy I have been advocating, and how the redemptive mode of critique I have been describing can help us meet them.

The Future as Praxis

Having spoken about the future as possibility, I now want to talk about it in more practical terms. Since this project began with an historical analysis of the conditions of secularism, it is only fitting that it end with an analysis of how those conditions are changing and probably will change in the coming decades. It goes without saying that we must be cautious in speaking about the future, and so my remarks should be construed as more tentative than usual. But I think we serve ourselves well if we try to anticipate and prepare for, and even aspire to change, what lies ahead. Therefore, this will be less an exercise in predicting the future and more an exercise in expanding our expectations of what is possible.

In a recent interview with Eduardo Mendieta, Habermas reflects on the amorphous collection of cultural forces summarized under the rubric of "globalization."[490]   One of the points to emerge from the discussion is the recognition that, globally speaking, the processes of modernization have now outrun the governing institutions of modernity. For this reason, globalization

---

[489] Jürgen Habermas, "Transcendence from Within, Transcendence in this World," in *Religion and Rationality: Essays on Reason, God and Modernity*, ed. Eduardo Mendieta (The MIT Press, 2002), 69.
[490] Habermas, "A Conversation About God and the World: Interview with Eduardo Mendieta," in *Religion and Rationality*, 147 – 67.

entails a number of problems. For example, there seem to be no mechanisms with which to regulate the forces of modernization, especially the market capitalism which is superseding the power of nation-states to control, and the distorting communication of mass media which is arguably producing an uncritical appropriation of consumer culture and reducing public opinion to a tool of market research which then bleeds into politics. As public discourse increasingly transcends national boundaries, the question of how to order it along rational-communicative lines becomes all the more pressing. Clearly, the public sphere, as a meta-topical phenomenon, was never limited to the nation-state, but the emergence of new communication and information technologies has facilitated an unprecedented expansion of the public sphere globally; and with this new expansion come new challenges. For example, the global public sphere is an amorphous collection of voices that cannot be mediated by the same institutions established for this purpose in the context of nation-states. This global public discourse seldom conforms to the ideals of communicative action; rather, it is a wild frontier in which a myriad of voices compete without criteria for genuine consensus. International media corporations now increasingly attempt to filter and distill this rough and ready 'discourse'. However, the transformation of the public sphere from a realm of intersubjective consensus to one of mass media and 'public opinion' (in the pollster's sense of 'market research') threatens to further distort an already cacophonous discourse. Habermas is aware of these challenges and observes, "[i]n a world still dominated by nation-states, there is no single regime capable of the kind of political action that could assume the 'global responsibility' demanded by moral points of view."[491] In *The Postnational Constellation*, he points toward a possible 'regime' capable of reining in the power of private corporations over public opinion and strengthening the power of the institutions of the traditional nation-state globally. But Habermas insists that we must do so via responsible political action, not through a missionary zeal to spread Western liberal ideals.[492]

Yet the desire to tame the global public discourse risks unilateralism if not undertaken carefully. And the increasing importance of religion as a cultural factor in this global discourse, and the 'clash of civilizations' rhetoric that often accompanies it, lends itself to a not-so-thinly veiled cultural imperialism found

---

[491] Habermas, 166.
[492] Habermas, 154.

among many of the proponents of the global state.[493] This impetus grows largely out of the assumption, latent in the globalization narrative, that modernity and now globalization "is the continuation of the Christian civilizing project, and that whatever stands in its way is 'oriental' despotism, Muslim fundamentalism, etc."[494] In other words, globalization is the secularized inheritance of Christianity that now confronts other religious forces that have not undergone enlightenment and are now unwilling to translate their political aspirations into publicly accessible, rational discourse. More often than not, unfortunately, the ensuing silence is interrupted with violence. Habermas, although more cautious in his appropriation of the civilizing narrative of modernity than others, nevertheless acknowledges the religious heritage of the project he is undertaking. In reflecting upon globalization and its links to Europe's Christian history he says, "This legacy, substantially unchanged, has been the object of continual critical reappropriation and reinterpretation. Up to this very day there is no alternative to it. And in light of the current challenges of a postnational constellation, we must draw sustenance now, as in the past, from this substance. Everything else is idle postmodern talk."[495] Nevertheless, it is vital, for Habermas, that this substance be translated into a universalistic language that can, in a non-authoritarian, multilateral way, present the Western accomplishments of human rights and liberal democracy to the rest of the world. The consequence of failure in this regard is further economic exploitation and violence. As Habermas emphasizes: "The mode for nondestructive secularization is translation. This is what the Western world, as the worldwide secularizing force, may learn from its own history. If it presents this complex image of itself to other cultures in a credible way, intercultural relations may find a language other than that of the military and the market alone."[496]

Under conditions of globalization, the ideal of the global citizen is relevant especially in connection with emergent religious voices in Western democracies. The narrative of globalization may well be different from the normative definition of 'global citizen' required to meet the above challenges. For example, the goal of globalization and presumably global citizenry is,

---

[493] Mendieta, the interviewer, mentions Fukuyama and Huntington as representative of this view.
[494] Mendieta in Habermas, 152.
[495] Habermas, 149.
[496] Habermas, "Faith and Knowledge," in *The Frankfurt School on Religion: Key Writings by the Major Thinkers*, 336.

ostensibly, to unify. We want to build consensus, tolerance, and stability. We tend to think that this paradigm is in everyone's best interests. The universalizing discourse of modernity is still with us, despite its more radical postmodern critics. The global citizen, as a part of this totalizing discourse, is optimistic about the prospects of enlightened self-interest and rational communication to build a better world. The question remains, however, whether such a totalizing discourse can accommodate particularity of the kind found in religious communities. In other words, must the global citizen be a secular citizen?

Like Habermas, I believe it is imperative to spread the liberal ideals of human rights globally in a way in which religious interlocutors can affirm. Religion is not necessarily a hindrance to this task if the global citizen is not construed as a secular citizen. That is to say, if we do not uncritically assume the broad contours of the secularization thesis in both its empirical and normative forms. In addition, religion may even be helpful within the global public discourse by dissipating the false aura of the obvious that surrounds secular worldviews and enshrines the priority of secular reasons in the public sphere. The assumptions of the secularization thesis are by no means universal, and sensitivity to religious concerns could go a long way toward fostering dialogue and building solidarity. I reiterate that this does not entail that one cannot advance the liberal ideals of human rights and the non-sectarian state, those formally secular aspects of our Enlightenment heritage defended by Habermas. Indeed, we need to articulate these values, defend them, and persuade others of their worth. It is my contention that sensitivity toward and dialogue with religious traditions will make this task more fruitful. As such, overcoming naïve secularism is crucial in a globalized world. Although, in my judgment, Habermas's delineation of postsecularism does not go far enough in the direction of including religious rationales for action within public debate, it does indicate, however indefinitely, the possibility of a formal secularization without naïve secularism. The global citizen, in our increasingly global public discourse with those who do not necessarily share our presuppositions, will be able to endorse the former only by overcoming the latter. Therefore, the global citizen should be a self-consciously postsecular citizen, but in even broader terms than Habermas allows. Not only should the postsecular citizen be able to translate religious language into the widest possible discourse, pragmatically construed, but she should also be able to equalize the burden that religious citizens bear in public discourse, thereby allowing them to participate without naïve secular*ism* being a requirement of admission to public debate. Only then will the goal of a postsecular society – to allow both religious and secular citizens to conceive of secularization as a "complementary learning system" inclusive of a plurality of discourses in the public sphere – be accomplished.

This point brings us to the increasing saliency of religious diversity. Building solidarity with those of robust religious convictions is going to be a major task for Western democracies over the coming decades. In Canada, the deliverances of the Bouchard-Taylor Commission[497] in Quebec remind us that we may not be as tolerant and multicultural in practice as we like to imagine. It also reminds us that philosophy can perhaps offer legislators some guidance when it comes to handling issues pertaining to religious diversity and its apparent conflict with Western democratic values. This simply reinforces the need for more philosophically informed analyses of our political culture. Again, liberal democracies cannot afford to be dismissive of religion in our current global climate. The secularization thesis in its strong articulation has not come to pass and we must deal with the current reality of religious pluralism. I believe that this pragmatist insight is a helpful corrective to Habermas. Again, this is not to say that the Enlightenment project is to be abandoned. Like Habermas, I think that we need to continue extending the liberal ideals realized only imperfectly since the Enlightenment. But we should bear two points in mind whether we are sympathetic to religion or not. First, the Enlightenment is not as secular as we might think. Habermas recognizes that many liberal ideals such as individual rights, liberty, and equality are secularized notions of ideals that originated, at least partially, in Christianity. Second, secularization is not as anti-religious as we might think. If secularization is a pragmatic response to religious pluralism, it does not necessarily presuppose or produce citizens with no religious commitments.[498]

However, the shape those commitments take are changing and will likely continue to do so. We have already noted some of these mutations via Taylor's useful terminology of "ontological indeterminacy" and "subtler languages," but there is more to be said in this regard. There are, no doubt, as Taylor notes, a plethora of spiritual options that do not conform to any particular orthodoxy or

---

[497] Gérard Bouchard and Charles Taylor, *Building the Future: A Time for Reconciliation*, *Abridged Report*, The Consultation Commission on Accommodation Practices Related to Cultural Differences (Government of Québec, 2008).
[498] See Jeffrey Stout, *Democracy and Tradition* (Princeton, NJ: Princeton University Press, 2004), 98.

institutional affiliation. Ecclesiastical institutions may be called upon to perform various rites of passage, but the moral instruction they offer is less likely to find unquestioning allegiance in an age that is more suspicious of authority. Granted, this is a generalized statement and probably admits some exceptions, nevertheless, I think it more or less accurately describes mainline Catholic and Protestant believers' attitudes since the 1960s. (I can do no better than direct readers to Taylor's chapter "The Age of Authenticity" in *A Secular Age* for more detail.) If my assumption is correct, we encounter a trend toward the de-institutionalization of religion. In chapter 4, we saw that Rorty envisions a future in which religion is pruned back to the parish level. In other words, religion will not disappear; it will simply cease to be a purveyor of public morality. Thus, religion will be more like poetry; it will provide a means of expressing the numinous in our lives. This qualified form of secularization is certainly a possible outcome of the de-institutionalizing trend, even though the presence of parishes implies that there is still a place for communal worship, instead of the purely private, romantic expression of religiosity. However, I am not sure that such an outcome is inevitable. As we have seen, Rorty himself provides an alternative vision in "Looking Backwards from the Year 2096." In the preceding, I have tried to articulate a public role for religion that moves beyond the *Kulturkampf* rhetoric; a religiosity that neither enforces orthodoxy on a pluralistic public nor dictates a morality that claims inherent superiority. Still, it is difficult to see how such a transformed religiosity could speak to the wider public without some institutional structure, although it would need to change significantly. Nevertheless, the trend toward de-institutionalization is real and invites speculation about how religiosity in the West might survive the atrophy of the institutions that have housed it for so long. We know that religion is remarkably resilient and it has already surpassed the half-life predicted by the atheists of the nineteenth century. Moreover, movements toward de-institutionalization within Christianity are nothing new. As Habermas observes, "All the great world religions were familiar with anti-clerical revival movements that criticized existing institutions, or with mystical movements, or the subjectivism of highly emotional forms of devotion, of which Pietism is an example for us."[499] However, the rise of information technologies exacerbate this trend by linking people together through ever vaster networks of meta-topical 'space', making the idea of assembling in a particular topical location almost

---

[499] Habermas, 152.

quaint, especially among youth for whom the internet is the preferred delivery system for just about everything, including spirituality.

The communications landscape has certainly changed since 1962 when Habermas wrote *The Structural Transformation of the Public Sphere.* In my first chapter, I quoted James Bohman who claims that globalization and new information technologies "make it at least possible to consider whether democracy is undergoing another great transformation, of the order of the invention of representative democracy and its institutions of voting and parliamentary assemblies in early modern European societies."[500] The volume in which Bohman's essay appears is especially concerned with how to think about communication not only "after Habermas" but also after the telecommunications revolution. Importantly, these changes to the public sphere, the vast expansion of the meta-topical space to which I alluded, also affect religion because it too may be understood, as Mendieta suggests, "as a form of human communication, and as such ... impacted by the transformations in the means and modes of communication."[501] He asks: "Is it possible that we may be witnessing the obsolescence of older forms of human interaction, and the birth of new ones that might catalyze the birth of new religions, new churches, new forms of piety and prayer?"[502] Habermas is reticent to answer this question, because he says it can only be answered "from within."[503] As one who has been an insider, it is my judgment that the future that Mendieta envisions is already upon us. If we are not witnessing completely new religions, we are at the very least witnessing mutations of the old ones. Whether these mutations are desirable or not is, of course, an open question. For his part, Habermas is dismissive of most new forms of spirituality as "a symptom of ego weakness and regression, the expression of a yearning for an impossible return to mythical forms of thought, magical practices, and closed worldviews, that the Church overcame in its battle against 'the heathens.'"[504] Here, I surmise, he has in mind what is usually called "New Age" spirituality and not specifically new forms of Christian religious expression facilitated by the new media. However, contemporary Christianity is

---

[500] James Bohman, "Expanding dialogue: the Internet, the public sphere and prospects for transnational democracy" in *After Habermas: New Perspectives on the Public Sphere*, ed. Nick Crossley and John Michael Roberts (Oxford: Blackwell, 2004), 131.
[501] Mendieta in Habermas, 151.
[502] Mendieta in Habermas, 151.
[503] Habermas, 151.
[504] Habermas, 152.

not immune from the kind of magical thinking to which he alludes. Some very influential manifestations of Christianity today – usually branded as 'charismatic' – are combinations of de-institutionalization, subjectivism, pietism, and supernaturalism. In effect, they combine the various trends under discussion. They also tend to be more media and technology savvy than their more traditional counterparts. In my judgment, this correlation is significant and supports the notion that the changes within communication, and the public sphere itself, will manifest themselves in religious organization and devotion. If not all of these changes are positive, there is at least potential in the coming decades for a more socially aware, politically engaged, and less strident Christian public presence. Even Habermas admits that "history teaches us that religious sects can be very innovative. So maybe not everything on the market is Californian claptrap and neopaganism."[505] It is heartening to see Habermas so eloquently defending the achievements of Christian civilization! Nevertheless, his point about the dangers of the market mentality with respect to religion is well taken. Furthermore, he notes that "In a homogenizing media society, everything loses its gravity, perhaps even institutionalized Christianity itself."[506] Ironically, for Habermas currently, if secularization wins the day, it will not be the achievement of atheistic intellectuals, or even rationality, but yet another conquest by the market. I agree with him. However, I remain optimistic that religion will survive as a form of culture long into the future. What form it will take is a matter of speculation, but I hope that it will continue to play a redemptive role. Perhaps part of this role, as I have suggested, will be to offer a critique of the processes of modernization that tend to dehumanize us. And this would also involve asking the question: are the mutations in religiosity facilitated by new technological means of communication an unqualified good? It is ironic that a secularist like Habermas should remind us that there is much within the Christian tradition that ought to be preserved. Again, I find myself in agreement with him.

In this chapter I have tried to articulate a role for religious language in public that even Habermas would recognize as offering a redemptive critique of the pathologies that he locates within modernity. In the course of articulating such a role, I have argued for a number of points. Firstly, I contend that Habermas, despite his emphasis on the form/content distinction and his effort to

---

[505] Habermas, 152.
[506] Habermas, 152.

confine his theorizing to procedural matters, nevertheless employs a number of substantive assumptions of his own. These assumptions include the autonomy and rationality of agents upon which his normative theory of communicative action and also his political theory depend. These assumptions function, for Habermas, as substantive commitments and rest uneasily with many of the totalizing, metaphysically overdetermined assumptions of materialism. Habermas's attempt to reconcile the materialistic picture of humanity with our phenomenological experience of ourselves as rational actors remains promissory. Insofar, as he maintains his commitment to the indispensability of these phenomenological features for any coherent account of rationality, his commitment to the assumption that we are in fact autonomous, rational actors can be aptly described as a fiduciary commitment.

Secondly, I have argued that we need not do metaphysics in order to talk meaningfully about the substantive commitments that both religious and secular citizens share. Here I express some sympathy with Habermas's postmetaphysical perspective over and against Meyer's criticisms. I argue that construing the differences between religious perspectives and secular ones in metaphysical terms—as 'heavy' and 'light' for example—plays into the hands of the subtraction story of secularization. Moreover, when it comes to the public sphere, such a construal helps justify the exclusion of religious language. Too often the presence of religion in the public sphere is seen as the presence of idiosyncratic beliefs about what lies 'beyond' the immanent frame, rather than the presence of religious citizens who are capable of giving arguments. However, even if the premises in their arguments are perceived as idiosyncratic by secularists, religious arguments certainly enjoy no monopoly on idiosyncratic premises, as I have argued at length. Therefore, they ought not to be excluded simply on that basis.

But there is a sense in which religious views are open to transcendence in a way that secular views are not. However, this 'transcendence' need not be construed metaphysically, as necessitating a reality or realm 'beyond' the immanent frame. Rather, one can speak phenomenologically about 'boundary conditions' that both secular and religious people experience, albeit articulated in different ways. It is not the case that modernity makes it impossible for people to experience these boundary conditions; it simply makes it more difficult to experience them *as* religious. Nonetheless, Taylor has identified articulations of these experiences in 'ontologically indeterminate' ways in many modern thinkers. Simply because one does not express these experiences in the language of dogmatic religion, it does not follow that one cannot express them by means of a 'subtler language'. I suggest that Habermas, insofar as his understanding of the ideal speech situation can be described as 'transcendent' under our revised definition, is also describing this collective phenomenology in subtle, ontologically indeterminate ways. As such, the role his theory plays, namely that of redemptive critique, shares many commonalities with the way some religious citizens understand their own societal role.

Finally, I suggest some practical ways in which religion can more fully embrace this role in the near future, ways that avoid the dangers of dogmatism that Habermas rightly criticizes. Perhaps those with religious imagination can envision ways that they can contribute to public discourse without dogmatism or institutional heavy-handedness. In other words, I am sympathetic to Habermas's criticism of religious dogmatism. I simply urge him to consider that there are other ways to imagine a public role for religion, including some that are in the spirit of his own project of redemptive critique.

Conclusion: The Way Forward

In this project, I have attempted a sympathetic critique of Habermas and other liberal theorists with respect to the role of religion in public discourse. In my judgment, the standard liberal view – that religion ought to be disallowed on contractarian grounds or, at the very least, that its expression be frowned upon by civically responsible citizens – is rapidly becoming antiquated in a globalized context. Nevertheless, I have sought to preserve the valuable insights of contemporary liberalism, namely state neutrality with respect to religion and the secular monopoly on power. Every citizen, regardless of religious adherence or lack thereof, must in principle understand the justification of the law, and maintaining the secularity of the state has historically been an affective measure for achieving such an outcome. Moreover, citizens should justify their reasons for supporting or opposing the exercise of public power. However, unlike many liberal theorists, I doubt that citizens will always agree or even agree for the same reasons, reasons that enjoy consensus for being 'secular' in some sense. As I have argued above, it is not clear to me in what sense secular reasons count as more 'public' or 'accessible' than any reasons, religious or otherwise, deemed 'private.' These terms do not seem to be doing any real work, aside from signaling in an *ad hoc* way which premises are likely to find support from secular liberals and which are not. But such disagreement over premises is much deeper and cannot be adequately captured by merely labeling reasons either 'public' or 'private.' A larger narrative needs to be told, and I have attempted to flesh out some of that narrative above.

Similarly, one cannot simply demarcate secular from religious reasons by claiming that the former are *prima facie* rational whereas the latter are not. Given the phenomenological factors in the way that secularists and believers experience the world, which I have outlined, it appears naïve to say that the secularist person appeals to pure reason, unconditioned by history and the shift in worldviews felt especially since the Enlightenment. The narrative that Taylor and others have articulated, in my judgment, casts doubt on the primacy of reason in the ascent of secularism; other factors, affective and normative, played a more heightened role than the typical self-portrait of secularism would lead one to believe. Again, to say that secular reasons are uniquely rational, and therefore public, is to oversimplify the case and underestimate the role that so-called private affections and moralizing play in justifying the secular outlook.

Historically, liberalism has had the advantage of mining the best affective and moral traditions of both humanism and Christianity and neither should be identified as its exclusive provenance. Secular*ism*, in oversimplifying its own narrative and claiming exclusive access to the public sphere, runs the serious risk of impoverishing liberalism by cutting it off from traditions that have sustained it historically. This is not to say that secularism is simply parasitic on a more substantive tradition, like Christianity. On the contrary, I have argued that secularism is itself a substantive tradition that is by no means as thin as many of its proponents suggest. And the contributions of this substantive tradition to liberalism have yielded some genuine insights, such as the formal secularity of the state. What I want to maintain, however, is that all of the best insights of the secular tradition can be preserved without imposing secular*ism*. Ironically, democracy without secularism leaves us with a more liberal public sphere.

Let me say some more about rationality and argument. I am not defending the position that secularists and religionists mean something different by 'reason' such that there is no way to adjudicate among various arguments in the public sphere. Nor am I suggesting that secularists and religionists necessarily disagree about the importance of giving reasons in public debate. In practice, such may be the case at various times, but nothing I have argued suggests a necessary incommensurability. Rather, what I have said is in line with standard argumentation theory: namely, that when it comes to non-trivial arguments it is exceedingly difficult find premises that are held in common. Consensus on the most interesting philosophical and political issues, perhaps especially the ones we care about most deeply, is going to be a rarity. As such, it seems strange to stake the success of liberalism on consensus, as liberal theorists like Habermas and Rawls seem to do. In those terms, the dialectical process is always going to be a failure. I have suggested that we abandon the notion of consensus, especially with respect to religious arguments, as a criterion for 'publicly accessible reasons.' In the case of religious reasons, such a criterion is a red herring because religious reasons enjoy no monopoly on being disputed. There are many disputed premises that are explicitly non-religious, say, Marxist premises or libertarian premises to take two ends of the political spectrum. But, of course, the fact that they are disputed is not an adequate reason to disqualify them from public debate. Therefore, they have the right to vie for support just like more mainstream political views. I fail to see a relevant difference in the case of religious premises.

To be sure, there are religious citizens who are content to have their views remain 'private' and have no interest in arguing for them. And there are others who want to impose their views on a diverse polity without offering any reasons for them. I have argued that if religious citizens want to fully participate in public debate they must offer something by way of argument for their position. Here I agree with Habermas and most liberal theorists. But I think religious citizens should feel free to couch their reasons in religious language, whereas Habermas insists on translation. Since I have argued at length for why I think the translation requirement should be relaxed, I will not repeat those arguments here. I simply want to clarify what I see to be the role of rational argumentation in public debate. I do not see the goal of argumentation to be consensus as such, not that I am opposed to consensus in principle; I just think it unlikely in most cases. Because I do not think that consensus is likely to emerge from debate, I certainly do not think it will emerge *prior* to debate when we all translate our premises into a universal language that commands rational assent. It is a fact that we are going to have different reasons and different premises in our arguments regardless of whether we are religious or secular. Clearly this does not entail that religious citizens who enter into the exchange of reasons ascribe less value to the exercise of reason in public debate than their secular counterparts. Reason, after all, is largely a formal discipline that most of us understand and follow albeit imperfectly in practice. We typically do not disagree on the question of whether or not we owe each other reasons or arguments. Rather it is the type of reason, or the content of the argument (what the premises say) that is often controversial. It is at this level where our arguments can reach a dialectical stalemate. Nevertheless, there are moves we can make to attempt to overcome these stalemates.

Pragmatically speaking, translation, where possible, is a worthwhile strategy for religious citizens to employ. If one can faithfully preserve the content and force of one's argument by translating it into terms that one's interlocutor might find more convincing, all well and good. I am quite happy to concede the utility of translation where it exists, although I recognize that such translation is often trickier than Habermas and Rawls and Rorty seem to assume. But the pragmatist will employ translation when useful. Thus, I do not object to translation into secular terms *per se*, rather I have argued specifically against conceptualizing it as a contractarian obligation. Instead, I argue it should be construed pragmatically, a position I read Habermas to actually support in some of his more nuanced statements of the translation requirement.

Another useful strategy to avoid conversation-stopping is Stout's immanent critique. This strategy is advantageous because, unlike the way translation is typically employed, immanent critique makes allowance for all manner of premises and recognizes that reasons come rhetorically packaged in ways that are not simply incidental to the argument, but essential to it. Thus, a secularist can appreciate that a religious person's political position on a given issue is deeply rooted in a theological tradition. Immanent critique also gives the secularist motivation to become familiar with that theological tradition in order to better understand her religious interlocutor's position and so also to mine the theological tradition for reasons that might be uniquely persuasive to someone informed by that tradition. So the giving of reasons plays a central role, but reason is not construed as set of secular premises to be enforced on a pluralistic discourse, but as a dialectical process that works pragmatically with that pluralistic discourse. Again, the goal is not to bring about some idealized rational consensus, but to achieve a workable basis for political praxis that satisfies the need to give reasons while recognizing the legitimacy of diverse reasons within the polity.

In this project, it has not been my intent to defend any particular religion or even the ideal of 'religion' in general, whatever that might mean. Nevertheless, I do make points that are often made in a more explicitly apologetic context. I do think that Christianity has played an influential and positive role in the formation of modern liberalism. I do not gloss over the wars of religion or the various problematic theologies that contributed to Christianity's alienation from the public sphere. But I do think that many of the virtues espoused by liberalism find their precedent in the New Testament and that the religious tolerance that Locke advocated, for example, did not emerge as a novel secular creation, but was indebted to Christian thinkers, particularly theological minorities, that had made the case even earlier. But this seems to be a modest point, one to which a secularist could easily assent in the interest of intellectual honesty.

Also with respect to the secularization thesis, the point I make is fairly modest. I do not claim that religions are resilient because some particular religion or aspect of religion generally, is true, although one cannot rule that possibility out entirely. I speculate that religion continues to offer something to humanity and that is why it persists. But an atheist like Habermas can also state that religion has an existential pull that eludes even the best secular accounts of our humanity. This point may be more controversial, but I think it is defensible and have offered various versions of it above.

I also make the point that religion, particularly Christianity, is more rationally respectable than many secularists seem to assume. I think that something like Reformed epistemology, spoken of mostly in relation to Wolterstorff, is sound; namely that religious persons are entitled to their religious belief in the absence of successful defeaters. This position informs how I construe rational entitlement and provides a healthy corrective, in my judgment, to the evidentialism presupposed in a liberal theory like that of Rawls. Moreover, it fits quite well with a pragmatist understanding of how we justify our beliefs. Of course, the proponent of the secularization thesis may be correct that religion is irrational and will eventually be upstaged by a complete science, but a lot of work would have to be done to show that. Judging from the contemporary scene in philosophy of religion, however, there is not the debate over the rational propriety of religious belief that there used to be. Both believers and atheists have taken the position that religious belief is rational in the absence of successful defeaters. Of course, there is still lively debate about potential defeaters and whether they succeed (variations on the problem of evil are popular candidates), but there is a rare consensus on the rational propriety of belief that does not seem to be reflected outside philosophy of religion. Part of what I have sought to do in this project is to make the fruit of contemporary philosophy of religion relevant to political philosophy. Wolterstorff has made some important headway here, but the application of religious epistemology to political philosophy has remained largely unexplored. I hope to have made some contribution to that effort.

I also suggest that Christianity continues to make a contribution to the moral underpinnings of the liberal state in a way that some secularists deny. Again, the point here is exceedingly modest. I do not claim that Christianity is the best or the only moral foundation for liberal society. Nor do I argue the more conservative position that liberalism is simply parasitic on its religious legacy as do some neo-traditionalist thinkers. I give due weight to Stout's suggestion that a moral foundation other than Western monotheism may be the preferred vehicle for the sustenance of the liberal virtues, and I am quite a bit more optimistic than Wolterstorff about the prospects of a secular morality that can do more or less everything that Christian morality has done historically, namely provide a hospitable environment for what he calls the culture of human rights. However, it is also undeniable in my judgment that Christianity has made significant contributions to liberal democracy. If I have overstated Christianity's contribution at all in my narrative it is only to compensate for the understatement, or indeed, absence of statement, that I find in shorthand secular narratives that often serve as the basis for political theory.

None of this is to let religion off the hook for some of its more problematic features, such as the dogmatism in which much of religion trades. Democracy does not have any room for the dogmatism often exhibited by religious adherents. As an inherently open-ended and revisable system, democracy must subject all ideas to scrutiny and criticism; no ideology is immune in the marketplace of ideas. As such, religious persons who are sensitive to the democratic process must abandon dogmatism and consent to have their beliefs placed on equal footing with other ideologies. This means that they must also abandon any privilege of privacy their beliefs might have enjoyed before entry into the public sphere. I agree with the secularist that surrender of dogmatism and the privilege of privacy are reasonable demands for participation in the democratic process. But religion need not be dogmatic.

I am aware that some who defend religion are guilty of defining religion in such abstract terms that it escapes the charges of its critics but fails to resemble anything that anyone actually believes or practices. I have tried to avoid this moving target fallacy in what I have written. I am realistic about what religion actually looks like in practice, while also being open to what religion could be; a religiosity that transcends the culture wars and transforms itself into something less dogmatic and authoritarian. I have articulated what I think such a religion would look like and what redemptive role it could play in the political realm. We all have a stake in hoping that this more liberal form of religion ultimately replaces various forms of fundamentalism. In this respect, liberalism itself is a powerful moderating force and needs to be supported as a means of overcoming tribal ways of thinking. But enforcing secularism will only strengthen those elements within religion that are antagonistic to liberalism and prolong the culture war mentality that infects much of the political discourse when it comes to the discussion of religion in public. Therefore, it is also in the interests of secularists to foster a more open dialogue.

The wider cultural context in which I have written this thesis is one of religious resurgence in the public consciousness and a secularist backlash against it. Both sides in the debate are frequently dogmatic and often lack a rudimentary understanding of the others' point of view. The current wave of atheistic propaganda is particularly culpable in this regard. Although it presents itself as the vanguard of science, the goal of much of this literature, in my judgment, is political; it seeks to paint religion as irrational because such a strategy, in their view, pays politically. They can say, in effect, "if the religious believe nonsense about science, we can't trust them to think clearly about public policy. We should just tell them to keep out of it." I think such a strategy backfires and simply reinforces the polarization that exists between religious and secular citizens. If secularists and religionists made a more honest effort to understand each others' positions, arguments, motivations, hopes, fears, and convictions, we might make some progress toward solidarity, not because we blithely ignore each others' differences, but because we are willing to argue about them in good faith. This project, in a modest way, strives to be such an honest effort and hopefully it succeeds.

Samenvatting

Democratie zonder secularisme: een pragmatistische kritiek op Habermas.

Deze dissertatie is een onderzoek naar de plaats van religieuze taal in publieke discussies. De consensuspositie is dat het goed is voor zowel religie als de politiek wanneer de twee domeinen gescheiden blijven. De staat behoort seculier te zijn, d.w.z. neutraal te staan tegenover verschillende religies. Dit voorkomt dat één religie een monopoliepositie krijgt en biedt aan het individu de gelegenheid om zijn eigen religie, indien aanwezig, te praktiseren. Hoewel een idealisering, is dit een algemeen principe dat de meeste voorstanders van een liberale democratie op een of andere manier anvaarden. Echter, onder het dunne vernis van deze consensus liggen diepe en complexe onderwerpen verscholen waarover overtuigde democraten met elkaar van mening verschillen. Dit onderzoek gaat over precies zulke onderwerpen.

Meer specifiek gaat het over deze onderwerpen 'in gesprek met' het werk van Jürgen Habermas. Habermas staat in filosofische kringen bekend wegens zijn theorie van communicatief handelen, die een uitgewerkte articulatie en verdediging biedt van de principes van de Verlichting. Habermas is overtuigd van de kracht van het geven van redenen, van het vermogen van de menselijke rationaliteit om een consensus te bereiken door de dwangeloze dwang van het betere argument. Voor hem is het rationele argument de enige legitieme kracht in de politiek. Echter, wil rationaliteit haar werk kunnen doen, dan moet zij publiek toegankelijk zijn en moet haar legitimiteit erkend worden door alle burgers, ongeacht hun religie.

Recentelijk heeft Habermas zijn positie met betrekking tot religieuze taal in het publieke domein echter afgezwakt. Mijn dissertatie traceert deze ontwikkeling en ik verbind daar vergaande conclusies aan.

Hoofdstuk 1 biedt een correctie op de 'subtraction theory' (om Charles Taylors term te gebruiken) aangaande moderne secularisatie. Ik betoog dat secularisatie niet identiek is aan Habermas' stelling, die hij ontleent aan Max Weber, over de 'onttovering van de wereld'. Mijn stelling is dat secularisatie het beste begrepen kan worden als antwoord op het gegeven van het religieuze pluralisme. Om dit te onderbouwen neem ik de lezer mee op een historische excursie door de vroeg moderne periode—de periode waarin Habermas en anderen het ontstaan van het publieke domein situeren. Omdat Habermas zichzelf plaatst in de traditie van het Verlichtingssecularisme, is het nuttig de vraag te stellen of het seculiere criterium voor participatie aan de politiek wel echt van de Verlichting afkomstig is. Ik betoog dat dit niet zo is en dat de stelling dat secularisme voortkomt uit de Verlichting, of zelfs dat de Verlichting de terugtrekking van religie uit het publieke leven heeft bevorderd, voorbijgaat aan belangrijke feiten betreffende de grondleggers van het Verlichtingsdenken en de politieke nazaat daarvan, het liberalisme.

Na in hoofdstuk 1 te hebben betoogd dat Habermas' vroege kritische theorie de 'subtraction theory' van secularisatie aan boord neemt, ga ik in hoofdstuk 2 door op dit thema omdat deze theorie op gespannen voet staat met Habermas' vertalingsvereiste ('translation requirement') volgens welke religieuze individuen hun particuliere geloofstaal dienen te vertalen in een verondersteld universele seculiere taal. Habermas stelt dat seculiere taal ons verplicht tot minder overtuigingen, en dus een betere garantie biedt voor consensus in het publieke domein. En dit is zo, volgens hem, omdat religieuze individuen additionele commitments hebben, zwaardere metafysische bagage met zich meetorsen, wat hun epistemische situatie lastiger maakt dan die van de secularist. Mijn betoog hiertegen is dat deze positie de 'subtraction theory' veronderstelt en dat deze theorie geen oog heeft voor de substantiële commitments van de secularist.

In hoofdstuk 3 onderzoek ik meer concreet hoe Habermas zich de vertalingsvereiste voorstelt in de politieke praktijk. Ik doe dat door een vergelijking te maken met Rawls, die, net als Habermas, een normatieve theorie heeft ontwikkeld over hoe in een democratie rationele discussies zouden moeten worden gevoerd. Ondanks verschillen, beschouwen beiden consensus als het doel van elke discussie en het doel van democratische discussies moet volgens hen rationele consensus zijn. Ik breng een aantal redenen naar voren om te denken dat dit onjuist is.

Zowel Habermas als Rawls insisteren dat uitsluitend 'publieke' of 'publiek toegankelijke' redenen tellen in een seculiere democratie. Bovendien stellen ze dat publieke redenen seculiere redenen zijn. Een paradigmatisch voorbeeld van een 'private reden' is een religieuze reden, en zulke redenen hebben geen rechtvaardigende potentie in een seculiere democratie. Dit stellen zij zo, omdat burgers zowel de scheppers als de geadresseerden zijn van de wet.

Iedere burger moet als burger de rechtvaardiging of onderbouwing van een wet kunnen begrijpen—en dus moet die rechtvaardiging/onderbouwing publiek, seculier en universeel zijn, en niet privaat en sektarisch. Dit geldt m.n. voor wat Rawls de 'principles of basic justice' noemt, maar ook voor de onderbouwing van het recht van de staat om bepaalde vrijheden in te perken.

Zowel Habermas als Rawls vatten de vertalingsvereiste in Kantiaanse termen als een verplichting die geldt voor alle rationele personen in een democratie, minstens op institutioneel niveau, waar de staat dwingmacht heeft. In hoofdstuk 3 betoog ik dat dit vereiste op een zwakkere manier moet worden geconstrueerd, meer in pragmatische termen. Ik ontwikkel argumenten die beogen aan te tonen dat dit zwakkere vereiste enerzijds evenveel bescherming biedt aan zowel seculiere burgers als aan religieuze minderheden als de standaard liberale theorie dat doet, maar anderzijds de ruimte vergroot voor religieuze burgers om hun bijdrage aan het publieke debat te vatten in religieuze termen.

Blijkens zijn meer recente werk heeft Habermas dit punt erkend en heeft hij zijn vertalingsvereiste herzien. Hij zegt nu dat burgers in de informele publieke sfeer (d.w.z. de sfeer van de opinievorming) ook religieuze redenen naar voren mogen brengen, maar dat zij zich in de formele publieke sfeer (het parlement) dienen te beperken tot seculiere redenen. Hij denkt dat dit 'institutional translation proviso' het probleem voorkomt dat religieuze burgers in een democratie worden uitgesloten van politieke participatie, terwijl het tevens de neutraliteit van de staat waarborgt. In een bepaald opzicht heeft dit proviso kracht. De wetten in een pluralistische samenleving moeten niet een bepaalde religieuze traditie bevoordelen. De taal in de wet moet zo neutraal zijn als mogelijk.

In het laatste deel van hoofdstuk 3 onderzoek ik Habermas' poging om een zodanig evenwicht te vinden tussen religieuze en seculiere burgers, dat de politieke participatie van de eersten niet wordt aangetast. Veel in wat hij zegt, acht ik loffelijk, maar betoog tevens dat zijn bijgestelde vertalingsvereiste verder dient te worden versoepeld.

Mijn kritiek op Habermas in de voorgaande hoofdstukken is geïnspireerd door de pragmatistische traditie. Dit roept wel de vraag op of pragmatisten zichzelf zien als denkers die ruimte bieden aan religieuze burgers om hun politieke argumenten te gieten in een religieus idioom. In hoofdstuk 4 onderzoek ik twee pragmatisten: Richard Rorty en Jeffrey Stout. Geen van beiden beschouwt zichzelf als religieus, maar Rorty staat veel minder open voor het idee van religieuze argumenten in het publieke domein dan Stout. Illustratief hiervoor is Rorty's essay "Religion as a Conversation Stopper" waarin hij betoogt dat religie moet worden geweerd uit het publieke domein. Hij doet dat door het bekende publiek/privéonderscheid te verdedigen en religie in het privédomein te plaatsen. Na nauwkeurige analyse blijkt echter dat Rorty de term 'privé' gebruikt in de betekenis van 'niet gedeeld door het brede publiek.' Anders gezegd, hij omarmt het standaard liberalisme. Echter, ik laat zien dat er problemen kleven aan de notie van 'publiek gedeelde' of 'gezamenlijk aanvaarde' premissen. Bovendien stelt het pragmatisme de notie van een ideale consensus ter discussie. De pragmatist weet dat er feitelijk verschil van mening is over de premissen in politieke argumenten, en vermoedelijk zijn niet alle meningsverschillen verkeerd, ook al functioneren sommige als conversatiestoppers. Immers, het publieke domein is niet een eindeloze discussiearena. Conversaties worden gestopt, en één van de hoogst geprezen democratische praktijken, namelijk: stemmen, is een conversatiestopper. Het is daarom moeilijk in te zien waarom publiek verschil van mening over religie wel een slechte zaak zou zijn, terwijl publiek verschil van mening in het algemeen dat niet is.

Ik concludeer daarom dat niets in de traditie van het Amerikaanse pragmatisme religieuze bijdragen aan het publieke debat diskwalificeert. Ik betoog dat Rorty's claim dat religie een conversatiestopper is, alleen geldig is voor geloofsuitspraken die onkritisch op gezag teruggaan. Rorty erkent nu ook dat het "Jeffersonian compromise", dat hij ooit verdedigde, onhoudbaar is. Hij biedt geen principe waarmee religie uit de publieke sfeer kan worden geweerd en heeft de verwijzing naar Rawls en Habermas als voorbeelden laten vallen. Hij is echter niettemin van mening dat gewoonten en gebruik een beroep op religie in sommige gevallen moeten zien te voorkomen, bijv. wanneer het gaat om de rechten van homo's. Hij wil nog steeds de religieuze burger ertoe pressen zijn argumenten op een seculiere manier te verwoorden. Naar mijn oordeel heeft zulk een oproep tot vertaling weinig zeggingskracht zonder een robuuste notie van rationaliteit. En die notie is er niet. Ik betoog vervolgens, met een voorbehoud, dat Stouts methode van immanente kritiek meer mogelijkheden biedt voor de 'abnormale conversaties' die onvermijdelijk zijn in een pluralistische democratie. Ik concludeer daarom dat pragmatisme een bondgenoot kan zijn voor de stelling dat religieuze burgers de gelegenheid moeten krijgen om deel te nemen aan het publieke debat in de taal van hun traditie.

In het slothoofdstuk verbreed ik het argument van de voorgaande hoofdstukken in deze zin dat ik betoog dat Habermas, niettegenstaande zijn focus op procedures, zelf menig substantiële assumptie maakt. Zijn politieke filosofie, bijvoorbeeld, hangt aan de assumptie dat personen autonome, rationele actoren zijn. Tegelijk is hij er zich van bewust dat het heersende materialistische paradigma, met haar deterministische wereldbeeld, de politieke notie van verantwoordelijk handelen ondermijnt. Daarom geeft Habermas zich moeite om het moderne wetenschappelijke beeld van de mens te verzoenen met de fenomenologische ervaring van onszelf als rationele actoren—een ervaring waarop de liberale politieke theorie is gebaseerd. Om dat doel te bereiken, kiest Habermas voor een niet-reductief materialisme. Maar de verzoening die hij zoekt, is vooralsnog slechts een belofte. Ik betoog daarom dat zijn commitment aan autonomie eerder substantieel is dan procedureel—en dat het daarom als een geloofscommitment kan worden beschouwd.

Tenslotte doe ik enkele praktische suggesties over hoe religie deze andere rol zou kunnen spelen in de toekomst en hoe de politiek open kan blijven voor inzichten uit deze hoek. Ik herhaal mijn punt dat men datgene wat distinctief is aan het moderne liberalisme kan handhaven zonder een ideologisch secularisme te hoeven aanvaarden. De formele seculariteit van het politieke domein is een waardevol aspect van het liberalisme. Maar die kan worden geaffirmeerd zonder naïef secularisme aan te hangen. Ik sta positief tegenover Habermas' kritiek op religieus dogmatisme. Wel geef ik hem te overwegen dat er andere manieren zijn om zich de publieke rol van religie in te denken dan dogmatisme, waaronder ook enige die goed passen bij zijn eigen project van bevrijdende kritiek. Bijvoorbeeld, religieuze burgers kunnen gebruik maken van pragmatische vertaling en immanente kritiek en daardoor abnormale conversaties mogelijk maken. Ze kunnen ook een correctief bieden voor de pathologische aspecten van de moderniteit die Habermas zelf ook kritiseert—en aldus bijdragen aan bevrijdende kritiek. Ik concludeer dat geen van deze activiteiten een bedreiging vormt voor discursieve democratieën. Integendeel, deze activiteiten zijn verenigbaar met Habermas' eigen project om het huidige antagonistische politieke discours te overstijgen. Hoewel we misschien nooit een ideale communicatieve situatie zullen bereiken, kunnen we wel leren om te gaan met de politiek van veelvoudige identiteiten zonder religieus sektarisme of ideologisch secularisme.

Bibliography

Adorno, Theodor. "Meditations on Metaphysics." In *The Frankfurt School on Religion: Key Writings by the Major Thinkers*. Edited by Eduardo Mendieta, 175 – 209. Routledge, 2005.

-------- "Progress." In *How Can One Live after Auschwitz*. Edited by Rolf Tiedemann, 126 – 45. Stanford, CA: Stanford University Press, 2002.

Audi, Robert and Nicholas Wolterstorff. *Religion in the Public Square: The Place of Religious Convictions in Political Debate.* Rowman & Littlefield Publishers, Inc., 1996.

Benedict XVI, *Spe Salvi*, http://www.vatican.va/holy_father/benedict_xvi/encyclicals/documents/hf_ben-xvi_enc_20071130_spe-salvi_en.html (accessed August 16, 2010).

Bohman, James. "Expanding dialogue: the Internet, the public sphere and prospects for transnational democracy." In *After Habermas: New Perspectives on the Public Sphere*. Edited by Nick Crossley and John Michael Roberts, 131 – 55. Wiley-Blackwell, 2004.

-------- and William Rehg. "Jürgen Habermas." *Stanford Encyclopedia of Philosophy*, http://plato.stanford.edu/entries/habermas/#DiaBetNatRel (accessed August 13, 2010).

Borradori, Giovanna. *Philosophy in a Time of Terror: Dialogues with Jurgen Habermas and Jacques Derrida.* Chicago: University Of Chicago Press, 2004.

Bouchard, Gérard and Charles Taylor. *Building the Future: A Time for Reconciliation*, *Abridged Report.* The Consultation Commission on Accommodation Practices Related to Cultural Differences. Government of Québec, 2008.

Buckley, Michael J. S.J. *At the Origins of Modern Atheism*. New Haven, CT: Yale University Press, 1990.

Calhoun, Craig. "Introduction: Habermas and the Public Sphere" In *Habermas and the Public Sphere*. Edited by Craig Calhoun, 1 – 48. Cambridge, MA: The MIT Press, 1992.

Cooke, Maeve. "A Secular State for a Postsecular Society? Postmetaphysical Political Theory and the Place of Religion." *Constellations*, 14.2 (2007): 224 – 38.

-------- *Language and Reason: A Study of Habermas's Pragmatics*. Cambridge, MA: The MIT Press, 1994.

Dann, Elijah G. *After Rorty: The Possibilities for Ethics and Religious Belief*. London: Continuum, 2006.

Enns, Phil. "Habermas, Democracy and Religious Reasons." *The Heythrop Journal*, LI (2010): 582 – 93.

Fish, Stanley. "Does Reason Know What It Is Missing?" http://opinionator.blogs.nytimes.com/2010/04/12/does-reason-know-what-it-is-missing/?emc=etal (accessed August 16, 2010).

Garnham, Nicholas. "The Media and the Public Sphere." In *Habermas and the Public Sphere*, edited by Craig Calhoun, 359 -- 76. Cambridge, MA: MIT Press, 1992.

Glaude, Eddie S. *Exodus!: religion, race, and nation in early nineteenth-century Black America*. Chicago: University of Chicago Press, 2000.

Habermas, Jürgen. "The Boundary between Faith and Knowledge: On the Reception and Contemporary Importance of Kant's Philosophy of Religion." In *Between Naturalism and Religion: Philosophical Essays*. Translated by Ciaran Cronin, 209 – 47. Polity, 2008.

-------- "Prepolitical Foundations of the Constitutional State?" In *Between Naturalism and Religion: Philosophical Essays*. Translated by Ciaran Cronin, 101 – 13. Polity, 2008.

-------- "Religion in the Public Sphere: Cognitive Presuppositions for the 'Public Use of Reason' by Religious and Secular Citizens." In *Between Naturalism and Religion: Philosophical Essays*. Translated by Ciaran Cronin, 114 – 47. Polity, 2008.

-------- "Equal Treatment of Cultures and the Limits of Postmodern Liberalism." In *Between Naturalism and Religion: Philosophical Essays*. Translated by Ciaran Cronin, 271 – 311. Polity, 2008.

-------- "Religious Tolerance as Pacemaker for Cultural Rights." In *Between Naturalism and Religion: Philosophical Essays*. Translated by Ciaran Cronin, 251 – 70. Polity, 2008.

-------- and Joseph Ratzinger. *The Dialectics of Secularization: On Reason and Religion*. Edited by Florian Schuller and translated by Brian McNeil, C.R.V. San Francisco: Ignatius Press, 2006.

-------- "Faith and Knowledge." In *The Frankfurt School on Religion: Key Writings by the Major Thinkers*. Edited by Eduardo Mendieta, 327 -- 37. Routledge, 2005.

-------- "Richard Rorty's Pragmatic Turn." In *Truth: Engagements Across Philosophical Traditions*. Edited by José Medina and David Wood, 109 – 129. Wiley-Blackwell, 2005.

-------- "Transcendence from Within, Transcendence in this World." In *Religion and Rationality: Essays on Reason, God and Modernity*. Edited by Eduardo Mendieta, 67 – 94. Cambridge, MA: The MIT Press, 2002.

-------- "A Conversation About God and the World: Interview with Eduardo Mendieta." In *Religion and Rationality*. Edited by Eduardo Mendieta, 147 – 67. Cambridge, MA: The MIT Press, 2002.

-------- *The Structural Transformation of the Public Sphere: An Inquiry into a Category of Bourgeois Society*. Translated by Thomas Burger and Fredrick Lawrence. Cambridge, MA: The MIT Press, 1991.

-------- *The Theory of Communicative Action, Vol. 1: Reason and the Rationalization of Society.* Translated by Thomas McCarthy. Beacon Press, 1985.

-------- *The Theory of Communicative Action, Vol. 2: Lifeworld and System: A Critique of Functionalist Reason.* Translated by Thomas McCarthy. Beacon Press, 1985.

-------- "The Hermeneutical Claim to Universality." In *Contemporary Hermeneutics: Hermeneutics as Method, Philosophy, and Critique.* Edited by Josef Bleicher, 181 – 211. London: Routledge and Kegan Paul, 1980.

Hart, Hendrik. "The Consequences of Liberalism: Ideological Domination in Rorty's Public/Private Split." In *Towards an Ethics of Community: Negotiations of Difference in a Pluralist Society.* Edited by James H. Olthuis, 37 – 50. Wilfrid Laurier Univ. Press, 2000.

Hösle, Vittorio. "Review Essay: A Metaphysical History of Atheism." *Symposium*, 14. 1 (Spring, 2001): 52 – 65.

Jaspers, Karl. *Way to Wisdom: An Introduction to Philosophy.* Translated by Ralph Manheim. New Haven, CT: Yale University Press, 1954.

Johnson, Mark. *Moral Imagination: Implications of Cognitive Science for Ethics.* Chicago: University of Chicago Press, 1993.

Kuipers, Ronald A. "An Inteview with Charles Taylor." In *'God Is Dead' and I Don't Feel So Good Myself: Theological Engagements With the New Atheism.* Edited by Andrew David, Christopher J. Keller, and Jon Stanley, 120 – 28. Cascade Books, 2010.

--------"Faith as the Art of the Possible: Invigorating Religious Tradition in an Amnesiac Society." In *'God Is Dead' and I Don't Feel So Good Myself: Theological Engagements With the New Atheism.* Edited by Andrew David, Christopher J. Keller, and Jon Stanley, 145 – 56. Cascade Books, 2010.

-------- "Stout's Democracy without Secularism: But is it a Tradition?" *Contemporary Pragmatism*, 3.1 (June, 2006): 85 – 104.

-------- *Critical Faith: Toward a Renewed Understanding of Religious Life and its Public Accountability*. Rodopi, 2002.

-------- "Singular Interruptions: Rortian Liberalism and the Ethics of Deconstruction." In *Knowing Other-wise: Philosophy at the threshold of spirituality*. Edited by James H. Olthuis, 105 – 130. New York: Fordham University Press, 1997.

-------- "Excellence and the Emersonian Perfectionist: An Interview with Jeffrey Stout, part 1" *The Other Journal*, http://www.theotherjournal.com/article.php?id=864 (accessed August 13, 2010).

Lalonde, Marc P. *Critical Theology and the Challenge of Jürgen Habermas: Toward a Critical Theory of Religious Insight.* New York: Peter Lang Publishing, 1999.

Locke, John. *An Essay Concerning Human Understanding*. Edited by Peter Nidditch. Oxford University Press, USA, 1979.

Loptson, Peter. *Philosophy, History, and Myth: Essays and Talks*. University Press of America, 2002.

Mill, John Stuart and Jeremy Bentham, *Utilitarianism and Other Essays*. Edited by Alan Ryan. Penguin Classics, 1987.

Moltmann, Jürgen. *The Future of Creation: Collected Essays*. Fortress Press, 2007.

Meyer, William J. "Private Faith or Public Religion? An Assessment of Habermas's Changing View of Religion." *The Journal of Religion* 75. 3 (1995): 371 – 391.

Newman, Jay. *On Religious Freedom*. Ottawa: University of Ottawa Press, 1991.

Parker, Kim Ian. *The Biblical Politics of John Locke*. Wilfrid Laurier Univ. Press, 2004.

Popkin, Richard H. *The History of Scepticism: From Savonarola to Bayle*, Rev Exp. Oxford University Press, USA, 2003.

Rawls, John. *Political Liberalism*. Columbia University Press, 1993.

Romanell, Patrick. Introduction to *A Letter Concerning Toleration* by John Locke, 5 – 11. New Jersey: Prentice Hall, 1950.

Rorty, Richard. "Solidarity or Objectivity." In *The Rorty Reader*. Edited by Christopher J. Voparil and Richard J. Bernstein. Wiley-Blackwell, 2010.

-------- *Philosophy and the Mirror of Nature, Thirtieth Anniversary Edition*. Princeton University Press, 2009.

-------- "Religion in the Public Sphere: A Reconsideration," *Journal of Religious Ethics*, 31.1 (2003): 141 – 49.

-------- "Pragmatism as Romantic Polytheism." In *Pragmatism and Religion: Classical Sources and Original Essays*. Edited by Stuart E. Rosenbaum, 118 – 26. University of Illinois Press, 2003.

-------- "Religion As Conversation-stopper." In *Philosophy and Social Hope*, 168 – 74. Penguin, 2000.

-------- "Looking Backwards from the Year 2096." In *Philosophy and Social Hope*, 243 – 51. Penguin, 2000.

-------- *Objectivity, Relativism, and Truth: Philosophical Papers*. Cambridge University Press, 1990.

-------- *Contingency, irony, and solidarity.* Cambridge University Press, 1989.

Ryan, Alan. Introduction to *Utilitarianism and Other Essays* by John Stuart Mill and Jeremy Bentham, 7 -- 63. Penguin Classics, 1987.

Sheehan, Jonathan. "Framing the Middle." http://www.ssrc.org/blogs/immanent_frame/2008/01/14/framing-the-middle/ (accessed August 13, 2010).

Smith, Norman Kemp. Preface to the second edition of the *Critique of Pure Reason* by Immanuel Kant. New York: St. Martin's Press, 1968.

Stout, Jeffrey. "Comments on Six Responses to *Democracy and Tradition*." *Journal of Religious Ethics*, 33.4 (2005): 709 – 44.

-------- *Democracy and Tradition.* Princeton University Press, 2005.

--------- "How Charity Transcends the Culture Wars: Eugene Rogers and Others on Same-Sex Marriage." *Journal of Religious Ethics*, 31.2 (2003): 169 – 180.

Taubes, Jacob. *The Political Theology of Paul.* Translated by Dana Hollander. Stanford University Press, 2004.

Taylor, Charles. *A Secular Age.* Belknap Press of Harvard University Press, 2007.

-------- "Secularism and Critique." http://blogs.ssrc.org/tif/2008/04/24/secularism-and-critique/ (accessed August 13, 2010).

Van Leeuwen, Henry G. *The Problem of Certainty in English Thought 1630-1690.* Springer, 1970.

Waldron, Jeremy. *God, Locke, and Equality*. Cambridge: Cambridge University Press, 2002.

Warner, Michael. *The Letters of the Republic: Publication and the Public Sphere in Eighteenth-Century America*. Harvard University Press, 1992.

Weber, Max. "Science as a Vocation." In *Max Weber's 'science as a vocation'*. Edited by Peter Lassman, Irving Velody, and Herminio Martins, 3 – 32. Routledge, 1989.

Wellmer, Albrecht. "Adorno, Modernity, and the Sublime." In *The Actuality of Adorno*. Edited by Max Pensky, 112 – 134. Albany: State University of New York Press, 1997.

Wills, Gary. "The Day the Enlightenment Went Out." *New York Times*, November 4, 2004.

Wolterstorff, Nicholas. *Justice: Rights and Wrongs.* Princeton University Press, 2008.

-------- "Jeffrey Stout on Democracy and Its Contemporary Christian Critics." *Journal of Religious Ethics*, 33.4 (2005): 633 – 47.

-------- "An Engagement with Rorty." *Journal of Religious Ethics*, 31.1 (2003): 129 – 39.

-------- *John Locke and the Ethics of Belief*. Cambridge University Press, 1996.

Zagorin, Perez. *How the idea of religious toleration came to the West.* Princeton University Press, 2003.

Zaret, David. "Religion, Science and Printing in the Public Spheres in Seventeenth-Century England." In *Habermas and the Public Sphere*. Edited by Craig Calhoun, 212 – 35. Cambridge, MA: The MIT Press, 1992.

Zuidervaart, Lambert. *Social Philosophy after Adorno*. New York: Cambridge University Press, 2007.

www.ingramcontent.com/pod-product-compliance
Lightning Source LLC
Chambersburg PA
CBHW080730300426
44114CB00019B/2544